SPECIALISTS FROM ALL BRANCHES
of the social sciences have here
brought their knowledge to bear
upon the new and complex problems inherent in governmentally
sponsored economic growth. Central to the discussion are the questions of how the economic advancement of underdeveloped areas is
related to cultural, social, and political factors and what similarities
or differences exist between western European peoples and the
colored populations of Asia, Africa,
and Latin America as economic
and cultural changes take place.

Detailed accounts of the chief economic problems include an analysis
of capital formation and mobilization, inflation, and balance-of-pay-
ment difficulties. In the political
sphere the development of new
elites, the role of governmental
development plans, and the performance of technical assistance
agencies are described; and in the
domain of social and cultural problems the restructuring of class relations, the influence of migration,
the adoption of new skills and patterns of behavior, the over-all
change in cultural values, and the
resistance opposed to new techniques and a new way of life are
examined.

THE PROGRESS OF
UNDERDEVELOPED AREAS

EDITED BY BERT F. HOSELITZ

THE PROGRESS OF UNDERDEVELOPED AREAS

ALEXANDER GERSCHENKRON

ROBERT K. LAMB

OSCAR HANDLIN

W. T. EASTERBROOK

RALPH LINTON

MELVILLE J. HERSKOVITS

MARION J. LEVY

MORRIS E. OPLER

WALTER R. GOLDSCHMIDT

MORRIS WATNICK

JACOB VINER

SAMUEL P. HAYES, JR.

KONRAD BEKKER

H. S. BLOCH

GEORGE HAKIM

ALBERT O. HIRSCHMAN

THE UNIVERSITY OF CHICAGO PRESS · CHICAGO

THE
NORMAN WAIT HARRIS MEMORIAL FOUNDATION

The Twenty-seventh Institute

THE Harris Foundation Lectures at the University of Chicago have been made possible through the generosity of the heirs of Norman Wait Harris and Emma Gale Harris, who donated to the University a fund to be known as "The Norman Wait Harris Memorial Foundation" on January 27, 1923. The letter of gift contains the following statement:

The purpose of the foundation shall be the promotion of a better understanding on the part of American citizens of the other peoples of the world, thus establishing a basis for improved international relations and a more enlightened world-order. The aim shall always be to give accurate information, not to propagate opinion.

Annual Institutes have been held at the University of Chicago since the summer of 1924. The lectures contained in this volume were delivered at the twenty-seventh Institute, June 18–21, 1951. Previous volumes in this series are available to readers who wish to obtain the lectures presented in the past.

THE UNIVERSITY OF CHICAGO PRESS, CHICAGO 37
Cambridge University Press, London, N.W. 1, England

Copyright 1952 by The University of Chicago. All rights reserved
Published 1952. Composed and printed by THE UNIVERSITY OF
CHICAGO PRESS, *Chicago, Illinois, U.S.A.*

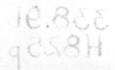

PREFACE

IN RECENT years interest on the part of social scientists in the problem of economic development and associated cultural changes has shown a steady increase. The reason for this has been partly the publicity given to the fourth point in President Truman's Inaugural Address of January, 1949, but partly also the preoccupation with developmental aid discussed and administered by the United Nations and its specialized agencies. In view of this great interest which has been aroused in this problem, which originates from the needs of making urgent practical policy decisions in this field, social scientists have been pressed into service. Their advice has been sought, and their intellectual and practical aid has been eagerly welcomed. But, as soon as social scientists reflected on the problems of economic development, they started to probe more deeply and began to ask questions which tended to lay bare some of the fundamental aspects of the conditions and accompanying circumstances of economic growth. The first two problems that required analysis were the elaboration of a conceptual and theoretical structure and the delineation of a general orientation. What is meant by economic development—and the derived concept "underdeveloped country"—and in what way, if any, are the policies associated with economic development at the present different from earlier practice? If there are "developed" or "advanced" countries in the present, they must have at some time been "underdeveloped," and the question may properly be asked whether and to what extent the past history of the economic development of the more advanced countries can serve as a model for the present and immediate future of "underdeveloped" countries.

It was obvious, therefore, that one way of reaching a general theoretical schema for the study of economic development consisted in the attempt of deriving generally valid propositions from the economic and social history of advanced countries. So long as this procedure was confined to the analysis and relation of purely or predominantly economic variables, it produced useful results the wider applicability of which became contingent upon the comparability of the over-all social and cultural framework of different human groups undergoing economic change. But the problem of comparability of different social and cultural frameworks, except in such general terms as to be operationally almost meaningless, imposed the need of supplementing the historical study with careful examination of factors belonging to the realms of social science in general. Thus it was found that the study of economic development not only extends into the field of history but also embraces areas of anthropology, sociology, and politics. Since the social institutions of populations in the process of development are closely related to those customarily designated as "primitive," a relevant aspect of the study of economic advancement consists in the determination of those culture traits which are hospitable and those which are inhospitable to innovation in the economic and technological fields. This observation comes close to an admission that, in the study of economic and technological development, the ultimate determinants of growth processes cannot fully be understood without crossing the line which separates economics from social anthropology.

A couple of simple examples will make this clear. Among the acknowledged factors crucial for the form and possibility of economic growth are the existence of innovations (i.e., the use of new methods of production) and the mobilization of real savings designed to serve as funds for the accumulation of capital which embodies these innovations in the form of new plants, machinery, tools, and other instruments. Now by means of economic analysis the mutual relations between these variables can be stated, and their relative magnitudes estimated and compared. But whether and what kind of innovations find a fruitful soil in a given society, what forms and mechanisms are most adequate to provide the real savings and make it possible to channel them into productive investment, cannot be answered by the economist, because the factors determining the rate of innovations, the disposal of income, and the form and rate of savings lie in the cultural and social conditions of a given population and not in their economy.

PREFACE

A second instance may be drawn from the area of developmental planning. Since planned development implies social accounting, an estimate of social costs may be made a conscious part of the development plan. Economic development, especially rapid development, is accompanied by social disorganization in many areas. But social disorganization implies many costs, some of which can be estimated in monetary terms. Industrialization especially, and the accompanying process of urbanization, may mean an increase in physical and mental ill-health, an increase in crime and other forms of conflict, the development of ethnic discrimination, and often the growth of those aspects of personal and group disorganization resulting from an increase in *anomie*. It calls for the establishment of new social services, new public utilities, and the vast enlargement of an administrative apparatus. Not all these social costs can be foreseen or estimated correctly, but the very recognition of these problems and their inclusion in some form in developmental plans means that such planning ceases to have a purely economic dimension. Developmental planning becomes, then, a procedure of analyzing social and cultural change and transforming its variables, wherever possible, into magnitudes that are quantifiable and hence measurable in economic terms. If this procedure is employed, the study of economic development breaks the bounds of traditional economics and spills over into the realm of general sociological analysis.

But, as has been pointed out earlier, the study of economic development not only represents a problem area in which lines between traditional social science disciplines must be crossed but also calls for procedures which permit the translation and adaptation of theoretical findings to practical policy. This is by no means a simple problem, because the objectives and means of the social scientist and the policy-maker are often diverse. The former is searching for general propositions and, normally, does not mind if his search takes him through lengthy speculations; the latter is concerned with finding very specific, workable answers to very specific concrete problems and usually must give these answers within a short, exactly prescribed time. A full-scale attack on the problem of economic development implies thus the building of bridges between social scientists of different specialties and interests, on the one hand, and between theoreticians and practical men of action, on the other.

The Twenty-seventh Institute of the Norman Wait Harris Memorial Foundation at the University of Chicago was devoted to throw light on these problems. Rather than summarizing anthropological, economic, and administrative knowledge pertinent to the process of economic growth, it was set up to determine and elucidate the issues which lead to fuller and better communication between specialists in several social science fields and between social scientists and public policy-makers. The participants represented the various social science disciplines as well as the public agencies engaged in technical aid programs, and the papers collected in this volume were presented at the various sessions of the Institute. Although written by specialists, they all manifest the view that economic development must be looked at as a problem area with dimensions in several social science fields. They all stress the human implications of technological and economic change, and they all display full awareness of the differences in culture, political and social structure, and systems of values and beliefs which are ever present in the study of economic and technological advancement.

My colleagues on the Committee of the Norman Wait Harris Memorial Foundation and in the Division of the Social Sciences at the University of Chicago have been liberal with aid and advice in planning the Institute. Miss Inez Gray has helped with typing the manuscript, and most valuable aid was given by Miss Elizabeth Sterenberg, who not only made all the technical arrangements for a successful Institute but also contributed in many ways in the preparation of this volume for publication. I have the pleasant duty of extending my sincere thanks to all these persons for their help. Most of all, I am indebted to the authors of the chapters of this volume for their generosity in preparing the papers and their patience with my editorial idiosyncrasies.

BERT F. HOSELITZ

UNIVERSITY OF CHICAGO
November 1951

TABLE OF CONTENTS

TABLE OF CONTENTS

PART I
THE HISTORICAL APPROACH TO ECONOMIC GROWTH

ECONOMIC BACKWARDNESS IN HISTORICAL PERSPECTIVE

By ALEXANDER GERSCHENKRON

INTRODUCTORY

A HISTORICAL approach to current problems calls perhaps for a word of explanation. Unlike so many of their predecessors, modern historians no longer announce to the world what inevitably will, or at least what ideally should, happen. We have grown modest. The prophetic fervor was bound to vanish together with the childlike faith in a perfectly comprehensible past whose flow was determined by some exceedingly simple and general historical law. Between Seneca's assertion of the absolute certainty of our knowledge of the past and Goethe's description of history as a book eternally kept under seven seals, between the *omnia certa sunt* of the one and the *ignorabimus* of the other, modern historical relativism moves gingerly. Modern historians realize full well that comprehension of the past—and that perforce means the past itself—changes perpetually with the historian's emphasis, interest, and point of view. The search is no longer for a determination of the course of human events as ubiquitous and invariant as that of the course of the planets. The iron necessity of historical processes has been discarded. But along with what John Stuart Mill once called "the slavery of antecedent circumstances" have been demolished the great bridges between the past and the future upon which the nineteenth-century mind used to travel so safely and so confidently.

Does this mean that history cannot contribute anything to the understanding of current problems? Historical research consists essentially in application to empirical material of various sets of empirically derived hypothetical generalizations and in testing the closeness of the resulting fit, in the hope that in this way certain uniformities, certain typical situations, and certain typical relationships among individual factors in these situations can be ascertained. None of these lends itself to easy extrapolations. All that can be achieved is the extraction from the vast storehouse of the past sets of intelligent questions that may be addressed to current materials. The importance of this contribution should not be exaggerated. But it should not be underrated either. For the quality of our understanding of current problems depends largely on the broadness of our frame of reference. Insularity is a limitation on comprehension. But insularity in thinking is not peculiar to any special geographic area. Furthermore, it is not only a spatial but also a temporal problem. All decisions in the field of economic policies are essentially decisions with regard to combinations of a number of relevant factors. And the historians' contribution consists in pointing at *potentially* relevant factors and at *potentially* significant combinations among them which could not be easily perceived within a more limited sphere of experience. These are the questions. The answers themselves, however, are a different matter. No past experience, however rich, and no historical research, however thorough, can save the living generation the creative task of finding their own answers and shaping their own future. The following remarks, therefore, purport to do no more than to point at some relationships which existed in the past and the consideration of which in current discussions might prove useful.

THE ELEMENTS OF BACKWARDNESS

A good deal of our thinking about industrialization of backward countries is dominated—consciously or unconsciously—by the grand Marxian generalization according to which it is the history of advanced or established industrial countries which traces out the road of development for the more backward countries. "The industrially more developed country presents to the less developed country a picture of the latter's future."[1] There is little doubt that in some broad sense this generalization has validity. It is meaningful to say that Germany, between the middle and the end of the last century, followed the road which England began to tread at an earlier time. But one

1. Karl Marx, *Das Kapital* (1st ed.), Vol. I, Preface.

should beware of accepting such a generalization too whole-heartedly. For the half-truth that it contains is likely to conceal the existence of the other half, that is to say, that in a number of most important respects the development of a backward country may, by the very virtue of its backwardness, tend to differ fundamentally from that of an advanced country.

It is the main proposition of this paper that in a number of important historical instances industrialization processes, when at length launched in a backward country, showed considerable differences, as compared with more advanced countries, not only with regard to the speed of the development (i.e., the rate of industrial growth), but also with respect to the productive and organizational structures of industry which emerged from those processes. Furthermore, these differences in speed and character of the industrial development were to a considerable extent the result of application of institutional instruments for which there was little or no counterpart in an established industrial country. In addition, the intellectual climate, within which industrialization proceeded, its "spirit" or "ideology," differed considerably as among advanced and backward countries. Finally, the extent to which these attributes of backwardness occurred in individual instances appears to have varied directly with the degree of backwardness and the natural industrial potentialities of the countries concerned.

Let us first describe in general terms a few basic elements in the industrialization processes of backward countries as synthe-sized from the available historical information on economic development of European countries[2] in the nineteenth century and up until the beginning of the first World War. Thereupon, on the basis of concrete examples, more will be said on the effects of what may be called "relative backwardness" upon the course of industrial development in individual countries.

The typical situation in a backward country prior to the initiation of considerable industrialization processes may be described as characterized by the tension between the actual

2. It would have been extremely desirable to transcend the European experience at least by including some references to the industrialization of Japan. Unfortunately, the writer's ignorance of Japanese economic history has effectively barred him from thus broadening the scope of his observations.

state of economic activities in the country and the existing obstacles to industrial development, on the one hand, and the great promise inherent in such a development, on the other. The extent of opportunities that industrialization presents varied, or course, with the individual country's endowment of natural resources. Furthermore, no industrialization seemed possible, and hence no "tension" existed, as long as certain formidable institutional obstacles (such as, for example, the serfdom of the peasantry or far-reaching absence of political unification) remained. Assuming an adequate endowment of usable resources as given, and assuming that the great blocks to industrialization had been removed, the opportunities inherent in industrialization may be said to vary directly with the backwardness of the country. Industrialization always seemed the more promising the greater the backlog of technological innovations which the backward country could take over from the more advanced country. Borrowed technology, so much and so rightly stressed by Veblen, was one of the primary factors assuring a high speed of development in a backward country entering the stage of industrialization. There always has been the inevitable tendency to deride the backward country on account of its lack of originality. German mining engineers of the sixteenth century accused the English of being but slavish imitators of German methods, and the English fully reciprocated these charges in the fifties and sixties of the past century. In our own days, Soviet Russia has been said to have been altogether imitative in its industrial development, and the Russians have retorted by making extraordinary and extravagant claims. But all these superficialities tend to blur the basic fact that the contingency of large imports of foreign machinery and of foreign know-how and the concomitant opportunities for rapid industrialization with the passage of time increasingly widened the gulf between economic potentialities and economic actualities in backward countries.

The industrialization prospects of an underdeveloped country are frequently judged, and judged adversely, in terms of cheapness of labor in terms of capital goods and of the resulting difficulty in substituting scarce capital for abundant labor. Sometimes, on the contrary, the cheapness of labor in a backward country is said to aid greatly in the processes of industrialization. The actual situation, however, is more complex than would appear on the basis of simple models. In reality, conditions will vary from industry to industry and from country to country. But the overriding fact to consider is that industrial labor in the sense of a stable, reliable, and disciplined group that has cut the umbilical cord connecting it with the land and has become suitable for utilization in factories is not abundant but extremely scarce in a backward country. Creation of an industrial labor force that really deserves its name is a most difficult and protracted process. The history of Russian industry provides some striking illustrations in this respect. Many a German industrial laborer of the nineteenth century had been raised in the strict discipline of a *Junker* estate which presumably made him more amenable to accept the rigors of factory rules. And, yet, the difficulties were great, and one may recall the admiring and envious glances which, toward the very end of the century, German writers, like Schulze-Gaevernitz, kept casting across the Channel at the English industrial worker, "the man of the future . . . [who,] born and educated for the machine, . . . does not find his equal in the past." In our days, reports from industries in India repeat in a still more exaggerated form the past predicaments of European industrializations in the field of labor supply.

Under these conditions the statement may be hazarded that, to the extent that industrialization took place, it was largely by application of the most modern and efficient techniques that backward countries could hope to achieve success, particularly if their industrialization proceeded in the face of competition from the advanced country. The advantages inherent in the use of technologically superior equipment were not counteracted but reinforced by its labor-saving effect. This seems to explain the tendency on the part of backward countries to concentrate at a relatively early point of their industrialization on promotion of such branches of industrial activities in which recent technological progress had been particularly rapid; while the more advanced countries, either from inertia or from unwillingness to require or impose sacrifices implicit in a large investment program, were more hesitant to carry out continual modernizations of their plant. Clearly, there are limits to such a policy, one of them being the inability of a backward country to extend them to lines of output where very special technological skills are required. Backward countries (although not the United States) were slow to assimilate production of modern machine tools. But a branch like iron and steel production does provide a very clear example of the tendency to introduce most modern innovations, and it is instructive to see, for example, how German blast furnaces so very soon become superior to the English ones, while in the early years of this century blast furnaces in still more backward Russia (South) were in the process of outstripping in equipment their German counterparts. Conversely, in the nineteenth century, England's superiority in cotton textile output was challenged neither by Germany nor by any other country.

To a considerable extent (as in the case of blast furnaces just cited) utilization of modern techniques required, in nineteenth-century conditions, increases in the average size of plant. Stress on bigness in this sense can be found in the history of most countries on the European continent. But industrialization of backward countries in Europe reveals a tendency toward bigness in another sense. The use of the term "industrial revolution" has been exposed to a good many justifiable strictures. But, if industrial revolution is conceived as denoting no more than cases of sudden considerable increases in the rate of industrial growth, there is little doubt that in several important instances, industrial development began in such a sudden, eruptive, that is, "revolutionary," way.

The discontinuity was not accidental. As likely as not the period of stagnation (in the "physiocratic" sense of a period of low rate of growth) can be terminated and industrialization processes begun only if the industrialization movement can proceed, as it were, along a broad front, starting simultaneously along many lines of economic activities. This is partly the result of the existence of complementarity and indivisibilities in economic processes. Railroads cannot be built unless coal mines are opened up at the same time; building half a railroad will not do if an inland center is to be connected with a port city. Fruits of industrial progress in certain lines are received as external economies by other branches of industry whose progress in turn accords benefts to the former. In viewing the economic history of Europe in the nineteenth century, the impression is very strong that only when industrial development could commence on a large scale did the tension between the pre-industrialization conditions and the benefts that may be expected from industrialization become sufficiently strong to overcome the existing obstacles and to liberate the forces that made for industrial progress.

This aspect of the development may be conceived in terms of Toynbee's relation between challenge and response. Toynbee's general observation that very frequently small challenges do not produce any responses and that the volume of response begins to grow very rapidly (at least up to a point) as the volume of the challenge increases seems to be quite applicable here. The challege, that is to say, the "tension," must be considerable before a response in terms of industrial development will materialize.

The foregoing sketch purported to list a number of basic factors which historically were peculiar to economic situations in backward countries and made for higher speed of growth and different productive structure of industries in backward as compared with more advanced countries. The effect of these basic factors was, however, greatly reinforced by the use in backward countries of certain institutional instruments and the acceptance of specific industrialization ideologies. In the following, some of these specific factors and their mode of operation on various levels of backwardness is discussed.

THE BANKS

The history of the Second Empire in France provides rather striking illustrations of these processes. The advent of Napoleon III terminated a long period of relative economic stagnation which had begun with the restoration of the Bourbons and which in some sense and to some extent was the result of the industrial policies pursued by Napoleon I. Through a policy of reduction of tariff duties and elimination of import prohibitions, culminating in the Cobden-Chevalier treaty of 1860, the French government destroyed the hothouse in which French industry had been kept for decades and exposed it to the stimulating atmosphere of international competition. By abolishing monopoly profits in the stagnating coal and iron production, French industry at length received profitable access to basic industrial raw materials.

To a not inconsiderable extent the fine industrial development of France under Napleon III must be attributed to that determined effort to untie the strait jacket in which weak governments and strong vested interests had inclosed the French economy. But along with these essentially, though not exclusively, negative policies of the government, French industry received a powerful positive impetus from a different quarter. The reference is to the development of industrial banking under Napoleon III.

The importance of that development has seldom been fully appreciated. Nor has it been properly understood as emanating from the specific conditions of a relatively backward economy. In particular, the story of the Crédit Mobilier of the brothers Pereire is often regarded as a dramatic but, on the whole, rather insignificant episode. All too often, as, for instance, in the powerful novels of Émile Zola, the actual significance of the developments is almost completely submerged in the description of speculative fever, corruption, and immorality which accompanied them. It seems to be much better in accord with the facts to speak of a truly momentous role of investment banking of the period for the economic history of France and of large portions of the Continent.

In saying that, one has in mind, of course, the immediate effects of creating financial organizations designed to build thousands of miles of railroads, drill mines, erect factories, pierce canals, construct ports, and modernize cities. The ventures of the Pereires and of a few others did all that in France and beyond the boundaries of France over vast areas stretching from Spain to Russia. This tremendous change in economic scenery took place only a few years after a great statesman and a great historian of the July monarchy assured the country that there was no need to reduce the duties on iron because the sheltered French iron production was quite able to cope with the iron needs of the railroads on the basis of his estimate of a prospective annual increase in construction by some fifteen to twenty miles.

But no less important than the actual economic accomplishments of a few men of great entrepreneurial vigor was their effect on their environment. The Crédit Mobilier was from the beginning engaged in a most violent conflict with the representatives of "old wealth" in French banking, most notably with the Rothschilds. It was this conflict that had sapped the force of the institution and was primarily responsible for its eventual collapse in 1867. But what is so seldom realized is that in the course of this conflict the "new wealth" succeeded in forcing the "old wealth" to adopt the policies of its opponents. The limitation of old wealth in banking policies to flotations of government loans and foreign-exchange transactions could not be maintained in the face of the new competitors. When the Rothschilds prevented the Pereires from establishing the Austrian Credit Anstalt, they succeeded only because they became willing to establish the bank themselves and to conduct it not as an old-fashioned banking enterprise but as a *crédit mobilier*, that is, as a bank devoted to railroadization and industrialization of the country.

This conversion of the old wealth to the creed of the new wealth points out the direction of the most far-reaching effects of the Crédit Mobilier. Occasional ventures of that sort had been in existence in Belgium, Germany, and France herself. But it was the great eruptive effect of the Pereires that profoundly influenced the history of Continental banking in Europe from the second half of the past century onward. The number of banks in various countries shaped upon the image of the Pereire bank was considerable. But more important than their slavish imitations was the creative adaptation of the basic idea of the Pereires and its incorporation in the new type of bank, the *universal bank*, which in Germany, along with most other countries on the Continent, became the dominant form of banking. The difference between banks of the *crédit mobilier* type and commercial banks in the advanced industrial country of the time (i.e., England) was absolute. Between the English bank essentially designed to serve as a source of short-term capital and a bank designed to finance the long-run investment needs of the economy there was a complete gulf. The German banks, which may be taken as a paragon of the type of the *universal bank*, successfully combined the basic idea of the *crédit mobilier* with the short-term activities of commercial banks.

They were as a result infinitely sounder financial institutions than the Crédit Mobilier, with its enormously swollen industrial portfolio, which greatly exceeded its capital, and its dependence on favorable developments on the stock exchange for continuation of its activities. But the German banks, and along with them the Austrian and Italian banks, established the closest possible relations with industrial enterprises. A German bank, as the saying went, accompanied an industrial enterprise from the cradle to the grave, from establishment to liquidation throughout all the vicissitudes of its existence. Through the device of formally short-term but in reality long-term current account credits and through developments of the institution of the supervisory boards to the position of most powerful organs within corporate organizations, the banks acquired a formidable degree of ascendancy over industrial enterprises, which extended far beyond the sphere of financial control into that of entrepreneurial and managerial decisions.

It cannot be the purpose of this presentation to go into details of this development. All that is necessary is to relate its origins and its effects to the subject under discussion. The industrialization of England had proceeded without any substantial utilization of banking for long-term investment purposes. The more gradual character of the industrialization process, and the more considerable accumulation of capital, first from earnings in trade and modernized agriculture and later from industry itself, obviated the pressure for developing any special institutional devices for provision of long-term capital to industry. By contrast, in a relatively backward country capital is scarce and diffused, the distrust of industrial activities is considerable, and, f.nally, there is greater pressure for bigness in industrial processes because of the scope of the industrialization movement, larger average size of plant, and the concentration of industrialization processes on branches of relatively high ratios of capital to output. To these should be added the scarcity of entrepreneurial talent in the backward country.

It is the pressure of these circumstances which essentially gave rise to the divergent development in banking over large portions of the Continent as against England. The Continental practices in the f.eld of industrial investment banking must be conceived as specific instruments of industrialization in a backward country. It is here essentially that lies the historical and geographic locus of theories of economic development that assign a central role to processes of forced saving by money-creating activities of the banks. As will be shown presently, however, use of such instruments must be regarded as speci..c, not to backward countries in general, but rather to countries whose backwardness does not exceed certain limits. And even within the latter for a rather long time it was mere collection and distribution of available funds in which the banks were primarily engaged. This circumstance, of course, did not detract from the paramount importance of such activities on the part of the banks during the earlier industrialization periods with their desperate shortages of capital for industrial ventures.

The effects of these policies were far-reaching. All the basic tendencies inherent in industrial development in backward countries were greatly emphasized and mangified by deliberate attitudes on the part of the banks. From the outset of this evolution the banks were primarily attracted to certain lines of production to the neglect, if not virtual exclusion, of others. To consider Germany until the outbreak of World War I, it was essentially coal-mining, iron- and steelmaking, electrical and general engineering, and heavy chemical output which became the primary sphere of activities of German banks. The textile industry, the leather industry, and the foodstuff-producing industries remained on the fringes of the banks' interest. To use a modern terminology, it was heavy rather than light industry to which the attention was devoted.

Furthermore, the effects were not confined to the productive structure of industry. They extended to its organizational structure. The last three decades of the nineteenth century were marked by a rapid concentration movement in banking. This process indeed went on in very much the same way on the other side of the English Channel. But in Britain, because of the different nature of relations between banks and industry, the process was not paralleled by a similar development in industry.

It was different in Germany. The momentum shown by the cartelization movement of German industry cannot be fully explained, except as the natural result of the amalgamation of German banks. It was the mergers in the field of banking that kept placing banks in the positions of controlling competing enterprises. The banks refused to tolerate fractricidal struggles among their children. From the vantage point of centralized control they were at all times quick to perceive profitable opportunities of cartelization and amalgamation of industrial enterprises. In the process the average size of plant kept growing, and at the same time the interests of the banks and their assistance were even more than before devoted to those branches of industry where cartelization opportunities were rife.

Germany thus had derived full advantages from being a relatively late arrival in the field of industrial development, that is to say, from having been preceded by England. But, as a result, German industrial economy, because of specific methods used in the catching-up process, developed along lines not insignificantly different from those in England.

THE STATE

The German experience can be generalized. Similar developments took place in Austria, or rather in the western sections of the Austrian-Hungarian Empire, in Italy, in Switzerland, in France, in Belgium, and in other countries, even though there were not inconsiderable differences as among the individual countries. But it certainly cannot be generalized for the European continent as a whole, and this for two reasons: (*a*) because of the existence of certain backward countries where no comparable features of industrial development can be discovered and (*b*) because of the existence of countries where the basic elements of backwardness appear in such an accentuated form as to lead to the use of essentially different institutional instruments of industrialization.

Little need be said with reference to the first type of countries. The industrial development of Denmark may serve as an appropriate illustration. Surely, that country was still very backward as the nineteenth century entered upon its second half. Yet, no comparable sudden spurts of industrialization and no peculiar emphasis on heavy industries could be observed. The reasons must be sought, on the one hand, in the paucity of the country's natural resources and, on the other hand, in the great opportunities for agricultural improvement that were inherent in the proximity of the English market. The peculiar response did not materialize because of the absence of the challenge.

Russia may be considered as the clearest instance of the second type of country. The characteristic feature of economic conditions in Russia was not only that the great spurt of modern industrialization came in the middle of the eighties of the last century, that is to say, more than three decades after the beginning of rapid industrialization in Germany; even more important was the fact that at the starting point the level of economic development in Russia had been incomparably lower than that of countries such as Germany or Austria.

The main reason for the abysmal economic backwardness of Russia was the preservation of serfdom until the emancipation of 1861. In a certain sense, this very fact may be attributed to the play of a curious mechanism of economic backwardness, and a few words of explanation may be in order. In the course of its process of territorial expansion which over a few centuries transferred the small duchy of Moscow into the huge land mass of modern Russia, the country became increasingly involved in military conflicts with the West. This involvement revealed a curious internal conflict between the tasks of the Russian government which were "modern" in the contemporaneous sense of the word and the hopelessly backward economy of the country on which the military policies had to be based. As a result, the economic development in Russia at several important junctures assumed the form of a peculiar series of sequences: (1) Basic was the fact that the state, moved by its military interest, assumed the role of the primary agent propelling the economic progress in the country. (2) The fact that economic development thus became a function of military exigencies imparted a peculiarly jerky character to the course of that development; it proceeded fast whenever military necessities were pressing and subsided as the military pressures relaxed. (3) This mode of economic progress by fits and starts implied that, whenever a considerable upsurge of economic activities was required, a very formidable burden was placed on the shoulders of the generations whose life-span happened to coincide with the period of intensified development. (4) In order to exact effectively the great sacrifices it required, the government had to subject the reluctant population to a number of severe measures of oppression lest the burdens imposed be evaded by escape to the frontier regions in the southeast and east. (5) Precisely because of the magnitude of the governmental exactions, a period of rapid development was very likely to give way to prolonged stagnation, because the great effort had been pushed beyond the limits of physical endurance of the population, and prolonged periods of economic stagnation were the inevitable consequences.

The sequences just mentioned present in a schematic way a pattern of Russian economic development in past centuries which fits best the period of the great reforms under Peter the Great, but whose applicability is by no means confined to that period.

What must strike the observer of this development is its curiously paradoxical course. While trying, as Russia did under Peter the Great, to adopt Western techniques, to raise the levels of output and the skills of the population to levels more closely approaching those of the West, Russia by virtue of this very effort was in some other respects thrown further away from the West. Broadly speaking, placing the trammels of serfdom upon the Russian peasantry must be understood as the obverse side of the processes of Westernization. Peter the Great did not institute serfdom in Russia, but perhaps more than anyone else he did succeed in making it effective. When in subsequent periods, partly because of point (2) and partly because of point (5) above, the state withdrew from active promotion of economic development, and the nobility emancipated itself from its service obligations to the government, peasant serfdom was divested of its connection with economic development. What once was an indirect obligation to the state became a pure obligation toward the nobility and as such became by far the most important retarding factor in Russia's economic development.

Readers of Toynbee's may wish to regard this process, ending as it did with the emancipation of the peasantry, as an expression of the "withdrawal and return" sequence. Alternatively they may justifiably prefer to place it under the heading of "arrested civilizations." At any rate, the challenge-response mechanism is certainly useful in thinking about sequences of that nature. It should be noted, however, that the problem is not simply one of "quantitative" relationship between the volume of the challenge and that of the response. The crucial point is that the magnitude of the challenge changes the *quality* of the response and, by so doing, not only injects powerful retarding factors into the economic process but also more likely leads to a number of undesirable noneconomic consequences. To this aspect, which is most relevant to the current problem of industrialization of backward countries, we shall advert again in the concluding remarks of this paper.

To return to Russian industrialization in the eighties and the nineties of the past century, it may be said that in one sense it can be conceived of as a recurrence of a previous pattern of economic development in the country, that is to say, with regard to the role of the state in that development. This distinguishes rather clearly the type of Russian industrialization from its German or Austrian counterpart.

Emancipation of the peasants, despite its manifold deficiencies, was an absolute prerequisite for industrialization. As such it was a negative action of the state designed to remove obstacles that had been earlier created by the state itself and in this sense fully comparable to acts such as the agrarian reforms in Germany or the policies of Napoleon III which have been mentioned earlier. Similarly, the great judicial and administrative reforms of the sixties were in the nature of creating a suitable framework for industrial development rather than promoting it directly.

The main point of interest here is that, unlike the case of western Europe, actions of this sort did not per se lead to an upsurge of individual activities in the country; and for almost a quarter of a century after the emancipation the rate of industrial growth remained relatively low. The great industrial upswing came when, from the middle of the eighties on, the railroad-building of the state assumed unprecedented proportions and became the main lever of a rapid industrialization policy. Through multifarious devices such as preferential orders to domestic producers of railroad materials, high prices, subsidies, credits, and profit guaranties to new industrial enterprises, the government succeeded in maintaining a high and, in fact, increasing rate of growth until the end of the century. Concomitantly, the Russian taxation system was reorganized, and the finacing of industrialization policies was thus provided for, while the stabilization of the ruble and the introduction of the gold standrd assured foreign participation in the development of Russian industry.

The basic elements of a backward economy were, on the whole, the same in Russia of the nineties and in Germany of the fifties. But quantitatively the differences were formidable. The scarcity of capital in Russia was such that no banking system could conceivably succeed in attracting sufficient funds to finance a large-scale industrialization; the standards of honesty in business were so disastrously low, the general distrust of the public so great, that no bank could have hoped to attract even such small capital funds as were available, and no bank could have successfully engaged in long-term credit policies in an economy where fraudulent bankruptcy had been almost elevated to the rank of a general business practice. Supply of capital for the needs of industrialization required the compulsory machinery of the government, which, through its taxation policies, succeeded in directing incomes from consumption to investment. There is no doubt that the government as an *agens movens* of industrialization discharged its role in a far less than perfectly efficient manner. Incompetence and corruption of bureaucracy were great. The amount of waste that accompanied the process was formidable. But, when all is said and done, the great success of the policies pursued under Vyshnegradski and Witte is undeniable, and what matters primarily from the point of view of this paper is the similarity not only in the origins but also in the effects of the policies pursued by the state in Russia. The Russian government of the nineties did not evince any interest in "light industry." Its whole attention was centered on output of basic industrial materials and on machinery production; like the banks in Germany, the Russian bureaucracy was primarily interested in large-scale enterprises and in amalgamations and co-ordinated policies among the industrial enterprises which it favored or had helped to create. Clearly, a good deal of the government's interest in industrialization was predicated upon its military policies. But these policies only reinforced and accentuated the basic tendencies of industrialization in conditions of economic backwardness.

Perhaps nothing serves to emphasize more these basic uniformities in the situation and the dependence of actual institutional instruments used on the degree of backwardness of the country than a comparison of policies pursued within the two halves of the Austrian-Hungarian monarchy, that is to say, within one and the same political body. The Austrian part of the monarchy was backward in relation to, say, Germany, but it was at all times much more advanced than its Hungarian counterpart. Accordingly, in Austria proper the banks could successfully devote themselves to the promotion of industrial activities. But across the Leitha Mountains, in Hungary, the activities of the banks proved altogether inadequate, and around the turn of the century the Hungarian government embarked upon vigorous policies of industrialization. Originally, the government showed a considerable interest in developing the textile industry of the region. And it is instructive to watch how, under the pressure of what the French like to call the "logic of things," the basic uniformities asserted themselves and how the generous government subsidies were more and more deflected from textile industries to promotion of "heavy industries."

THE GRADATIONS OF BACKWARDNESS

To return to the basic German-Russian paradigm: What has been said in the foregoing does not exhaust the pattern of parallels. The question remains as to the effects of successful industrializations, that is to say, of gradual diminution of backwardness.

At the turn of the century, if not somewhat earlier, changes became apparent in the relationship between the German banks and the German industry. As the former industrial infants had grown to strong manhood, the original undisputed ascendancy of the banks over industrial enterprises could no longer be maintained. This process of liberation of industry from the decades of tutelage expressed itself in a variety of ways. Increasingly, industrial enterprises transformed connection with a single bank into co-operation with several banks. As the former industrial protectorates became economically sovereign, they embarked upon the policy of changing alliances with regard to the banks. Many an industrial giant, such as the electrical engineering industry, which could not have developed but for the aid and entrepreneurial daring of the banks, began to establish its own banks. The conditions of capital scarcity to which the German banks owed their historical position were no longer present. Germany had become a developed industrial country. But the specific features engendered by a process of industrialization in conditions of backwardness were to remain, and so was the close relation between banks and industry, even though the master-servant relation gave way to co-operation among equals and sometimes was even reversed.

In Russia the magnificent period of industrial development of the nineties was cut short by the 1900 depression and the following years of war and civil strife. But, when Russia emerged from the revolutionary years 1905–6 and again achieved a high rate of industrial growth in the years 1907–14, the character of the industrialization processes had changed greatly. Railroad construction by the government continued but on a much smaller scale both absolutely and even more so relatively to the increased industrial output. Certain increases in military expenditures that took place could not begin to compensate for the reduced significance of railroad-building. The conclusion is inescapable that in that last period of industrialization under a prerevolutionary government the significance of the state was very greatly reduced.

At the same time the traditional pattern of Russian economic development happily failed to work itself out. The retrenchment of government activities led not to stagnation but to a continuation of industrial growth. Russian industry had reached a stage where it could throw away the crutches of government support and begin to walk independently—and, yet, very much less independently than in contemporaneous Germany, for at least to some extent the role of the retreating government was taken over by the banks.

A great transformation had taken place with regard to the latter during the fifty years that had elapsed since the emancipation. Commercial banks had been founded. Since it was the government that had fulfilled the function of industrial banks, the Russian banks, precisely because of the backwardness of the country, were organized as "deposit banks," thus resembling very much the type of banking in England. But, as industrial development proceeded apace and as capital accumulation increased as a result of this development, the standards of business behavior were growingly Westernized. The paralyzing atmosphere of distrust began to vanish, and the foundation was laid for the emergence of a different type of bank. Gradually, the Moscow "deposit" banks were overshadowed by the development of the St. Petersburg banks that were conducted upon principles that were characteristic not of English but of German banking. In short, after the economic backwardness of Russia had been reduced by state-sponsored industrialization processes, use of a different instrument of industrialization, suitable to the new "stage of backwardness," became applicable.

IDEOLOGIES OF DELAYED INDUSTRIALIZATIONS

Before drawing some general conclusions, a last differential aspect of industrialization in circumstances of economic backwardness should be mentioned. So far, important differences with regard to the character of industrial developments and its institutional vehicles were related to conditions and degrees of backwardness. A few words remain to be said on the ideological climate within which such industrializations proceeded.

Again we may revert to the instructive story of French industrialization under Napoleon III. A large proportion of the men who reached positions of economic and financial influence upon Napoleon's advent to power were not isolated individuals. They belonged to a rather well-defined group. They were not Bonapartists but Saint-Simonian socialists. The fact that a man like Isaac Pereire, who contributed so much, perhaps more than any other single person, to the spread of the modern capitalist system in France should have been—and should have remained to the end of his days—an ardent admirer of Saint-Simonian doctrines is on the face of it surprising. It becomes much less so if a few pertinent relationships are considered.

It could be argued that Saint-Simon was in reality far removed from being a socialist; that in his vision of an industrial society he hardly distinguished between laborers and employers; and that he considered the appropriate political form for his society of the future some kind of corporate state in which the "leaders of industry" would exercise major political functions. Yet arguments of that sort would hardly explain much. Saint-Simon had a profound interest in what he used to call the "most numerous and most suffering classes"; more importantly, Saint-Simonian doctrines, as expanded and redefined by the followers of the master (particularly by Bazard), incorporated into the system a good many socialist ideas, including abolition of inheritance and establishment of a system of planned economy designed to direct and to develop the economy of the country. And it was this interpretation of the doctrines which the Pereires accepted.

It is more relevant to point to the stress laid by Saint-Simon and his followers upon industrialization and the great task they had assigned to banks as an instrument of organization and development of the economy. This, no doubt, greatly appealed to the creators of the Crédit Mobilier, who liked to think of their institution as of a "bank to a higher power"and of themselves as "missionaries" rather than bankers. That Saint-Simon's stress upon the role to be played by the banks in economic development revealed a truly amazing—and altogether "un-utopian"—insight into the problems of that development is as true as the fact that Saint-Simonian ideas most decisively influenced the course of economic events inside and outside France. But the question remains: Why was the socialist garment draped around an essentially capitalist idea? And why was it the socialist form that was so readily accepted by the greatest capitalist entrepreneurs France ever possessed?

It would seem that the answer must again be given in terms of basic conditions of backwardness. Saint-Simon, the friend of J. B. Say, was never far removed from ideas of laissez faire policies. Chevalier, the co-author of the Franco-English treaty of commerce of 1860 that ushered in the great period of European free trade, had been an ardent Saint-Simonian. And yet under French conditions a laissez faire ideology was altogether inadequate as a spiritual vehicle of an industrialization program.

To break through the barriers of stagnation in a backward country, to ignite the imaginations of men, and to place their energies in the service of economic development, a stronger medicine is needed than the promise of better allocation of resources or even of the lower price of bread. Under such conditions even the businessman, even the classical daring and innovating entrepreneur, needs a more powerful stimulus than the prospect of high profits. What is needed to move the mountains of routine and prejudice is faith—faith, in the words of Saint-Simon, that the golden age lies not behind but ahead of mankind. It was not for nothing that Saint-Simon devoted his last years to the formulation of a new creed, the "New Christianity," and suffered Auguste Comte to break with him over this "betrayal of true science." What sufficed in England did not suffice in France.

Shortly before his death Saint-Simon urged Rouget de Lisle, the aged author of the "Marseillaise," to compose a new anthem, an "Industrial Marseillaise." Rouget de Lisle complied. In the new hymn the man who once had called upon "enfants de la patrie" to wage ruthless war upon the tyrants and their mercenary cohorts addresses himself to "enfants de l'industrie" —the "true nobles"—who would assure the "happiness of all" by spreading industrial arts and by submitting the world to the peaceful "laws of industry."

Ricardo is not known to have inspired anyone to change "God Save the King" into "God Save Industry." No one would want to detract from the force of John Bright's passionate eloquence, but in an advanced country rational arguments in favor of industrialization policies need not be supplemented by a quasi-religious fervor. Buckle was not far wrong when in a famous passage of his *History* he presented the conversion of public opinion in England to free trade as achieved by the force of incontrovertible logic. In a backward country the great and sudden industrialization effort calls for a New Deal in emotions. Those carrying out the great transformation as well as those on whom it imposes burdens must feel, in the words of Matthew Arnold, that

> . . . Clearing a stage
> Scattering the past about
> Comes the new age.

Capitalist industrialization under the auspices of socialist ideologies may be, after all, less surprising a phenomenon than would appear at first sight.

Similarly, Friedrich List's industrialization theories may be largely conceived as an attempt, by a man whose personal ties to Saint-Simonians had been very strong, to translate the inspirational message of Saint-Simonism into a language that would be accepted in the German environment, where the lack of both a preceding political revolution and a national unification rendered nationalist sentiment a much more suitable ideology of industrialization than the socialism of Saint-Simon's.

After what has been just said it will perhaps not be found

astonishing that, in the Russian industrialization of the 1890's, orthodox Marxism can be said to have performed a very similar function. Nothing reconciled the Russian intelligentsia more to the advent of capitalism in the country and to the destruction of its old faith in the *mir* and the *artel* than a system of ideas which presented the capitalist industrialization of the country as the result of an iron law of historical development. It is this connection which largely explains the power wielded by Marxist thought in Russia of the period when it extended to men like Struve and in some sense even Miliukov, whose Weltanschauung was altogether alien to the ideas of Marxian socialism. In conditions of Russian "absolute" backwardness again a much more powerful ideology was required to grease the intellectual and emotional wheels of industrialization than either in France or in Germany. The institutional gradations of backwardness seem to find their counterpart in men's thinking about backwardness and the way in which it can be abolished.

CONCLUDING REMARKS

The story of European industrialization in the nineteenth century would seem to yield a few points of view which may be helpful for appreciation of present-day problems.

1. If the spurtlike character of the past century's industrialization on the European continent is conceived of as the result of the specific pre-industrial situations in backward countries and if it is understood that pressures for high-speed industrializations are inherent in those situations, it should become easier to appreciate the oft-expressed desires in this direction on the part of the governments of those countries. Slogans like "Factories quick!" which played such a large part in the discussions of the pertinent portions of the International Trade Organization charter, may then appear less unreasonable.

2. Similarly, the tendencies in backward countries to concentrate much of their efforts on introduction of the most modern and expensive technology, their stress on large-scale plant, and their interest in developing investment goods industries need not necessarily be regarded as flowing mainly from a quest for prestige and economic megalomania.

3. What makes it so difficult for an advanced country to appraise properly the industrialization policies of its less fortunate brethren is the fact that in every instance of industrialization imitation of the evolution in advanced countries appears in combination with different, indigenously determined elements. If it is not always easy for advanced countries to accept the former, it is even more difficult for them to acquiesce in the latter. This is particularly true of the institutional instruments used in carrying out industrial developments and even more so of "ideologies" which accompany it. What can be derived from a historical review is a strong sense for the significance of the native elements in industrializations of backward countries.

A journey through the last century may, by destroying what Bertrand Russell once called the "dogmatism of the untravelled," help in formulating a broader and more enlightened view of the pertinent problems and in replacing the absolute notions of what is "right" and what is "wrong" by a more flexible and relativistic approach.

It is, of course, not suggested here that current policies vis-à-vis backward areas should be formulated on the basis of the general experience of the past century without taking into account, in each individual instance, the degree of endowment with natural resources, the climactic disabilities, the strength of institutional obstacles to industrialization, the pattern of foreign trade, and other pertinent factors. But what is even more important from the point of view of this paper is the fact that, useful as the "lessons" of the nineteenth century may be, they cannot properly be applied without understanding the climate of the present century, which in so many ways has added new and momentous aspects to the problems concerned.

Since the present problem of industrialization of backward areas largely concerns non-European countries, there is the question of the effects of their specific pre-industrial cultural development upon their industrialization potentialities. Anthropological research of such cultural patterns has tended to come to rather pessimistic conclusions in this respect. But perhaps such conclusions are unduly lacking in dynamic perspective. At any rate, they do not deal with the individual factors involved in terms of their specific changeabilities. At the same time, past Russian experience does show how quickly in the last decades of the past century a pattern of life that had been so strongly opposed to industrial values and that tended to consider any nonagricultural economic activity as unnatural and sinful began to give way to very different attitudes. In particular, the rapid emergence of native entrepreneurs with peasant-serf backgrounds should give pause to those who stress so greatly the disabling lack of entrepreneurial qualities in backward civilizations. Yet, there are other problems.

In certain extensive backward areas the very fact that industrial development has been so long delayed has created, along with unprecedented opportunities for technological progress, also great obstacles to industrialization. Industrial progress is arduous and expensive; medical progress is cheaper and easier of accomplishment. To the extent that the latter has preceded the former by a considerable span of time and has resulted in formidable overpopulation, industrial revolutions may be defeated by Malthusian counterrevolutions.

Closely related to the preceding but enormously more momentous in its effects is the fact that great delays in industrialization tend to allow time for social tensions to develop and to assume sinister proportions. As a mild example, the case of Mexico may be cited, where the established banks have been reluctant to co-operate in industrialization activities that are sponsored by a government whose radical hue they distrust. But the real case in point overshadowing everything else in scope and importance is, of course, that of Soviet Russia.

If what has been said in the preceding pages has validity, the Soviet industrialization undoubtedly contains all the basic elements that were common to the industrializations of backward countries in the nineteenth century. The stress on heavy industry and oversized plant is, as such, by no means peculiar to Soviet Russia. But what is true is that in Soviet Russia those common features of industrialization processes have been magnified and distorted out of all proportions.

The problem is as much a political as it is an economic one. The Soviet government can be properly described as a product of the country's economic backwardness. Had serfdom been abolished by Catherine the Great or at the time of the Decembrists' uprising in 1825, the peasant discontent, the driving force and the earnest of success of the Russian Revolution, would never have assumed disastrous proportions, while the economic development of the country would have proceeded in a much more gradual fashion. If anything is a "grounded historical assumption," this would seem to be one: the delayed industrial revolution was responsible for a political revolution in the course of which the power fell in the hands of a dictatorial government to which in the long run the vast majority of the population was opposed. It is one thing for such a government to gain power in a moment of great crisis; it is another to maintain this power for a long period. Whatever the strength of the army and the ubiquitousness of the secret police which such a government may have at its disposal, it would be naïve to believe that those instruments of physical oppression can suffice. Such a government can maintain itself in power only if it succeeds in making people believe that it performs an important social function which could not be discharged in its absence.

Industrialization provided such a function for the Soviet government. All the basic factors in the situation of the country pressed in that direction. By reverting to a pattern of economic development that should have remained confined to a long-bygone age, by substituting collectivization for serfdom, and by pushing up the rate of investment to the maximum point within the limits of endurance of the population, the Soviet government did what no government relying on the consent of the governed could have done. That these policies, after having led through a period of violent struggles, have resulted in permanent day-to-day friction between the government and the population is undeniable. But, paradoxical as it may sound, these policies at the same time have secured some broad acquiescence on the part of the population. If all the forces of the population can be kept engaged in the processes of industrialization and if this industrialization can be justified by the promise of happiness and abundance for future generations and—much more importantly—by the menace of military aggression from beyond the boundaries, the dictatorial government will find its power broadly unchallenged. And the vindication of a threatening war is easily produced, as is shown by the history of the last five years. Economic backwardness, rapid industrialization, ruthless exercise of dictatorial power, and the danger of war have become inextricably intertwined in Soviet Russia.

This is not the place to elaborate this point further with regard to Soviet Russia. The problem at hand is not Soviet Russia but the problem of attitudes toward industrialization of backward countries. If the Soviet experience teaches anything, it is that it demonstrates *ad oculos* the formidable dangers inherent in our time in the existence of economic backwardness. There are no four-lane highways through the parks of industrial progress. The road may lead from backwardness to dictatorship and from dictatorship to war. In conditions of a "bipolar world" this sinister sequence is modified and aggrandized by deliberate imitation of Soviet policies by other backward countries and by the latter's voluntary or involuntary incorporation in the Soviet orbit.

Thus, conclusions can be drawn from the historical experience of both centuries. The paramount lesson of the twentieth century is that the problems of backward nations are not exclusively their own. They are just as much problems of the advanced countries. It is not only Russia but the whole world that pays the price for the failure to emancipate the Russian peasants and to embark upon industrialization policies at an early time. Advanced countries cannot afford to ignore economic backwardness.

But the lesson of the nineteenth century is that the policies toward the backward countries are unlikely to be successful if they ignore the basic peculiarities of economic backwardness. Only by frankly recognizing their existence and strength and by attempting to develop fully rather than to stifle what Keynes once called the "possibilities of things" can the experience of the nineteenth century be used to avert the threat presented by its successor.

POLITICAL ELITES AND THE PROCESS OF ECONOMIC DEVELOPMENT

By ROBERT K. LAMB

T HE struggle now going on around the globe is about the terms on which people in underdeveloped countries are going to organize their societies so as to live in an industrial age. Their elites are seeking, as did the American Revolutionary elite, to form new nation-states for the sake of national development. The struggle of these peoples for self-determination is complicated by the fact that the world is polarizing around two great powers, exponents of two very different answers to this global problem.

The American answers are those of an elite forced by events to form a commercial nation-state; the Russian answers are those of an elite forced by events to form an industrial nation-state.

These answers arise from the conditions surrounding these two revolutions, more than a hundred and twenty-five years apart, and from the measures taken by the American and Russian elites during the formation of these two nations. The United States, like the Union of Soviet Socialist Republics, was in many senses an underdeveloped country when it was transformed into a new nation-state by a revolution led by a new elite. This paper shows how circumstances attendant upon the organization of these two nation-states have contributed to the present polarization of the world and what this means for people in underdeveloped countries today who are seeking to organize their societies so as to live with machines.

The present aligning of the world between Russia and the United States is recent, but the roots go back a long way. Only since 1914 has the economic center of the world capitalist community shifted from London to New York; the political capital only shifted to Washington in 1939. By these recent shifts we

Americans became the heirs to the world-wide political and economic responsibilities carried for nearly two centuries by the British Empire and the London metropolitan economy. The Russians, the first challengers of the Anglo-American coalition who operate outside the orbit of the London metropolitan economy, are heirs to a tradition at least as old as the French Revolution.

The challenge of the Russians to the Anglo-American coalition arises from the fact that they are organizing their own world metropolitan community around their answer to the global problem of how to live with machines. They say that a machine civilization needs a new society led by a new elite and that the value system for this society is communism.

The United States was organized to provide new answers as to how to live with the commercial revolution, at a time when machine civilization was just getting a start in Britain and before either country had faced the implications of the industrial revolution for the organization of nation-states. This country, by a century and a half of development of the industrial revolution within a commercial society, has become the greatest exponent of private enterprise as the answer to how to live with machines. We head a coalition of allied nations seeking to defend this way of life and hold this leadership as the oldest nation in the world still living under its original system of political, social, and economic organization.

The contrast between the type of nation-state formed by the new Russian elite outside the Old World economy and the types of nation-states developed by English and Americans, or Germans, Italians, or Japanese, inside the London economy becomes fundamental to our understanding of the issues arising in today's polarized world. To instal a complex of modern technology into the isolated Russia of 1917 called for the development of highly organized new institutions and new techniques under the direction of a whole new range of social, political, and economic leadership, a new Soviet elite. The old methods of organizing national elites as decision-makers for commercial nation-states were too difficult for, and perhaps unavailable to, a country which had driven out or destroyed its relatively small aristocracy and business class and wanted to become a great industrial nation quickly.

Before we start to explore the conditions surrounding the American and Russian revolutions and the measures taken by the elites of these two countries during the formation of these two nations, I propose to discuss certain definitions. For example, what is an elite? Why is a discussion of elites linked in this paper to a metropolis? What is a world metropolitan community, and how does an elite in a given metropolis come to leadership of such a community?

"Metropolis," as here used, means an urban center where major decisions are made for a larger community—a surrounding city-state, nation-state, or world metropolitan community. Those who occupy the strategic points of decision-making in a metropolis and control its decisions are here called its "elite," regardless of whether these strategic points over which they preside are economic, social, or political. The elite in a metropolis is only part of the larger body of elite needed to direct the affairs of a whole community; but, because of its central position, it tends to preside over the major decisions for that community.

Elites, in the process of organizing or reorganizing city-states, nation-states, or world metropolitan communities, must work with the materials provided them by history and within the social situation they inherit. Their success depends upon their ability to transform these inherited factors into a new system directed toward their new goals. These new elites derive much of their strength and effectiveness from the history of their development as an elite in and around a given metropolis. This metropolitan center is a training ground for new elites, as it has been for oncoming generations of the old elite.

The role of a metropolis varies with the size of the community for which it serves as center; the size of such a metropolitan community depends in turn on its stage of development. London secured its position as the center of an emergent national and international metropolitan economy not only by reason of its role as Britain's capital but as the heir to a series of European city-states. This development runs back at least to the Fourth Crusade, when the Venetians diverted the Crusaders to an attack on Constantinople and spread commercialism in expanding waves, decade by decade, throughout Europe.

To see the commercial revolution in perspective, we need to understand how European commercial city-states were formed, how side by side with them nation-states arose, how in a few instances the two forms were merged, and how one commercial nation-state, Britain, became the center of the world's metropolitan economy.

City-states have generally been commercial communities whose close interpersonal relations give them great internal strength and hence require a minimum of formal political or social institutions. Their elites are usually closely knit by intermarriages and name their members to political positions in the ruling oligarchy. Economically, they depend on long lines of communication, with markets and borrowers around the world, and so are vulnerable to sudden crises such as overtook the Bardi and Peruzzi in Florence when Edward III of England went bankrupt in the fourteenth century. Nation-states provide a national political economy over which the elite can exercise more complete control but only by greater concern with military and diplomatic problems.

A national elite, by merging the forms of city-state and nation-state, can introduce rule by oligarchy into a constitutional monarchy and give their nation a social flexibility not common to absolute monarchies. Since nation-states derived from feudal principalities, and these in turn from the manorial system, nationalism carries with it feudal principles of rights and obligations different from the contractual relationships inherent in the commercial city-state. Feudalism also carries with it the principles of the aristocratic landed family system, with its emphasis on primogeniture.

The absolute monarchy is the feudal family "writ large" and endowed with the "divine right of kings." It becomes, in turn, the defender of a system of nobility, even while it tries to bend the nobles to the king's will; it defends especially the inheritance rights of the landed gentry, as we can see by a rereading of Sir Robert Filmer's *Patriarcha*, to which Locke's *First Treatise on Government* is an answer. The mercantile family, by contrast, builds itself around the family firm; this attempt by the family group to perpetuate itself established the firm as one of the forerunners of the corporation. Firms help to reinsure the ventures of family members but suffer from the handicaps of unlimited liability. The joint-stock and limited liability companies are attempts to spread the risks to others inside and outside the group. Merger of the nation-state and city-state systems gives the national elite new flexibility by permitting it to manipulate national sovereignty so as to experiment with new forms of organization of power and control.

When the commercial operations of a nation-state expand to the proportions of a world metropolitan community, the elite must assume new and greater responsibilities. Yet an expanding commercial community lends itself to manipulation and control by an elite trained to rule a combined imperial and metropolitan economic system.

The transformation of the London metropolitan economy after 1689 into the leading contender for the role of capital of a world metropolitan community depended upon the formation a hundred years earlier of a new group among the English elite, trained in the struggle against Spain, who combined in a national coalition leaders of English political, social, and economic affairs, centered on the commerce of the City of London. In 1689, by overthrowing the Stuarts, who tied England to the absolute monarchies of the Continent, and by bringing in William and Mary as constitutional monarchs, the English created a new-model nation-state directed toward the goals of the commercial revolution. When elites come to power in periods of crisis, they do so in part by their ability to rally the community around a drive for new goals and by their skill in propounding a new value system acceptable usually to a majority of the community. This system of ideas and aims provides the framework within which the elite organizes a new structure of power and control. Because of the formal organization of political institutions, we are familiar with the political structure of society (at least its *formal* structure) but relatively unfamiliar with the structure of economic and social power and control.

To see the connection of ideas and social structure, consider the relation to the Revolution of 1689 of Locke's *Treatises on Government*, and the Declaration of Right, wherein the ideas about "life, liberty, and property," "social contract," and the right of revolution as an "appeal to heaven" are set forth. These are the justifications of the political, economic, and social measures of the Glorious Revolution. Read the pamphlets and correspondence Locke and his friends wrote on the reform of the coinage, formation of the Bank of England, and reorganization of the East India Company and the Board of Trade and Plantations; and remember that within the generation between 1689 and 1720 the English elite established a national bank based on a funded national debt, a national money market tied to a national treasury, and a political party system operating through a national parliament.

The American elite, with whom we are particularly concerned in this paper, were the direct heirs of the British Whig revolution and the exponents of the value system of Locke and his friends. They laid down in the Declaration of Independence, the Constitution, and the Bill of Rights the rules under which we still operate, rules for protecting "life, liberty, and property," to use Locke's phrase, for which Jefferson substituted "life, liberty, and the pursuit of happiness." These are the rules whereby the elite of a national political economy can administer a private enterprise system and a market economy. They are based upon contractual relationships between men. In the century and a half since we ratified our written Constitution the British have more than once altered their unwritten constitution to adjust Britain's political economy to the demands of its political parties, looking toward state intervention and, more recently, toward socialism. The American value system, still based on "the pursuit of happiness," has enabled this country to become the rallying point for all other nations within the orbit of the Anglo-American coalition.

The values of the American patriots grew out of the Whig Revolution of 1689, but the British Whigs of 1760 had lost not only their revolutionary zeal but their ability to work together. Had the Whig coalition been able to hold power, the American

Revolution might have been postponed, perhaps indefinitely, and the United States might have become a British dominion, as Franklin hoped it would. The growth of a series of city-states in the North American colonies required a new plan for organizing the London metropolitan economy; the simultaneous defeat of the French around the globe, but especially in India, confronted the British Whig party with great imperial decisions at just that time when its own family coalition was falling apart. Many of these British families operated in the colonies through American Whig friends and relatives who considered independence only as a last resort. The Walpoles and other leading Whigs were working with Franklin to try to put together an international consortium which would support an American confederation; these maneuvers depended upon an alliance with France and the restoration of the Whigs to British cabinet control. Their failure ended the hopes of Americans for dominion status.

By 1774, therefore, the problem of the American elite was how to found a separate commercial nation-state within the orbit of the London metropolitan economy. The Americans realized between 1774 and 1776, when they declared their independence, that the ingredients needed for forming a new American nation were independence, alliance, and confederation. In short, they must work out a close-knit national political economy around the Continental Congress and persuade nations rivaling London's political economy to enter into alliances with them if they were to secure even *political* independence from the metropolis. With victory they could hope to negotiate to return within London's orbit.

To achieve such a new national system, they must alter their own social structure as an elite. The development of each elite requires some system of social mobility and some method for self-perpetuation; the means whereby elites maintain themselves differ markedly from one society to another; they express the style of each elite and their solutions to the problems confronting them. Like most early aristocracies, the American elite (including merchants and landed gentry) were bound together by the family system and its extended-kinship groups. These families dominated the towns and counties of each original colony and gave each little city-state its own indigenous aristocracy. As the Revolution approached, this divided into a "prerogative party" supporting the royal governor and forming a majority of his council, opposed by a "country party" of patriots who dominated the local assemblies. Often the patriots were as aristocratic as the king's supporters; many were large landholders and speculators in frontier lands, whose sons became leading merchants. Their interests, however, were more closely tied to the soil and shipping of the colonies than to the mother-country. In various colonies the "prerogative party" was heavily dependent on official positions granted by royal governors, and in many colonies the patriots were especially offended by payment of official salaries out of royal fees and customs dues and not by grant of the assemblies.

Until the Revolution began, these quarrels were localized, colony by colony, although the committees of correspondence did their best to spread them. After the Revolution started, the scale of operations of the new American elite was enlarged from that of the original colonies to national and even international proportions; division of function was called for, and what had been hitherto a fairly homogeneous elite began to divide into subelites responsible for political, economic, and social decision-making. During the Revolution and down through the Federalist administrations of Washington and Adams, a majority of the elite were aristocrats trained by tradition to play many roles as magistrate, legislator, soldier, frontiersman, merchant, and often farmer and surveyor.

In the years before the Revolution and increasingly during and after the Revolution, a new elite was emerging, largely self-made. To be sure, most of these men owed their rise to favors from the aristocracy. The war, however, called for new methods of tying groups of men together outside the family system, and insurance companies or offices, joint privateering ventures, speculative land companies, and many other devices became the forerunners of banks and joint-stock corporations. The British had kept a tight rein on corporation charters and had abolished one Colonial bank after another. The protection of a new nation-state was needed to set the new and more impersonal trend into full motion.

The American Revolutionary elite, who aimed at adapting the social institutions inherited from the British to the needs of a continental political economy, had to invent or develop new social institutions—new at least in the form used in the United States: political parties based on a broad franchise, corporations deriving their sovereignty from individual states and not from the federal government, religious organizations guaranteed freedom of worship, and other voluntary associations whose freedom of speech and right of assembly were insured by the Bill of Rights. Above all, the American elite established the interdependent system of executive, legislative, and judicial institutions of our new commercial nation-state. They created a national bank, a national foreign office (the State Department), and national military and naval establishments. By the time the Washington administration was launched under the new Constitution, the elite had evolved a *new-model* nation-state, a republic which has stood the test of time. As its greatest bulwark, they lodged decisions about its national sovereignty in a Supreme Court composed of judges chosen for life. In the United States the symbol of the Constitution as the sovereign law replaced the sovereign king; divine right of kings was no longer the means for justifying the hereditary privileges of primogeniture and a closed aristocracy. The social contract holds American society together.

To run this new-model nation-state called, however, for the creation of a new-model elite. As division of function increased, so did the problem of how to maintain social cohesion. Here, Americans owe much to Jefferson's establishment of an open-ended aristocracy giving leadership to the pursuit of life, liberty, and property. In Virginia, Jefferson pressed for the removal of primogeniture, and by the national election of 1800 he defeated the Federalists and destroyed their national party, advocates of rule by aristocracy. He did not destroy Hamilton's centralized system of control over the national political economy, but he did change its base from that of a more-or-less closed aristocracy of extended-kinship groups. Jefferson, by the Louisiana Purchase and the formation of the Democratic-Republican party as the successor to the Federalists' power, shifted the foundation of the American political economy for a century afterward and based it on the individual property-holder and the family-sized farm. A new and mobile American elite grew from the merger of the Hamiltonian economic and the Jeffersonian political principles. A social elite set the standards for admission to an aristocracy of breeding and wealth, a political elite controlled the new party system, and an economic elite provided the wherewithal to maintain control of the political economy of the United States in the hands of a coalition of these three groups working together.

By 1815, when the United States negotiated a junior economic partnership in the London metropolitan economy, both Britain and America were faced by the problem of how to incorporate the industrial revolution within the commercial revolution. Insular Britain and continental America had each to work out a different solution, and these differences go far to explain the roles their elites have played in the world from 1815 to the present time. Just as the limited resources of the British Isles had long since forced the British elite to develop maritime commerce and naval power, so now, as industry grew, its products were diverted toward the development of overseas markets which were in turn tied to the London metropolitan economy. Thus the industrial revolution served to reinforce the commercial revolution as a means for making London the commercial capital of the world community. The industrial revolution combined also with the political effects of the American and French revolutions to force Britain to adjust her imperial structure and to alter her social structure, reducing the role of her landlords and increasing the political influence of her industrial magnates (of course, industrialists continued to buy landed estates and become landlords). These shifts in political and economic power were signalized by the Reform Acts of 1832 and 1867 and by the repeal of the Corn Laws. Such measures gave Britain a new flexibility, that of a middle-class democracy, led by an elite combining landlords, merchants, and industrialists, operating a world-wide market economy. A place could be found among the nobility for successful members of the rising elite. Securely above and beyond the social grading system stood the British royal family, whose personal sovereignty held the empire together. This social grading system ran remarkably serenely until the eve of the first World War, when the Labour party appeared and began to tear the social fabric.

The continental American economy had no need throughout the nineteenth century for such a close-knit social structure as that dominated by the British aristocracy. Momentum drew American society together. Centralization was not something the Americans had constantly to strive for; theirs was no globe-girdling empire like the British. Developing within a continent so vast and so well supplied with natural resources, the American people developed an industrial system inside a commercial economy and created a new national metropolitan community directed by an expanding elite centered economically in New York and politically in Washington. They did this, however, with the aid of loans from the London metropolitan economy and continued to hold their junior economic partnership within the British Empire down to 1914, supplying Britain with the bulk of its cotton, wheat, and many other raw materials. So long as this subordinate relationship continued, the United States was one of the two chief pillars of the London metropolitan economy, the other being India.

Until the American Civil War most great industrial fortunes represented the investment of surplus accumulated in commerce (many of them in trade with China and India following the lead of Britain), and those family fortunes have dominated the Atlantic seaboard cities until quite recently. The railway revolution starting in 1830 shifted this balance somewhat; railway financing called for widespread development of the corporate device and encouraged speculation in railway securities.

The northern Civil War economy produced an economic transformation comparable only to that of the American Revolutionary war economy in our previous history. Out of it came the National Banking Act of 1863 and the Fourteenth Amendment to the Constitution, later interpreted by the Supreme Court as conferring increasing federal protection on the person of the individual corporation, as if the Constitution had intended to protect its rights rather than those of the human individual. This reinterpretation of the Constitution, although undoubtedly in the spirit of John Marshall's decisions regarding the "contract clause," represents a great shift in the American system of values since the American Revolution. The corporate revolution which it made possible has rendered the political economy of the United States increasingly less flexible; the ensuing growth of big business has called for parallel growth of big government and big labor.

However inflexible the continental economy of the United States was becoming by 1914, its industrial power and its huge domestic market made it a massive challenger operating within the London metropolitan economy. Americans returned to large-scale foreign trade after the Spanish-American War, capturing British markets in the Orient with petroleum and other mass produced goods and invading Europe and other continents with efficient American machinery and machine tools developed for the mass markets of our continental economy. Because of the intimate financial and commercial connections maintained between Britain and the United States, Americans enjoyed a status approaching that of citizens of a British dominion but with an unexampled political independence. The crisis of 1914 enabled Anglo-American bankers and statesmen to reverse the terms of the economic partnership, raising the United States to senior economic partner.

The coming of peace showed the duality which is basic to the American political economy: our isolationism and our expansionism; we owe them both—in large measure—to our continental opportunities. The American "melting pot" has brought to our shores millions of people who are only too glad to turn their backs on the countries of their origin; their children, often ashamed of their parents' immigrant status, have frequently become advocates of "isolationism," as they are bound to be also strong supporters of expansionism in "the pursuit of happiness." The Republican party won the national elections of 1920 by advocating "minding our own business" and staying out of the League of Nations, at a time when some of the most prominent Republican international lawyers and financiers were working to prop up the economies of Europe.

As the heirs to the London metropolitan economy our bankers were obligated to salvage their wartime investment in Allied victory. As members of an American elite whose training for generations had been concentrated on the development of a continental economy, they wanted to assume a minimum of the world-wide political responsibilities so long carried by the elite of the British Empire. Throughout the postwar decade of the 1920's, the American people and their leaders tried to turn their backs on the rest of the world and concentrate on the expansion of America's capacity to produce and consume the products of our great continental industrial system. Yet year by year it was increasingly apparent that the economic center of the world metropolitan community had shifted from London to New York and that the political center was shifting to Washington.

The American elite realized correctly that the American people and the political economy of the United States were not ready for these responsibilities, but they found more and more of them thrust upon this country. The market crash of 1929 revealed how truly unready we were, and its international repercussions led to the release of fascism as a threat to world peace.

Our economic unreadiness was aggravated by the decline of the London metroplitan economy. If the commercial system centered on Britain was no longer operable by an island people whose needs for imports were necessarily high, how could a continental economy like the United States become the hub of a world commercial system? Our political unreadiness was revealed by our dismay at the rise of fascism. If the constitutional systems exported by Britain and America could be so easily overthrown in advanced countries like Germany, Italy, and Japan, what hope was there that less-developed countries could make constitutionalism work? Although, before the outbreak of fascism, there had been a hundred years of imitation of Anglo-American forms of political and economic organization, parliamentary or congressional democracy had not worked outside the Anglo-Saxon world with anything like the efficiency of its master-models. The exceptions were small countries like those of Scandinavia and elsewhere, which had usually grafted the forms on their own native patterns developed before the industrial revolution.

Within the orbit of the Anglo-American metropolitan community, however, one after another of the new nations has imitated, with wide variations, the Anglo-American models of nation-states organized for private enterprise. They have entered into the commercial framework and the market economy centered on London but have attempted to modify it to fit the goals of their elites. All of these larger nations except Britain, America, and France have been formed as new nation-states since the second half of the nineteenth century began and so have imported the industrial revolution as a large-scale complex unit. None of these new nations except the British dominions has held a relationship to London in any way comparable to that of the United States. Starting with the German *Zollverein*, each nation has tried to maintain a measure of national independence from the London metropolitan economy; but the failure of Napoleon's continental system insured that none of these rival European nations could have a market large enough to threaten the British commercial system without war, and this showdown was postponed until 1914.

The case of France deserves brief separate consideration. Its revolution ended the domination of Europe by absolute monarchy, although it did not destroy the influence of European feudal aristocratic families even in France. The French elite in the period between 1789 and 1815 paved the way for the ultimate victory of constitutional monarchies and republics throughout the Continent and established the first modern European nation-state within the London metropolitan economy. Because the French Revolution and especially Napoleon's land reform required a balance in France between peasant small holdings and Parisian metropolitanism as the basis for social equilibrium, the French post-revolutionary elite never produced a serious threat to the British metropolitan economy. The French revolutionary tradition kept her in ferment throughout the nineteenth century, but in no case did these crises transform

France into an aggressive modern nation-state comparable to Germany, Italy, or Japan. After 1870 the French lost the territories bordering on Germany needed to make France a first-rate industrial power but stabilized their political economy so successfully as to become the bankers for many eastern European countries and especially for czarist Russia; France played this role as the satellite of the London metropolitan economy.

It remained for the elites of Germany, Italy, and Japan, in a series of national crises around the year 1870, to develop a new type of aggressive nation-state. In each case an elite, organized around a semifeudal aristocracy, produced a modern nation-state and imported from abroad the nineteenth century-forms of social, political, and economic life necessary to create modern industrial societies.

We can hardly exaggerate the importance of the date at which these new nation-states were formed. New mass-production methods in steelmaking were replacing iron with steel products, and electrical engineers were developing the dynamo and the central power station experimentally during the early years of life of these new nations. The massive effect of the complex of modern industrial capitalism which they took over insured the rapid economic growth of their national societies. These peoples were heavily agrarian at the time their new nations were formed. None of these nations had enjoyed the advantages of a long period of commercial expansion in modern times such as characterized the histories of Britain, France, and the United States (although Italy during the Renaissance and Germany during the days of the Hanseatic League had an earlier city-state development). Each had a relatively rigid social hierarchy in which the ruling classes had long been accustomed to impose their authority on the underlying population. By enabling a feudalistic aristocracy with military traditions to control a highly developed system of commercial and industrial capitalism, and by subordinating the new business elite to them, these nations confronted the world with three aggressive and expansive new competitors.

So long as they could expand at the expense of weaker peoples (e.g., the expansion of Germany into the Balkans, of Italy into North Africa, and of Japan into East Asia), no showdown developed between the Anglo-American coalition and these challengers. Once they found themselves checked diplomatically and militarily, however, their appearance of constitutionalism disappeared through a merger of feudal, commercial, and industrial elements into one monolithic totalitarian regime; and their aggressive tendencies took the path of military adventure. Two world wars were required to destroy their challenge to the Anglo-American system of economic, social, and political organization.

The removal of these challengers within the Anglo-American orbit cost the British their rank as a first-rate power and left the United States to confront the Soviet metropolitan challenge.

If we pause, in our analysis of the effort of men to learn to live with the machine, to ask ourselves what it signified to have Britain lose her leadership of the world metropolitan community, we must conclude that the commercial revolution was over and that the underdeveloped nations of the globe were ready to domesticate the industrial revolution for themselves. By this we mean that commercialism had tied the peoples of the globe together in a network of trading relationships which centered on London and made them all—in varying degrees—members of a world-wide market economy. Through this market for goods and services the social systems of one people after another were transformed; they ceased to operate self-contained village societies and began to direct their efforts toward production for the market and purchase of many goods, even necessities, from outside their local economies. For the most part, except in the advanced countries of Europe and its offspring nations, the commercial revolution carried with it only a limited number of industrial accompaniments: a few railroads, some motor roads, and the equipment for modern urban living in a few larger communities, in one underdeveloped country or another.

The rise of nationalism among these underdeveloped countries after the first World War led to increasing demand for their national self-sufficiency. Nationalism, especially when embodied in tariff barriers and other restraints on international trade, was the enemy of the London metropolitan economy.

Britain's aggressive form of free trade was a kind of imperialism, requiring other nations to tie themselves to the British commercial system for the mutual benefit of all participants. Refusal of other nations to play the game deprived Britain of her leadership.

Britain's loss of world leadership marked also the end of European political and economic domination of the other nations of the globe. Britain had acted as the pivot around which all those European nations with interests in underdeveloped countries had organized their economic and political lives. The acceptance by the United States during the second World War of the political as well as the economic responsibilities previously borne by Britain has tended to obscure the degree of the crisis for Europe created by the passing of the world metropolitan economy centered on London. European nations, including Britain, still have great industrial capacity whose products are needed by the underdeveloped countries of the globe; but, unless those countries can buy European goods and especially European machinery on their own terms, they are prepared to go without or wait until they can produce their own.

The spread of the commercial and industrial revolutions around the globe has stirred one agrarian society after another into rapid social change. As these revolutions have moved along from countries like England and France, where the commercial revolution built modern democratic nation-states in settled agricultural nations, to virgin territories like those of the United States and the British Dominions, private enterprise systems have developed, populations have expanded to fill the vacant spaces, and new democratic societies have been formed. Feudalistic societies have been industralized and in the process have created trouble for their neighbors by the explosive mixture produced by combining authoritarianism with modern technology. Now the truly underdeveloped countries of the globe are on the move, and it is the spread of commerce and industry by the elites of Britain and Europe that has set them in motion.

The challenge of Soviet Russia arises from the fact that, at this juncture in world history when the underdeveloped countries of the globe are ready to domesticate the industrial revolution, the Russians have had thirty-five years of experience in industrializing their underdeveloped country. The Russians know the industrial revolution is today a complex entity which can be exported to the backward areas of the world, set up there, and made to run. They have developed a continental economy stretching from eastern Germany to Siberia, tied it together with hundreds of new urban centers, and organized at least its heavy industries along modern lines. They have centralized this society around the national metropolis of Moscow, which since the recent war is becoming the capital of its own Communist world metropolitan community. In the process they have drawn into their industrial society over a hundred peoples living within the borders of the Soviet Union and altered their traditional way of life.

To do this continent-wide job of urbanization and industrialization, the Soviet has developed a new kind of elite, the Communist party, to control an industrial society in which planned production has taken the place of private enterprise as the regulator of the economy. Lenin and his followers were building upon an ideological tradition derived from Karl Marx, Friedrich Engels, the philosophers of the Paris Commune of 1870, and many other socialist ideologies. The Bolsheviks built also upon the centuries-old foundations of communal living among the Russian people, as developed in the *mir*, the *artel*, and the Greek or Russian Orthodox church. These traditions emphasized collective responsibility for the individual, who in turn had the sins of omission and commission of the group on his own conscience. Just as the Anglo-Saxon owes a great debt to his heritage of individualism derived from individual responsibility for the group, developed in the folk-moot or town meeting, so the Russian is undoubtedly influenced by his recent emergence from a peasant past where these communal traditions were strong.

In addition to these deep-rooted social traditions, the fact that the Bolsheviks developed out of a long conspiratorial history of revolutionary action under the czars has left a deep mark on the Communist party. Likewise, the Communists operate within the general political history of Russia, where decentralization has been a recurring force, only offset by a recurring dictatorial centralism. The metropolitanism of Moscow, in other words, may have a somewhat different significance than the metropolitanism of London or New York; it may arise from Russia's deep need for central control to hold the country together to do the job its rulers have set it.

Political centralism in the West has sprung from the feudal system, by way of the divine right of kings, and has come to rest in national sovereignty. In a republic such as the United States the constitution as social contract is sovereign and gives sanction to the corporate groups which carry on its economic life. This tends to develop an economic hierarchy from the top down and a political system from the town or county up to the nation.

To understand these differences between the Russians and Americans, we have to revert to the conditions at the time of their revolutions. An American aristocracy only a century removed from many feudal forms, such as manorial landholding, emerged during the Revolution as an active economic, political, and social force for organizing a new nation-state and conferring power and control upon itself. By the development of the corporate form within which to inclose its economic activities, the American aristocracy pushed the commercial nation-state a new step forward. It created islands of economic sovereignty within a national political sovereignty. Economic, and to a considerable degree social, initiative has remained in these groups ever since. So long as they were operating within the framework of British commercialism, their emphasis was upon the market and upon a separation of government and business. Since America's coming of age, their assumption of increasing responsibility has taken the form of treating the workers, stockholders, distributors, and suppliers of their corporate systems as members of one great family, as we can see from the statements of the presidents of these corporations at their annual meetings. Their individualism produces a kind of paternalism (or industrial manorialism), and they continue reluctantly to endow the federal government with full social responsibility for the welfare of the individual citizen.

The fact that the Russians had had no such long history of development of their present social forms deprives us of direct parallels. It is worth noting, however, that the Russian industrial bureaucracy is not too different from that of the American. Each is dealing with comparable problems. Because the Russians have driven out those elements which had Western commercial traditions of individualism, the chief individualists are those old Bolsheviks who seized the initiative during the Russian revolution. For the most part, however, Russian decision-making is a collective party responsibility.

In the last analysis, we are discussing questions of power and control over decision-making. Ever since the American Revolution an elite have had the initiative in transforming this country economically, and they have been able to gain political sanction for their activities. It is this which has made the United States the greatest exponent of the private enterprise system. So long as they had responsibility only for the development of this continent, the fact that they were operating within the matrix of the British commercial revolution created a minimum of complications for the American elite. They were able to expand the industrial revolution in this framework without dangerous distortion of their methods of operation. The first World War changed all this. It changed it in many ways. The United States had been becoming more and more centralized in its operations around the economic capital of New York and the political capital of Washington. The war accelerated these trends and speeded up American industrialization so that, when peace came, there was no comparable industrial society on the globe.

The elite to conduct these continental, and increasingly global, operations was divided between an administrative hierarchy in business and government, whom we may call a "bureaucracy," and a limited number of men with initiative, whom we may call "entrepreneurs." The entrepreneurs were dedicated to control of a market economy, while the bureaucrats were increasingly interested in uninterrupted day-to-day operation of an industrial or governmental machine. In times of war and other social crises like the onset of the depression the interests of the two groups tended to merge in the running of what we may call a "mobilized economy." During intervals like that between 1920 and 1929, however, their ways diverged, and the entrepreneurs, operating in a speculative market for goods and services, produced a great boom and bust, at the same time that they were greatly enlarging the productive capacity of the American economy.

Since the beginning of the New Deal the distinction between political and economic leadership has been diminishing. More and more businessmen have been entering government, as they did during the first World War. The result is a new American political economy. This leadership has been thinking increasingly in global terms. It aspires to industrialize underdeveloped countries on its own terms. This means the use of development corporations and the acceptance by the peoples of these underdeveloped countries of some loss of sovereignty especially over those areas where the development corporations operate. The presence of such corporations tends to produce progressive social change in the surrounding areas as well as in the area directly controlled. Frequently those operating the American corporations have been unable to foresee the full consequences of their intervention. This is especially true of the effects of American sanitation of lowering the death rate and increasing the survival rate of small children. The accompanying pressures of population on resources and demand for higher standards of living frequently produce local political unrest and a demand by these American corporations for some form of American intervention.

The current contest between the Communist coalition and the Anglo-American coalition raises the question: Which coalition is more effective in industrializing the peoples of the underdeveloped areas of the globe?

Americans, as the heirs to the traditions of the London metropolitan economy, are trained in commercial techniques of trading for profit in underdeveloped areas. Since the first World War, with the decline of this world-wide commercial economy based on London, the rise of autarchy in the advanced nations, and nationalism in the more underdeveloped countries, the areas in which these commercial techniques are effective have shrunk and are continuing to shrink. These people all aspire to have balanced national economies, whether they are adequately supplied with local resources or not. Certain countries having critical raw materials or surpluses of foodstuffs for export can industrialize somewhat according to the old patterns, unless world mobilization curtails their imports of machinery. The international markets operating according to nineteenth-century patterns are not, however, going to industrialize the underdeveloped countries.

They are not because these countries are not satisfied to develop in the hit-or-miss fashion by which the industrial revolution was carried abroad by Britain and other commercial nations in the nineteenth century. They have seen the Russian continental economy industrialized in the last thirty-five years, and—however little they want to imitate the Russians politically—they want to industrailize in a hurry.

Spokesmen for these people in the United Nations and elsewhere indicate that their people do not want the Russians *or* the Americans to control the process. They want to industralize their own countries. Most of them have had all they want of foreign intervention. Technical assistance from abroad? Yes. Financial help? Yes. Materials and machinery? Yes. Yardsticks for measuring performance if further aid is to be given? Yes. Outside interference and control? No.

This calls for a new kind of foreign aid, administered through an international agency which attaches only the minimum number of safeguards. Acceptance of such a multilateral program for international economic development would call for as great adjustments in the Russian metropolitan economy as in our own. They are organized to incorporate adjacent nation-states into their orbit, as they have in the Balkans and Central Europe, on their own terms; the fact of contiguity has so far been indispensable to the Russian system. They have devised a continental metropolitan economy comparable to that of the United States in its expanse but comparable only to that of the American war economy in its form of organization.

The period since the depression began in the United States in

1929 has seen the growth in this country of a new type of economy. The American wartime economy temporarily abandoned many of the market devices and many of the rules of a peacetime capitalist economy in order to maximize output for military purposes. We could do this because the goods produced were designed to be blown up and thrown away. We could do it also because the American people would submit to this amount of regimentation during a temporary national emergency. The present defense mobilization presents new problems to the United States precisely because for the first time in our history we are talking about an emergency without a foreseeable end. We face such an emergency, I believe, because we have assumed responsibility for carrying the burdens of the Anglo-American world metropolitan economy at that moment in the world's history when this economy has a challenger from outside.

The strength of our metropolitan system lies in its expansionism. The more we adopt the attitude of "do to" and the less we use the methods of "do with," the more rigid our approach to the problems of other peoples becomes. We can already see what happens when a proposal like the Point IV program becomes involved with our military needs for strategic materials; the result is a report like "Partners for Progress," where the emphasis is upon ways of extracting necessary war goods from our underdeveloped neighbors around the globe. Most of us here can probably agree in general that a multilateral solution for the problems of underdeveloped areas is most desirable, but I will state it as my belief that we need to challenge the Russians to an economic competition for industrializing the underdeveloped areas of the globe through a multilateral program to be administered through the United Nations. We need to present this challenge to the United Nations and not merely to the Russians, and we need to offer it as the first step in a peaceful settlement of the current world conflict. I am naïve enough to believe that this is still within the realm of possibility. I am not so naïve as to think that this can be accomplished without changing the attitudes of the elites of both Russia and the United States.

It is my hope that, if the United States does not take the initiative, there are enough people in the United Nations who understand the need for multilateral programs of economic development to formulate a plan which the underdeveloped countries of the world can agree upon. This should then be presented to the Russians and to the United States for acceptance or rejection. These programs must relate the economic development of underdeveloped areas to the decentralization of power and control within the more advanced countries. The present centralization of decision-making in the metropolitan economies of both Russia and the United States is not healthy for peacetime operations.

A fully industrialized world is a world of regional metropolitan communities, interchanging scarce goods only until a chemical industry capable of developing and using atomic power produces synthetic goods cheaply enough to offset comparative advantage. This is the norm toward which we are moving, and, however long it is in coming, the growing pains as we develop toward it are sending tremors around the globe. The time has come for the advanced nations to recognize that they hold their comparative advantage "in trust."

Even sectional regions within the United States and other nations are confronted with this lesson: you cannot any longer get ahead by pushing the other fellow behind.

INTERNATIONAL MIGRATION AND THE ACQUISITION OF NEW SKILLS

By Oscar Handlin

THE period of international migration as we knew it down until the first World War seems quite definitely closed; and in that context the transfer of skills to underdeveloped areas through migration seems primarily a historical problem, one that was characteristic of a closed phase of our past. But since history, if it teaches at all, teaches by analogy, we may find problems analogous to those of the present in the past. In any case, we may be able through an examination of that earlier experience to throw light on certain matters of more general concern to social scientists.

Reviewing the experience of some three hundred years down to the first World War, I was most impressed by the constant faith shown both by individual enterprisers and by government planners that technical skills could be transferred without any substantial modification from one milieu to another; that the kind of abilities developed in one society could without any essential changes or adjustment be snatched out of their setting and applied in some society that was quite different. That faith obscured a genuine question whether a skill developed in a particular context and continuous with a particular social environment could be torn out of that context advantageously and moved to some other context—advantageously in the sense of a net gain to the society which loses the skill and to the society in which it is desired to be implanted.

To find the material for an answer to this question, I propose to examine very briefly a number of illustrative examples to see whether there is a basis for generalization as to the degree of success attained in such transfers and as to the nature of the encouraging or discouraging factors. I propose to draw these illustrations from the history of the United States, which was for a long time an underdeveloped area dependent on many kinds of technical assistance from the more developed cultures and economies of western Europe.

There were cases when these transfers were completely disastrous. Through the seventeenth-century records, for instance, move a whole series of shadowy, exotic figures—Greeks, Persians, Armenians, Poles, Germans, eastern Europeans of various kinds, as well as Frenchmen and Italians, sent to the new continent by hopeful enterprisers in the expectation that their skills in raising silk or making wine or manufacturing glass or the other desired commodities of trade could be put to use in the New World.[1] Generally the record mentions these people for a year or two before they fade away into an obscurity which is a sign of the lack of success of their enterprise. The lack of success is interesting, as is also the extent to which the mistakes were repeated over and over again throughout the seventeenth and the early part of the eighteenth centuries.

On a somewhat larger scale at the beginning of the eighteenth century was the attempt, partly financed by private enterprisers and partly by the crown itself, to develop a naval-stores industry in the Colonies with the aid of German Palatines, skilled artisans displaced by the religious wars and, to the number of almost five hundred, transplanted to New York. This is a well-known story—a story of successive failures, of the ultimate collapse of the enterprise, and of the dispersal of the colony.[2]

These illustrations reveal with some clarity the conditions under which the transfer of skill is unlikely to succeed. Here control of the transfer was entirely in the hands of the home government or of home companies which approached the problem with completely preconceived ideas as to the desirable commodities of trade and which attempted, in the light of immediate objectives of their own, to use the skills of the migrants without regard for the practical conditions of the colonies and the na-

1. *Records of the Virginia Company of London*, ed. Susan M. Kingsbury (Washington, 1906), I, 251, 252, 368, 466, 499, 633; also Louis Adamic, *Nation of Nations* (New York, 1945), p. 287.

2. Warren A. Knittle, *Early Eighteenth Century Palatine Emigration* (Philadelphia, 1937).

ture of the economy into which the migrants were moving. The fate of such ventures was more or less to be expected.

A second category of efforts to move skills achieved a continuing measure of success and offers a more positive model for examination. These cases involved the transfer by entrepreneurs of certain technical skills, often closely guarded secrets. In these movements the entrepreneurs who held these skills themselves came to the new country and were capable of applying those skills to the conditions of the new society by a continuing series of adjustments.

I have in mind such transfers as were made when the Dutch Jews, expelled from Brazil in the middle of the seventeenth century, brought the secrets of sugar manufacture to the West Indies; or when planters from the Barbados moved to South Carolina in the early eighteenth century and brought the techniques of rice and cotton planting with them. In the eighteenth century a series of moves brought to Rhode Island, again through Portuguese Jews, the secrets of the manufacture of spermaceti candles and formed the basis for a very significant extension of the industrial life and the commercial enterprises of that colony.[3] More familiar instances come from our own industrial history: the migration of Samuel Slater with the secrets of cotton manufacture; of the Schofields with the plans for woolen mills; and, in the nineteenth century, of a critical group of German families who introduced the techniques of the brewing, the printing, the optical, the chemical, and the piano industries.[4]

These transfers possessed a number of common characteristics. First, there was a very high economic value on the technique itself, which gave an enormous advantage to those

3. See Samuel Oppenheim, *An Early Jewish Colony in Western Guiana* ("Publications of the American Jewish Historical Society," Vol. XVI), pp. 97 ff., 138 ff.; Herbert I. Bloom, *A Study of Brazilian Jewish History, 1623–1654* ("Publications of the American Jewish Historical Society," Vol. XXXIII), p. 101; Lee M. Friedman, *Jewish Pioneers and Patriots* (Philadelphia, 1948), pp. 303 ff.; Edward McCrady, *History of South Carolina under the Proprietary Government, 1670–1719* (New York, 1897), p. 357.

4. Caroline F. Ware, *The Early New England Cotton Manufacture* (Boston, 1931), pp. 19, 21 ff.; Arthur Harrison Cole, *The American Wool Manufacture* (Cambridge, 1926), I, 88 ff.; Albert Bernhardt Faust, *The German Element in the United States* (New York, 1927), II, 74, 89, 108 ff., 113 ff.

who could carry the skill with them and apply it to the new conditions. Second, these industries often remained at the handicraft level at which the value of the skill was maximized. Finally, it is significant that when these industries expanded, the people who brought the skill with them were edged out by native entrepreneurs unless they were capable of revising their techniques so completely as to adjust to the needs of the new circumstances. It would seem, then, that the success of these transfers depended on the ability of the entrepreneur who controlled the skill to move along with it and to adapt it in application to the changing needs of the milieu.

A third type of transfer is perhaps the most enlightening of all. There have been occasions in which it was not the entrepreneur who moved but rather a large skilled labor force, compelled to apply its skills under new circumstances. The most instructive experience, I think, was that of the British who came to the United States in the last decades of the nineteenth century, roughly in the years from 1870 to 1900.[5] This move took place under the terms of a rather close relationship between the English and American economies in those years. There was a certain parallelism of development with a considerable lag on the part of the Americans. Close commercial ties and cultural similarities, of course, facilitated the transfer.

The calls upon skilled British labor came under three circumstances. The need sometimes arose when American industry moved into the production of high-quality goods that demanded particular skills as yet unavailable in the United States. After 1870, for instance, when the cotton mills began to produce more than the rough fabrics they had earlier, and when the woolen mills began to take up worsted manufacture, they called upon large numbers of Scottish and English laborers, holding out as an attraction a high wage differential that drew many immigrants across the Atlantic.

The second condition stimulating a transfer of skills was the occurrence of a difference in the pace of depressions and recovery from depressions in the two economies. In the 1860's,

5. In this account I have drawn upon a doctoral dissertation soon to be published: Rowland T. Berthoff, "British Immigrants in Industrial America" (Harvard University, 1951).

for instance, the coal industry in Scotland and Wales suffered consistently from hard times at a period when the American coal industry was expanding. In 1879 the depression in the United States ended much more decisively than in Great Britain; the iron and steel industry here recovered, while times were still slack in England; and English iron and steel workers were tempted to make the migration.

Finally, as a result of calculated tariff policies, large segments of English industry, including English workers, could be transferred to the New World. Thus, until 1890, the United States had been the largest buyer of Welsh tin; in that year it consumed 70 per cent of the Welsh output. The McKinley tariff then set such high rates that, within a decade, half of the Welsh mills were closed and had moved almost intact, with their labor force, to the United States.[6] The same thing happened in the silk and the lace and in a number of other industries.

In each case the imported skilled, technically equipped English, Scottish, and Welsh laborers were highly valued at first. In every instance, however, they proved only transitional as a labor force and were quickly replaced by other hands, often unskilled and with a somewhat different relationship to the productive processes. Sometimes the change came as a result of technological improvements which permitted industrialists to employ less skilled workers at lower cost. In the textiles, after the turn of the century, the ring frame and the Northrop loom were the means by which English and Scottish laborers gave way to Italian, Slavic, and Portuguese peoples. A somewhat similar development occurred in the coal industry after 1890 with the introduction of more extensive machinery and greater use of dynamiting.

But it was not simply low cost that created the growing preference of American managers for less skilled labor; it was also the fact that, as each industry grew, managers discovered a kind of technological conservatism in skilled immigrant labor that was resistant to change and that insisted on preserving old ways of production. At that point it was easier to train previous-

6. *Ibid.*, I, 124 ff.

ly unskilled labor than to utilize the outmoded techniques of the skilled immigrants.

In the coal industry, for instance, the careful practices of the Welsh and English miners in undercutting veins ran counter to the inclination of the managers to use dynamite extensively to blast out whole seams without the kind of preparation and without the kind of care familiar in the English coaling industries. In the steel industry, too, at every step that involved technological change after 1880, the managers discovered that it was simpler to teach new methods to completely unskilled labor than to induce the already skilled to alter the nature of their skill.[7] The skilled labor forces, brought in to serve a particular need that existed at the point of its introduction, having served that need, became obsolescent and found it difficult to adjust to the requirements of new conditions. It was fortunate in terms of the total development of American economy that American industry was able to slough off these people and to replace them with an alternative labor force.

I think a rather simple, perhaps an obvious, conclusion may be drawn from this very brief survey of the types of American experience with the introduction of technical skills through international migration. There is a kind of rough equilibrium among the available technical skills in a society, the social context within which those skills operate, and the rest of the economy that they influence. The injection of new skills is disruptive, but it can be stimulating under certain conditions, for example, when the economy is itself expanding and therefore makes room for the new skills without injuring the status or the situation of those who possess old skills. Then its impact is creative and not simply repetitive. But control of the skill must not be so rigid in terms of the preconceptions with which it is introduced that it cannot be discarded when it no longer fits the conditions it was intended to serve and, in that sense, becomes obsolete.

7. James Howard Bridge, *The Inside History of the Carnegie Steel Company* (New York, 1903), p. 81.

STATE CONTROL AND FREE ENTERPRISE
IN THEIR IMPACT ON ECONOMIC
GROWTH

By W. T. Easterbrook

MENTION was made the other day of difficulties present in the dealings of the United States with economically more advanced peoples—the handicap of similarity, the psychology of resentment. Someone suggested the notion of a continuum stretching from the very backward nations at the one extreme to the more economically advanced areas at the other. This could be seen as a horizontal line with, say, the Hopi well to the left and the modern industrial nation at the extreme right. It is with the right end that I am concerned, with Canada as a useful study in United States impact and in enterprise-state relationships. You can take it as a worm's-eye view if you wish.

While Canada cannot be regarded as economically backward, in her relations with the United States she faces problems in some respects not unlike those of the so-called backward areas. Her proximity to the United States and the power and weight of the United States economy have raised perplexing problems for Canadian statesmen and enterprisers for over a century; and much of the country's history can be written in terms of adjustment to United States moves which have rocked the North American boat.

It might be suggested that indications of friction and of tensions, which are on the increase (and this is not imaginary), raise questions about United States policy in other areas. Why is not the global potlatch paying off in terms of prestige? You might look at Canada as a case in point. If in her relations with the United States misunderstandings are common, it is difficult to expect better things where cultural differences are great. Signs of friction are most apparent when Canadian policy fails to hew to the United States line. When the minister of external affairs suggested not so long ago that Canada had a mind of her own, his statement invoked a very strenuous response from many presumably ill-informed sources on this side of the line; the reaction was sudden and, from a Canadian point of view, rather startling.

But, for better or worse, of all the forces shaping state-enterprise relationships in modern Canadian growth, the United States has been and is the most potent. An industrial revolution of some magnitude is under way in Canada today. The Laurentian Shield, which covers more than half the country and was once regarded as mainly barren rock, is the center of this revolution. Canada's rate of increase in capacity to produce measured in terms of the national product is roughly half that of the United States. Her population growth every ten years approximates the annual rate of increase in the population of her neighbor. And, yet, in their impact on Canada's economy, present-day developments are best described as cyclonic.

The economics of this growth is fairly simple—the application of massive technology to the strategic resources of modern industrialism which we have in embarrassing abundance. Political issues are raised which are much less simple, and these relate mainly to Canada's relation with the United States. A large bulk of Shield production is exported, and a few items provide the bulk of income from export trade. About two-thirds of Canada's income from export trade last year came from the United States, and about two-thirds of that income was based on forest products and metals. This makes for a high sensitivity to external market conditions and not always predictable commercial policies.

There is nothing new in this extreme vulnerability of the economy to outside influences or in the proportion of national income based on foreign trade, which is still roughly about one-third. What is new and not likely to be of passing consequence is the urgency of United States demand for a few basic materials. The delicate issues raised by the pricing policies of the newsprint industry are symptomatic of the increasingly close interrelationships of the two economies and of the political problems for government and enterprise which this relationship must involve.

These problems are rendered more difficult and pressing by the rate of United States economic penetration over the past few decades in the form not only of investment outlays but of direct influence and control over Canadian resource development and manufacturing capacity. Canada stands as a valuable if not much-publicized area of investment not only because of resource and market considerations but because of her safe, sane, and sober people and a political stability almost unequaled anywhere.

While this United States–backed boom is good for the Canadian pocketbook, it does raise the old specter of colonial status. It took a half-century following Confederation to establish her independence of the United Kingdom, even though this fact does not seem to be grasped in some circles. Now new and powerful forces are threatening to complete the cycle of colony to nation to colony.[1] The unpleasant fact facing Canadians is that in the past and again today the most important influences in Canada's economic life have been and are external. Her role continues to be one of adaptation to forces over which she has had little apparent control.

At one time Canada could play off the United Kingdom and the United States. This is illustrated in the history of her commercial policy. When one let her down or hit too hard, she could turn to the other, and it worked out pretty well. Now, with the United Kingdom's decline accentuated by one war too many, prospects for continuance of the mother-country's role as counterweight to the power and influence of the United States are becoming increasingly dim. At one time Canadians watched London for changes to come; now they worry about Washington, and many feel that they have something to worry about.

There was a period in Canadian history when the drive to nationhood promised the political and economic independence cherished by so many for so long. From 1867 to the first World

1. See H. A. Innis, *Great Britain, the United States and Canada* (Cust Foundation Lectures [Birmingham: University of Birmingham Press, 1948]), p. 4.

War there seemed to be every prospect of achieving a maturity which, to use a common platform expression, would place Canada on a par with the great free nations of the world. She has come a long way, and political independence is unquestioned, but the economic bases are so not firm or solid as once hoped.

Back of this drive to independence was the power of the state. Industrialism in the sense of large fixed investments and lengthening time horizons got its start back in the 1830's when decisions were made which launched Canada on a program of expansion from which there could be no turning back. Early state support in transportation and communications was designed to enable Canadian enterprise to capture the trade of the expanding United States Midwest and to strengthen Montreal's position against New York. The Act of Union of 1840 united the two central Canadian provinces, Ontario and Quebec, and provided a political base big enough and strong enough to attract and put to work the funds necessary for the advancement of a healthy enterprise system. So the canals of the 1840's and the early railways of the 1850's and 1860's were built, and they failed. There was no choice but to go on, and the only way to go was westward via a transcontinental system located to tap the resources of the prairies and the Pacific Coast. The outcome was Confederation and a larger and stronger national unit.

What followed could be described as a period of planned expansion, with a great deal of state control of a very direct sort over the rate and the course of growth from the 1870's to 1914. In this task of nation-building, the state played its part with few questions raised about the philosophy back of state action or the objectives sought. The state's function was to create by its power and support the sort of environment in which the businessman could take the ordinary risks to be faced in his pursuit of legitimate gain.

This role was assumed or accepted more or less by default. Only the state could provide the setting necessary to enterprise, and this because of the sheer magnitude of the task not only facing so small a population but equally pressing the absolute necessity of increasing the rate of expansion if areas to the west were not to be absorbed in the stronger westward-moving United States. A slow-measured rate of progress was out of the question, and without the trade and markets of western Canada the central provinces faced the prospect of being bottled up and sooner or later absorbed into the polity of their neighbor. Yet the risks were too great and the pace much too fast to permit enterprise to step out on its own. (I note in passing that there were more than long-run influences at work in shaping the role of the state. There were cyclical problems as well, but I cannot go into these at this time.)

This project of national independence was based on a very simple formula—the achievement of economic and political unity in a system bound together by its transcontinental railway network, with central industrial Canada selling its wares in the western provinces, and the West in turn deriving its income from the sale of agricultural produce in England and on the Continent, and all this behind a tariff wall which reduced United States competition and brought in sufficient customs revenues to finance much of the necessary capital construction. It was, on the whole, a nicely balanced system, an east-west economy geared to overseas markets, with American influence kept to a minimum in the interests of the British connection and the stable social system of French Canada.

However, trade and investment channels would not stay put, and new forces emerged to weaken this wheat-railway-tariff complex so painfully worked out. While, on the one hand, chaos in Europe and the economic weakness of the United Kingdom reduced the strength of east-west lines of trade, on the other, a large and expanding trade with the United States, sparked by the resources of the Shield, began in the interwar years of the twentieth century to exert an enormously strong south-north pull on the Canadian economy. And the state is caught in the position of attempting to preserve an economic unity the bases of which have been sadly weakened by these developments.

How to preserve a unity originally based on transcontinental railways, wheat, and tariffs is a prime political problem, and a recent Royal Commission on Railways was faced with the task of formulating policies in the face of divisive tendencies which find their origin in developments across the line. State support of railways and state sponsorship of overseas markets may help but not much. Once more, changing external circumstances demand adjustments, and these may well take the form of increasing state intervention in the area of Canadian-American relations.

Along with the presence of a more or less positive state, acting in the best liberal tradition, has gone the acceptance of bigness in enterprise organization. The degree of centralization in Canadian economic life, in transportation and finance, in industrial and marketing organization, is best described as extreme. First solidly established in central Canada, large-scale enterprise extended its operations over the Maritimes and the western provinces.

The industrialization of the Shield increased a degree of concentration already great, and, with the state as a more or less silent partner (although exerting a good deal of control), large-scale enterprise organizations acted as the spearhead of Canadian expansion, and they were big for the same reasons that the state was so important. The small-unit Maritimes, the prairie farmers, and individual enterprisers, in general, fitted more or less comfortably into an environment in which state and business bureaucracies made the rules.

Modern Canadian economic growth, then, has been based on a partnership of state and private enterprise working under pressures induced by close proximity to the United States and faced with all the obstacles present in a difficult resource and population distribution and by risks inherent in an economy so persistently vulnerable to influences over which there can be little if any control.

Earlier stages in Canadian economic history are not without interest in discussion of the growth aspects of state and private enterprise activity. There was, for example, a century-long conflict between state control and private organizations for possession of the resources of the northern half of the continent. A French state system over much of its history effectively opposed both the Hudson's Bay Company to the north of its territories and the competition of other enterprisers to the south. I shall not go into the details of this competitive struggle, but one point should be underlined—the real issue here was not that of state versus private control but the creation of an environment in which economic and political expansion could be achieved in the face of obstacles so great that only the big organization could operate for any period of time. The French form was the bigger and more powerful of the two. Where risks are great, only the biggest bureaucracy can carry on, and not uncommonly this has been the state. As risks lessen, the private form with state support is enabled to invest with some hope of commensurate return. It is only in unique environments that state action may retreat well into the background, with some allowance for lag in the process.

With the end of the continent-wide fur trade in 1821, the collapse of the transcontinental system based on the trade, and the emergence of regions showing great diversity in aim and outlook, new staples were looked to for providing the bases for expansion. The timber trade flourished until the 1840's and helped to support a growing population and an expanding agriculture; these in turn necessitated improvements in communications so vital in the long struggle for control of half a continent. I have already indicated the outcome—expenditures far beyond the powers of nascent enterprise and the need for the state to create a setting in which merchants, early manufacturers, and commercially minded farmers could live and have their being.

Although we have no studies of the Canadian central provinces comparable to the Hartz and Handlin studies of American states,[2] my impression is that the cycle of change from positive government to passive government and back again has no parallel in the Canadian provinces. The role of the government in shaping the contours of economic life was never seriously questioned in Upper Canada and, following 1837, not effectively opposed over the St. Lawrence region, nor, for that

2. Oscar Handlin and Mary Flug Handlin, *Commonwealth: A Study of the Role of Government in the American Economy* (New York: New York University Press, 1947), and Louis Hartz, *Economic Policy and Democratic Thought: Pennsylvania, 1776–1860* (Cambridge: Harvard University Press, 1948).

matter, has it faced serious opposition in Canada over the past century.

Lipson's sequence of planned economy to free enterprise to planning once more finds no application here in any respect.[3] I have suggested the reasons why, and they relate mainly to the position of Canada vis-à-vis the United States. Dreams did not come true; enterprise failed to attain stature and strength comparable to that of its neighbors; and, when national bankruptcy threatened, recourse to bigger doses of state support appeared as the only way out.

Fundamentally, this position has been one of balance between private and public sectors of the economy, and I see few signs of any radical upset in this relationship. Here and there provincial governments have shown indications of stepping beyond assigned limits, but these are minor ripples. The federal government has displayed, for some, disturbing welfare notions—the baby bonus, for instance—but, if there are any real threats to established ways of life from such moves as these, I have not been able to discover them.

This is not to ignore the presence of changes which impose considerable strain on the old balance of state and enterprise. The impact of two wars and preparation for a third and the closely related industrial boom based on the resources of the Shield bring with them new and strong demands for increased state intervention in the interests of internal unity and defense against economic penetration and military attack. But the same conditions promote bigness in enterprise, too, and I see no likelihood of other than a continuance of long-established working arrangements among power concentrations, private and public, in economic life. Only persistent failure to meet minimum demands for public welfare could upset the apple-cart, and, in view of Canada's resource position, this is best described as a remote possibility.

From this sketchy review of Canada's past and present, it may be suggested that comparisons of the virtues and weaknesses of state control and free enterprise do not help much in

3. E. Lipson, *The Growth of English Society: A Short Economic History* (New York: Henry Holt & Co., 1950).

the study of growth. They tend to draw attention from what, for the historian, at any rate, is a more urgent task—understanding the forces at work which explain the dominance of either form or the presence of partnership between them—and this means going back to conditions which appear to account for changes in the role and status of decision-makers in the private and public sectors of the economy.

There is implicit in the title of this paper the assumption of freedom of choice: once we know which is the better life, we have only to choose and act accordingly. Yet the dominance of either form is more than a matter of the wisdom and preferences of enlightened leadership; it raises the question of why there is a wider scope for decision-making at some times and in some places than in others. This is not to preach the old and empty doctrine of economic determinism but to argue that we need to know much more about the setting of economic activity before we can get at the conditions of enterprise freedom or lack of it.

It is only under highly favorable conditions that the area of choice is as wide as that commonly assumed in much contemporary discussion of the role of enterprise or state, and commonly such conditions have been notable mainly for their absence. This raises the question of why enterprise has been able to break through old forms, to overcome traditional ways of doing things in some areas and not in others, and why some periods of breakthrough are longer-lasting and more revolutionary in their impact. Not uncommonly the enterpriser has been held in check by the power and resistance of strongly established bureaucracies without his best interests at heart; occasionally he has come to terms; and on rare occasions he has come to dominate all aspects of society and to stamp it with his own image.

Most of the conditions of enterprise dominance were present over much of Canadian history, and in a check of the elements which one United Nations publication refers to as "pre-conditions of economic development" few appear to be missing.[4] Yet

4. See *Measures for the Economic Development of Underdeveloped Countries* (New York: United Nations, May, 1951), chap. iii.

there was one great difference between the Canadian setting and that of the United Kingdom in its period of unquestioned supremacy and of the United States following the Civil War. That difference was a matter of power and its corollary choice. While there is nothing inevitable about the process of private enterprise moving to the front, the state to the background, the necessary conditions were present in these areas, and the enterpriser did take over. It is misleading to assume that the same happy conditions existed elsewhere or are at present anywhere today.

I have suggested that in the comparatively weak and vulnerable economy of Canada the range of choice was at best limited and that there was never at any time the prospect of the enterpriser breaking out in a rash of rugged individualism. Defenses were necessary and took the form of bigness in enterprise and state.

Looking at the title of this paper again, I am not at all sure that historical or contemporary events provide any clear bases for comparison of the merits and drawbacks of either form. Certainly Canadian economic development fails to do so. There are examples of state activity ranging all the way from French experience following 1660 to the present Ontario Hydroelectric Commission, in which aggressive, innovational activity is there beyond question and, conversely, of private forms running from the Hudson's Bay Company before its reorganization to large-scale enterprise organizations possessing attributes commonly associated with bureaus of government.

Such units, big in relation to their sphere of activity, influence the rate of growth according to the whole set of conditions in which they operate and according to the scope and type of leadership. Commonly, sharp limitations on the freedom of action of state and private enterprise have been present, and some of these have been indicated in the preceding pages. What of the future? Is there any prospect of a break, sharp or gradual, from this long-continued emphasis on adaptation to external influences?

The current economic situation is not such as to suggest a marked change of this sort. Canada's sensitivity to economic changes in the United States will be, if anything, greater than in the past. In the political area the outcome is less clear, and in closing I suggest one possibility of some modification in Canada's traditional role of adaptive response to changes beyond her borders. As long as United States influence was mainly exerted by private enterprise in that country, Canadian moves took the form of more or less easy adjustment to such influence, and certainly signs of explosive tendencies were lacking. It is when government faces government across the line, when moves and countermoves rise to the level of higher politics, that Canadian nationalism begins for the first time to take on shape and meaning, a development which promises to be of the greatest consequence for Canadian-American relations in the future and, in turn, for the role of state and private enterprise in Canadian economic growth.

PART II

THE CULTURAL ASPECTS OF
ECONOMIC GROWTH

CULTURAL AND PERSONALITY FACTORS AFFECTING ECONOMIC GROWTH

By RALPH LINTON

I AM afraid that the title of this paper may arouse false expectations, since I expect to lay much more stress on culture than on personality in my discussion of factors influencing economic growth. The role of personality in relation to economic change is only one aspect of the interrelations of personality and culture. The study of these interrelations is still in its infancy, and the established facts, insofar as they bear upon our present problem, can be summarized briefly.

There is good evidence that any personality configuration which can be found in one society can be matched in any other. In the small "primitive" groups which anthropologists prefer to study, all personality types may not be present at all times, but any type can be relied upon to show up eventually. However, the frequencies of various personality types vary enormously from one society to another. Thus, a type which is the most frequent in one society may be so rare in another that individuals who show it are regarded as pathological. An anthropologist friend told me that, when he settled in a village in the Admiralties, the local natives pointed out one of their number as insane. As he came to know the man, he found him not only sane but much more likeable than any of the others. He discovered that he was regarded as insane because in an emergency, say, a drowning child, he would help a neighbor without waiting to drive a bargain as to how much he should get for the assistance.

In small, culturally homogeneous societies a large majority of members usually belong to one personality type, while other types are represented by scattered individuals. The basic personality type shows a close relation to the society's techniques of child care and to the demands which the society makes upon its adult members. From numerous clinical studies in our own society we know the effects of certain sorts of early experience on the developing personality. In each of the "primitive" societies studied to date, the methods of child-rearing have been such as might be expected to produce the basic personality type. Moreover, individuals with this sort of personality find themselves at home in the society's culture. They are able to accept its values and fulfil the obligations which it imposes with a minimum of psychological difficulty.

We do not know whether the same conclusions apply to large, heterogeneous societies such as modern nations. A modern nation always includes numerous communities and classes which may differ markedly in their customs. Although a number of interesting and suggestive books have been published on the subject of national character, none of them rests upon study of an adequate sample of individuals from the various sub-societies within the nation in question.

Fortunately, the question of national character is not of paramount importance for our present discussion. Individuals normally behave in accordance with the culture of their societies, and, given a knowledge of this culture, one can predict their reactions to most situations without knowledge of their personality configurations. Let us suppose, for example, that I am in Norway and have no change with which to tip a porter. I give him a hundred-kroner note, asking him to get it changed for me. On the basis of a knowledge of Norwegian culture, I can predict with a high degree of probability that he will be back with the change. If I did the same thing in Italy, I could predict with an even higher degree of probability that I would never see the porter again.

Most of the factors which effect the adoption and integration of new ideas by a society can be phrased more effectively in cultural than in psychological terms. If we know what a society's culture is, including its particular system of values and attitudes, we can predict with a fairly high degree of probability whether the bulk of its members will welcome or resist a particular innovation. We can also predict what parts of the society's economic or social system will be effected first and where the resulting disorganization will be most extensive. In any such predictions the circumstances surrounding the innovation, such as its source, external pressure toward its acceptance, and immediate utility, must, of course, be taken into account. The one variable which cannot be reduced to exact terms and which always interferes with exact prediction is the presence of particular individuals.

Our studies of the processes of culture change have revealed the extreme importance of innovators, persons who for some reason espouse a new idea and devote themselves energetically to "selling" it to their society. Both the motives and the personalities of such individuals appear to be varied, but it is safe to say that their personalities are rarely of the basic type. Opposed to them are, in most cases, a group of equally vigorous conservatives, persons who are contented with the status quo because, often unconsciously, they derive advantage from it. The social position, force of character, and intelligence of particular individuals belonging to one or the other of these groups may have a very real effect on patterns of economic growth. They not only may hasten or retard the growth itself but also may determine which of several possible lines it will follow.

In addition to the active innovators, the social disruption which inevitably accompanies extensive culture changes always brings to the fore numerous individuals who find the innovations congenial and are ready to exploit them. This is even more true in cases where the innovations are not congruous with the pre-existing culture than in those where they are. In fact, such persons are very frequently misfits in their societies, handicapped by atypical personalities. If the innovations are accepted, these former misfits become a new elite, and there is a strong tendency for them to transmit their advantage to their descendants, thus becoming the founders of a new hereditary ruling group. The current situation in Russia provides a good illustration for this.

Turning from questions of personality and its influence, there are two factors effecting economic growth which are universal. First, all societies and most individuals welcome improvement in their economic condition as long as such improvements do not involve more trouble than they are worth, that is, necessitate too many changes in established behavior patterns and controvert too many accepted values. In a research undertaken by sociologists some years ago, it was discovered that nearly everyone in our own society believes that he could live comfortably on an income one-third larger than that which he actually has. This attitude seemed to be present irrespective of the actual level of income. In the same way, all societies would like to improve their economic condition, although the ceilings which they would initially set for the improvement might vary greatly. Where a society no longer tries to improve economic conditions, this attitude can be traced to a series of past failures and frustrations.

One often hears that our own reservation Indians have no desire to improve their economic condition. Government experts will tell them how to breed cattle or get better crops by scientific methods, but they will go on as they are. If one follows back the history of the dealings of our Indians with the United States government, it is easy to understand the reason for such apathy. Tribe after tribe made a real effort to copy white ways when they were placed on reservations. They saw that the old life was ended and did their best to adapt. However, whenever a tribe got a communally owned cattle herd which could be a valuable source of income, stockmen who wanted the range brought pressure in Washington, and the tribe suddenly found its herd sold and the money "put in trust." If a tribe developed an irrigation project and brought new land under cultivation, presently an excuse would be found for expropriating this and moving the tribe to a still more submarginal territory. The Indians were frustrated and puzzled by changing government policies, in which the only consistent feature was that they always lost, and finally settled back into apathy and pauperism.

Unless a society has had adverse experiences of this sort, its members will be interested in improving their economic condition; but we must remember that many of the people whom we hope to help have had such experiences. Many colonial peoples and the sharecroppers and tenants who form a large part of the population in even independent "backward" nations know from sad experience that, every time their income increases, so do their rents and taxes. After each advertised economic advance they find themselves with very much the same standard of living they had before they underwent the trouble and uncertainty involved in practicing new techniques.

One also finds that the members of the average peasant community view any attempts to improve their economic condition which originate with their rulers with considerable and not unjustified suspicion. This holds whether the rulers are foreign imperialists or a native upper class. The peasant feels that anything which his rulers offer as a chance to improve his condition is probably much more to their advantage than to his own. Since his ruers have always mulcted him in the past, he assumes that they will continue to mulct him in the future. So much for the desire for economic betterment which is obviously basic to any attempt to improve economic conditions.

The second factor which is universally significant in connection with any attempt to improve economic conditions is the ability of any society's members to handle machines. In spite of a few humorous examples, as in the often-cited case of the African natives who, when given wheelbarrows to move earth, carried the loaded barrows on their heads, there is abundant evidence that the members of any society can be taught to use mechanical and even scientific techniques. Many of these techniques can be learned without any understanding of the principles involved. They do not even entail surrender of established beliefs in magic. I was in Cairo at the time when model-T Fords were in process of replacing donkeys as the preferred means of transportation. Around the radiator caps of most of the Fords were draped strings of large blue beads. These had previously been worn by donkeys to avert the evil eye, and the native drivers felt that they were equally necessary with the new carrier.

One of the greatest contributors to the diffusion of mechanical skills and technological ability has been the automobile. This contrivance seems to have a fascination for people everywhere. It has penetrated into many out-of-the-way parts of the world, bringing new crafts in its train. Since these frontier regions are where bad cars go when they die, it requires no mean degree of skill to keep them running, and I would back certain Polynesian and Swahili mechanics of my experience against nine-tenths of American garagemen for ingenuity and mechanical know-how.

It is obvious that any individual can learn mechanical skills more readily if his training is begun while he is young. People brought up with machines learn to use them almost unconsciously, while those who do not encounter them until they are adult have more trouble. People reared in societies which have a manipulative tradition also learn mechanical skills more readily than those from societies which are indifferent to good craftsmanship. Most of the unmechanized civilizations do have such a tradition, while it is by no means lacking among "primitive" groups. A friend of mine who had spent many years in the Arctic told me that, if an outboard motor got out of order, he simply found an Eskimo and turned it over to him. The Eskimo might never have seen an outboard motor before, but he would be delighted at the chance to take one to pieces and put it together again. It might take him several days, but, if there was anything broken or out of place, he would be sure to locate it. Similarly, Polynesians have a manipulative culture. In ancient times skilled craftsmen enjoyed great social prestige, and today much of this carries over to the mechanic.

Needless to say, in societies where the technology is crude, or where the social position of the skilled craftsman is low, it takes much longer to diffuse mechanical skills. Nevertheless, it can be done. We have abundant evidence that, as far as intelligence and learning ability are concerned, there is no group in the world which cannot be mechanized.

Unfortunately, industrialization presents another problem even more complicated than that of technical training. If modern machinery is to produce an improvement in economic conditions, it has to be operated by labor which will be on the job even though it is a wonderful day and the fish are biting. It is much easier to train an intelligent man to diagnose and repair an injury to a machine than to get him to spend day after day tightening Nut 36 on an assembly line.

There is a story, typical whether true or not, of an American in Mexico who bought a chair which a carpenter had brought to the market, liked it, and a few days later asked him to make five more on the same pattern. The carpenter promptly doubled the original price on the plea that he would get so bored doing the same thing five times. Boredom can be a deadly enemy of efficiency. If one reads the history of European mechanization, one will encounter numerous laments by English factory management over the unreliability of labor during the first half of the nineteenth century. Factory workers were kept at work only by the constant threat of starvation and the release provided by orgiastic Saturday nights and revivalistic Sundays.

In time, and with the aid of greatly shortened hours, European labor learned to put up with the monotony of factory work. It is a safe prediction that other labor can be trained to do so. It is also safe to predict that the assembly line is an intermediate step in the development of modern technology. Whenever it becomes cheaper to tighten Nut 36 by machinery than by hand, a machine will be substituted for a man. However, labor in most unmechanized societies is relatively cheap and will continue to be so for some time to come. Its training to monotony is one of the first problems to be solved in the drive for economic betterment.

In summary, every society would like to improve its economic position, and every society is capable of learning to operate the machines and follow the scientific procedures which might lead to such improvement. Let us turn now to the cultural and social factors which may operate to inhibit or retard economic growth.

The first and perhaps most important of these is unrestricted breeding. This is no more and no less natural than other features of human behavior. It is intimately wrapped up with the society's culture, and birth control is infinitely older and more widely distributed than the use of rubber. Where such relatively humane methods of keeping down population are not in use, the balance between societies and their food supply has, until recently, been maintained by periodic famines and plagues. What happens when modern science and charity step in to prevent these can be seen in the case of the Navaho.

When I first visited the Navaho in 1912, there were supposed to be about twenty thousand of them. Exact figures were lacking, since many of those living in the back districts could not be caught to be counted. Today there are over sixty thousand, with no signs of a letdown in the rate of increase. Since there are already enough Navajo to weave all the blankets and herd all the sheep for which white Americans can provide a market, no solution to the problem is in sight.

No matter what the degree of technological advance, unrestricted breeding accompanied by modern medical practices can only result in a steadily depressed standard of living, a situation in which the occasional sharp pangs of famine are replaced by constant dull hunger pains. At the same time, most of the unmechanized civilizations actually encourage unrestricted breeding. In societies where a woman's social importance depends upon the number of sons she produces or where a man's happiness in the next world is proportional to the number of descendants making sacrifices to his shade, the best lectures of Mrs. Sanger are likely to fall on deaf ears.

The problem of how to deal with human fertility is by no means limited to "backward" societies, so let us turn to cultural factors more immediately related to economic growth. Since culture change of any sort is heavily dependent upon individual initiative, the values which are attached in any society to individual industry and to individual accumulation of wealth will become important factors in determining the extent and direction of economic changes. If one goes over the whole range of the world's societies, one can find weird and wonderful patterns of ownership, wealth distribution, goods exchange, and other economic activities. Most members of this audience have probably heard of the Northwest Coast potlatches, in which a man humbles rivals by destroying his own property or of the amazingly intricate rules governing division of an Australian hunter's kill among his relatives. However, such cultural aberrations have little to do with the great oriental populations which are of paramount importance in the world of today and tomorrow. These groups have civilizations which are actually older than our own in most cases. They are habituated to city life and a mercantile economy even though this economy rests upon an economically depressed peasantry and hand industries. What these people need is mechanical skills and scientific techniques. On other aspects of economic life they are well able to take care of themselves. I have not heard of any suggestion in Washington that, as part of the Point IV program, we should send a delegation to Armenia to teach the natives how to trade.

Fortunately for any plans which we may have for encouraging economic growth, China, Southeast Asia, the Islamic cultures of the Near East, India, and, although these are often ignored, the high native civilizations of West Africa are all thoroughly familiar with trade, credit, banking, and private property. In the Islamic countries in particular, one is struck by the resemblance of these patterns to those of medieval Europe. China also seems familiar to an American in these respects. India avowedly has a different value system from the rest, but anyone who has done business there will recognize that indifference to economic gains is largely limited to ascetics.

In spite of these resemblances there are certain significant differences which can hardly fail to influence both the speed and the direction of economic growth. One of the most important of these is the varying patterns of individual as against communal ownership of land and other natural resources. Ownership always involves a conflict of values—the claims of the individual against those of the group. In the Near East in particular there are areas where the desire to give all families in a village equal economic opportunity results in the redistribution of village land every few years. At this time each family will get an allotment based on its size. A family which has grown from eight to ten will get more land this time than it did at the last division; one which has shrunk from eight to five, less. Whatever the social justice of such a practice, it robs the family of any incentive to improve the land it is working. It is, in effect, a renter from the community with no assurance of tenure.

Closely related to this is the practice, widespread even in some parts of Europe, of subdivision of land through inheritance. At the death of a landowner, his fields are divided as equitably as possible among his sons. Since all his land is not of equal value or usable for the same purposes, the desire to give every heir a fair share results in repeated fragmentation until a man may find himself owner of fifty or sixty tiny plots spread over an area of several square miles. Under such conditions individual ownership and use of modern machinery becomes uneconomic and, in practice, impossible.

To continue with cultural factors effecting possible improvements in agricultural techniques, one of the main initial blocks to improvement is the widespread institution of absentee landlords. The tenants of such landlords are nearly always sharecroppers rather than renters, and the oriental landlord really shares. The tenant usually pays anywhere from a quarter to a half or more of his crop each year for the privilege of remaining on the land. Under such circumstances it is hard to persuade him to expend the extra labor required to instal modern methods while he lacks the capital needed for fertilizer and modern tools. Only fundamental changes in the system of land tenure will make modern agricultural methods possible in most of the unmechanized civilizations.

Ownership of natural resources other than land, especially minerals, may also stand in the way of economic development. Government ownership is a long-established pattern in most of the civilizations under discussion. Mining claims are leased but never owned outright by the operators. In many cases the countries in question have not enough capital to modernize mining operations or the trained personnel required for this. At the same time, if they bring in foreign capital and experts, demagogues will immediately raise the cry that that party in power is selling the nation's birthright. The current difficulties over Iranian oil would be a case in point.

Another series of factors influencing economic growth are directly connected with social structure. One of the most important of these is the extent and nature of kin claims and the extent of the kin group. In all the unmechanized civilizations such groups are much more extensive and functionally much more important than they are among ourselves. In China and India, in particular, the ideal family is the "joint family." This is a technical term used to refer to a family which functions as a corporation and survives generation after generation without division of the family property. Members of such a family who do not live in the common establishment are expected to contribute part of their income to the family funds. In return, all members of the family are entitled to support and care in case of old age or disability.

Where the family structure is of this sort, economic improvement presents certain specific problems, while changes in the established economic system are unusually disruptive socially. Joint families function under the direction of the oldest living male, unless he is obviously senile, in which case the next oldest takes over, Their reactions thus tend to be highly conservative. Moreover, kin claims within the joint family are so strong that in the establishment of a new commercial or manufacturing enterprise they have to be given precedence over actual ability. All relatives have to be taken care of before outsiders can be employed in other than menial positions. This situation plagued the Imperial Chinese government, which recognized the inevitability of nepotism in administrative offices and did what it could to counter it by appointing administrators to provinces as far as possible from those in which their joint families lived. In recent times the Japanese have been able to work out a fairly effective adjustment between joint family claims and business efficiency. The families controlling large enterprises marry daughters to their most promising employees, who then take the family name. However, this method will not work everywhere. Even in Japan able young men are reluctant to become adoptive husbands, since it means separation from one's own family group and little control over one's wife.

On the other side of the picture, economic change is always destructive to a joint family system. This can be seen even in Europe, where the early Roman and Germanic families were not unlike the oriental joint families. Such families broke down under the impact of developing mercantilism with its increase in individual opportunity, while their complete destruction came with the rise of modern mechanized civilization. Here in the United States we have reached the low point in a process of breakdown of kin structure which has reduced our functional kin group to the primary, biologically determined one of parents and children. However, now that most skilled trades are becoming hereditary through union policy, and influence is becoming increasingly important for getting a start in a profession, we may expect a recognition of more extended kin ties and an increased persistence of family groups. It may be doubted whether the joint family pattern will re-establish itself as long as its usual function of providing social security is taken care of by government agencies and its other once important function of keeping working capital intact is invalidated by taxes and inflation.

It can be stated as a theorem, valid in a very high percentage of cases, that the greater the opportunities for individual economic profit provided by any social-cultural situation, the weaker the ties of extended kinship will become. Modernization of the unmechanized cultures, with their unexampled opportunities for individuals with intelligence and initiative, cannot fail to weaken or even destroy joint family patterns. This in turn will entail a whole series of problems for the societies in question. They must develop new mechanisms to provide for the economic and psychological needs now taken care of by family organization.

Social values connected with class structure may also have a profound effect on economic change. While the members of any group can learn to use machines, there are great differences in their eagerness to learn. Societies and even the members of different classes within a society may differ profoundly in their attitudes toward trade and work. In most of the unmechanized civilizations, including those of our own not very remote ancestors, the upper classes derived their wealth from either (1) ownership of land and exploitation of the peasants on it or (2) pre-emption of governmental posts and the consequent profits from salary and "squeeze." Most civilizations employ both sources of wealth, but ownership of land is, generally speaking, more important in Europe and government office more important in Asia, especially China. It is a curious and rarely recognized survival of this old culture pattern which makes western Europe and the United States the only places in the world where an honest and able man has to accept serious financial loss if he works for the government. Outside these regions the men who hold government office are the ones who get the largest incomes. Their salaries are huge in comparison with the earnings of craftsmen or even merchants and are supplemented by recognized and regulated graft.

Whatever the basis of wealth and power, one finds that in all the unmechanized civilizations the trader and the mechanic rank far down in the social scale. The farmer, while actually the worst exploited of all, is usually accorded a somewhat higher position socially, especially if he is a landowner. As a result, attempts at economic improvement are caught on the horns of a dilemma. Foreign experts sent in to implement such programs immediately arouse hostility and suspicion, but there are not enough native experts and little chance to train them. The upper classes, who are the only ones who can afford to give their sons a foreign education, prefer to have them trained in white-collar occupations, preferably law. Even when they do go into such fields as engineering, they prefer theory to practice and feel that any sort of manual work, even as a part of training, is socially degrading.

It may be added that members of the upper classes who are unconventional enough to take technical subjects in Western universities very often show a strong disinclination to return to their own countries when their training is complete. The type of mind which makes such aristocrats critical of the social values of their own civilizations seems to predispose them to appreciate the creature comforts of the West. Very much the same reluctance to return will be found among the students who have gone abroad for study under government scholarships or missionary auspices. Although this situation will no doubt be overcome eventually, lack of trained native personnel will continue to be one of the serious problems for some time to come.

Last among the cultural factors which influence economic growth is one which I mention with reluctance because of its very intangibility. Anyone who has been able to study several different societies at first hand will recognize that cultures differ markedly in their degree of integration: the extent to which the various elements of which they are composed are mutually adjusted and mutually interdependent for their successful functioning. There is no unit of measurement for these differences, and they are even difficult to describe, but they are very real nevertheless. They have important bearing on the way in which a society will function in stable situations and in those of cultural change and on its resilience under changing conditions.

There are some cultures which seem to be built like finely adjusted clock movements. Every element interlocks with every other in a way to delight the hearts of followers of the British functional school. Value systems and actual behavior patterns are consistent, and even the cosmology and mythology explain and reinforce the status quo. Such cultures are most commonly found in societies which have lived for a long time under relatively stable conditions. As long as these conditions remain unchanged, the cultures function smoothly, taking care of every need of the society and of its normal members and providing answers to all problems.

At the other end of the scale there are cultures which are so loosely organized and so full of both ideological and behavioral inconsistencies that one wonders how they are able to function at all. I have never forgotten an interview I once had with a noted Swedish economist who had been brought over by one of the foundations to study certain American social problems. After three months in the United States, most of which had been devoted to a study of labor conditions, he gave it as his considered opinion that the republic was about to collapse, since no society could survive such confusion in a fundamental feature of its economy. Such lack of organization is by no means limited to civilizations. It can also be found in relatively simple societies such as some of the American Indian tribes. Since some other Indian tribes show an extremely high degree of culture integration, study of what has happened to those of each type under white impact is instructive.

In closely integrated cultures the introduction of any new culture element immediately sets in train a series of obvious dislocations. Other things being equal, the closer the integration, the more extensive and immediate the dislocations. These changes give a preview of the social and psychological consequences of incorporating the new element into the culture. They become obvious before the new thing has been fully accepted and often are disconcerting enough to result in its rejection. After a few unfortunate experiences, a society of this sort is likely to set its face solidly against all change and, if it is in a politically subject position, to develop elaborate techniques to keep the existing culture intact and resist all outside attempts to change it. This situation can be seen in such societies as the Rio Grande Pueblos of our own Southwest and various Guatemalan Indian communities. Under the steadily increasing pressure exerted by changes in the community's environment, such things as the opening of roads, establishment of markets, settlement of more advanced groups near by, and so forth, the old culture is maintained with desperation until the pressure finally becomes too great, when it collapses, leaving the community little basis for reintegration and adjustment. It becomes a disorganized aggregate of individuals incapable of functioning as a unit and held together only by common language and common dislike of the outsider.

In contrast to this, loosely integrated societies usually show little resistance to new ideas, since the consequences of accepting them do not become obvious for some time. When they do become obvious, the new culture element has already gained a foothold and cannot be rejected without considerable inconvenience and loss. The tendency is then to extemporize, to use emergency measures which in time become crystallized. However, the society, having always been accustomed to inconsistencies and contradictions, finds little difficulty in putting up with a few more. Such societies show extreme resilience. Indian tribes such as the Comanche, whose culture has always shown this fundamental pattern, have been able to survive and increase in numbers in spite of defeat and loss of resources.

Under sufficient pressure, changes can be produced in any culture. Those which accompany alteration in fundamental economic patterns, whether of production, distribution, or ownership, are certain to be far-reaching and to result in disruption of the existing social system. Planners for betterment should realize this. They should also realize that the opposition of groups in power to plans for economic improvement may be selfish but certainly is not unintelligent in terms of self-interest. Such groups profit most heavily from the status quo, and any change in it means social and usually economic loss for them.

We know that in every society there are individuals whose personalities are such that they will be able to profit by the confusion following on any extensive changes in the society's economic system. When such changes occur, these individuals form a new power group. In course of time they become consolidated into a new ruling class, one which tends to take over the prestige symbols of its predecessor. We have seen this process repeated again and again during the recent, first mercantile and then technological, revolutions in Europe; and we may expect to see it occur in all the unmechanized civilizations as they are mechanized. From the point of view of the bulk of the population it will not be a matter of great importance whether the new ruling group rules under a capitalistic system or under a Communistic one. In either case the rulers will be managers and technical experts, and it will make little difference whether formal ownership of the property which they control is vested in the state, as under communism, or in a great body of small anonymous stockholders, as in our own emergent type of capitalism. Fundamental change in an economic system means a revolution, and any revolution, after the dust has settled, means a new set of rulers and a proletariat still in its familiar position at the bottom of the social and economic scale.

THE PROBLEM OF ADAPTING SOCIETIES
TO NEW TASKS

By MELVILLE J. HERSKOVITS

IN THE rapidly growing vocabulary of American social science a new term has come to be heard with increasing frequency in recent years—one might almost say in recent months. This is the term "manipulation." In this new use it applies where an individual or a group, working with the tools research has provided, moves into a social situation with the aim of altering patterns of thought and action so as to achieve a given practical end. It represents the logical working-out of those aims of physical science, prediction *and* control, which for so many years have been accepted by the students of human behavior and human institutions as the ends toward which they, as scientists, should strive.

In a general, prescientific sense, the process of manipulating human behavior and thus, to varied degrees, the course of human history is nothing very new. The action of the democratic process itself, in terms of argumentation and persuasion, represents an attempt to manipulate behavior and thought for given ends. The rule of the manifold historical autocracies, or the ways of diplomacy, bring to mind countless examples of manipulation of peoples and their political and social destinies. Cross-culturally, colonization, commerce, the slave trade to the New World, the missionary activities of the eighteenth and nineteenth centuries—all served as conscious or fortuitous instruments of induced change in belief systems, social organization, and many other phases of the lives of those on whom these forces impinged.

What distinguishes the prescientific procedures in bringing about change from the methods which the disciplines that study man, whether as an individual or as a member of a society, employ today is the new dimension that has been given all programs of action, the dimension of scientific method. On its most ubiquitous level we have applied scientific method to the manipulation of preferences for one product as against another through advertising. It can be seen in such other varied aspects of our life as labor-management relations, town-planning, public administration, fund-raising campaigns, the development of new industries, and education and child welfare.

These random examples of the application of science to problems of directed ends have been drawn from our own society. Certainly in such areas of public concern as education, child welfare, or public administration, they represent attempts to solve problems of importance. Or, where manipulation of one group by another within the same population is undertaken, it is still a process which operates within the conventions of our society as a whole. Common cues to behavior, a common historical background, and common language are shared by both groups. The basic motivating drives can be taken for granted; the area of agreement as to the values that shape ends is large. To put the matter in technical terms, this is intracultural manipulation, in which only such differences as exist between subcultural groups need be taken into account.

When we approach the problem of influencing peoples other than ourselves, the matter becomes vastly complicated. The area of prediction is narrowed by factors that do not enter where concern is with one's own culture, where the task is to predict behavior on the basis of reactions that fall within a reasonably well-recognized framework of total response patterns. For to adapt another society to new ways of living involves the formidable process of reshaping basic habits that are manifest both in belief and in behavior. It calls for an induced shift in preestablished ends and a directed reorientation of value systems. It requires, consequently, an intensive analysis of the existing relationships among the various aspects of culture—technological, economic, social, educational, political, religious, and aesthetic—before any kind of prediction can be made of the results that will follow the disturbance of the balance between them.

Here, then, we come on a primary factor in the problem that

has given rise to the discussions of this Institute. "In the areas of technical aid to underdeveloped countries," states the call for these meetings, "most attention has been paid so far to certain theoretical economic problems, whereas the relations between cultural changes and economic growth, as well as the aspects of the impact of the sociopolitical structure of underdeveloped countries on modernization, has received less attention." What kind of adjustments seem to be indicated when the technological and economic patterns of Europe and America are introduced into nonindustrialized areas? What are the psychocultural mechanisms that cause peoples having different ways of life to hold tenaciously to their established modes of behavior, especially in terms of the sanctions which give these ways of life meaning and value? With these propositions examined, we can consider some of the assumptions of the same order in our own culture that underlie programs aimed at benefiting other peoples. In this manner we will move beyond the unilateral position customarily taken in planning and implementing technical aid programs and lay a conceptual basis of a process of mutual helpfulness that is a prerequisite to their effective functioning.

Let us take a recurring situation under programs of economic development all over the world that has had to be faced by those in charge of operations calculated to bring the benefits of the technical proficiency of our industrialized economy to underdeveloped areas. This situation rarely, if ever, figures in discussions of those "theoretical economic problems" where considerations of large scope, such as basic resources, national income, labor pool, or location, determine the answers that set the goals for the operating missions. It concerns one of those elements in the total problem that has to do with the human factor in the equation, the element which, because of the operation of culturally prescribed motivations that lie outside the patterns of our own pecuniary economy, introduces unknowns that make for the gap between theoretically based prediction and actual achievement.

We here consider the problem of labor turnover. It is a commonplace that one of the greatest difficulties faced in the development of enterprises of any sort in underdeveloped areas, whether extractive, agricultural, or industrial, is that of holding workers to the job. Typically, what occurs is that men will take employment for a period of time and then, when money to meet certain specific wants is in hand, leave. Among numerous illustrations, that of the attempt to establish a textile plant near the native reserves of South Africa may be cited. Erected under the auspices of the South African Social and Economic Planning Commission, its purpose is to bring industry to the African and thus avoid some of the evils that have marked the migration of workers to the cities or that have followed their segregation in the mine compounds of the Rand. It is to be manned by Africans who are to be trained not only to operate the machines but eventually to assume managerial and technical posts.

The experiment is a continuing one, but it is recognized by those concerned with it that labor turnover is one of its most serious problems. Even though it is near the reserves, so that a native need not face the long separation from his wife and family that the man who goes to the cities or to the mines must contemplate, workers come and go. It is the same story—a man will work long enough to meet the limited goal set by the needs of his family unit. When he has earned enough for this, he leaves, to return to a mode of life that is in harmony with an economic system that existed before industrialization was introduced into the area, whereby subsistence and prestige wants are satisfied without reference to pecuniary considerations.

The problem of how to cope with this unstable labor market has had various answers. The imposition of taxes, payable only in currency, was attempted as an early solution. This method got roads built but could scarcely provide labor for large-scale, continuing undertakings. There has been wide recourse to contract labor, which permits the employer to compel a worker to stay on the job for a specified time. On the Firestone plantations in Liberia a policy of paying wage differential incentives to workers who remain on the job beyond a specified time has been instituted. First-class hospital facilities, good schools for the children of the laborers, and the attraction of well-built houses are additional incentives to facilitate a dependable labor supply.

It is argued that the incentive of a larger wage would only increase the difficulty, since, the more the worker earned in a given time, the sooner he would attain his objective, and consequently the sooner he would leave his job. The encouragement of a wider range of wants, in terms of an induced goal of a higher standard of living, is another longer-range solution that has been suggested. Yet, in the final analysis, despite the many methods formulated of inducing change in economic attitudes and behavior on the part of the existing and potential labor supply, the factor of pre-established custom dominates the labor scene, and the problem remains essentially unsolved.

What, then, are some of the special aspects of tradition that, rarely taken into account, may be considered as operative in these situations, rendering it difficult to achieve what would, on the face of it, seem to be a simple task of utilizing available labor power for the development of underdeveloped areas? We may turn to Africa for some insight into this perplexing problem. This is not because the problem as such is in any way peculiar to Africa but because the examples to be drawn point the difficulties encountered here, as elsewhere, in the development of a rich continent, so dynamic in its present-day political and economic orientations, yet about which so little is known in the United States.

The instance of an indigenous manufacturing system will give us something of the type of background against which proposals for economic development must be projected. It should be stressed that the instance is a regional example and is not to be taken as representative of Africa as a whole. No single instance could subsume the vast range of institutions, lying in all aspects of culture, that mark the many bodies of tradition found there. But if it is not to be taken as typical, neither is it to be thought of as atypical. It is useful, and it is here used because it highlights a problem.

Ironworking has, from very early times, been known throughout Negro Africa. There is good though not conclusive evidence that the technique was developed on that continent. Ironworkers are almost invariably members of a guild, membership in which is customarily based on family relationship, with the craft validated by supernatural sanctions. This is the pattern among the peoples of the Upper Volta River in French West Africa, where knives, hoes, and other iron implements are manufactured by members of such guilds. Yet because here, as in non-industrial societies the world over, the lines of specialization are blurred, these men are not the full-time specialists they would be in our society. They are, as a matter of fact, primarily agriculturalists, earning their living only partially by the sale of their products and working their forges principally during that part of the year, the dry season, when the fields are not cultivated.

This is a significant fact, for it is plain that they would have no difficulty in supporting themselves entirely by the manufacture of iron implements. Their numbers in relation to the total group of which they form a part are small. In one series of districts enumerated some twenty-five years ago, there were 60 ironworkers in a population of about 20,000; in another series, there were 39 of these specialists out of some 18,000 inhabitants. It is apparent that this number of ironworkers cannot begin to supply the demand for the implements they produce. This is why, for generations, hoes and bush knives have been imported from other tribes and why, more recently, trading firms have stocked implements on the native model made in Europe.

One does not have to pursue the matter further to perceive that motivations quite different from those obtaining in the economies of Europe and America are operative here. The question that would occur to one conditioned to the patterns of business enterprise in the Western world would be why these ironworkers do not take advantage of the obvious market at hand. Why do they not supply it by complete, full-time specialization and the training of more apprentices to enlarge their operations so that, as entrepreneurs in the strict sense, they could then hire these trained workers to increase further their production? And this is a fair question—fair, that is, for those who approach the problem in terms of current economic theory. All the conditions for the expansion of production are present, yet they are ignored. It is apparent that the answer lies outside the scope of economics as envisaged for our culture; that to reach a satisfactory explanation would require probing deep into what we know concerning the psychology of culture, as applicable to this particular situation. And since, in this case, we have nothing more to go on than the facts that have been provided us and are presented here, we can only have recourse to generalizations about the reasons why a people hold to such customary modes of behavior in the face of a patent economic opportunity—modes of behavior that seem logical, rational, and of self-evident worth to them, while to the outsider they seem so illogical and so irrational.

We shall return later to this point. For the moment the case we have cited will serve to illustrate how divergent from the conventions of societies with machine technologies and complex economies may be the systems of peoples living in underdeveloped areas. For we can ill afford to be unrealistic about the complexity of the problems of reconciliation involved in attempts to manipulate such peoples so as to achieve ends not envisaged by those whose ways of life are to be changed or not adaptable within the limits of possible variation of their culture.

If we examine the indigenous productive systems of the continent in more general terms—and much of what will be indicated is applicable to nonindustrialized societies outside Africa as well as to the peoples of that continent—we find that they present certain consistent characteristics that are highly relevant to the question we are considering. One of these has to do with the rhythm of work, a second with the way in which the available supply of labor is mobilized so that the economy can function, while a third concerns the motivations for labor, the factor of incentives. There are still other significant characteristics whose analysis must await more detailed presentation: the role of kinship groupings and sex division of labor in organizing and orienting the economics of production; the importance of supernatural sanctions governing ritual cycles for the service of deities or ancestors, when customary tasks are not performed; the influence of class stratification and native political structure on attempts to introduce new economic concepts and technical procedures.

Especially in the tropics, the zone where the greatest portion of technical aid to underdeveloped countries will be made available, the rhythm of work in indigenous societies is the rhythm of the seasons. This does not mean that there are no daily rhythms, but these do not dictate changes in economic activity as do the longer fluctuations of seasonal change. Just what time of the day men and women go to the field, or on just what days they will work, will be determined by them in terms of the demands of the day. It is the total job, however, that is of primary concern. If a crop is successfully harvested, it is of little moment just how the time necessary to grow it was allotted. This is to be seen in the instance of the ironworkers among the Volta River peoples, where these men, primarily agriculturalists, divide their time seasonally between the two types of activities in which they engage. It is to be seen in other societies where house-building or house-repairing, or the making of mats or mortars or other utensils and the like is deferred until the dry season. It is likewise apparent when cycles of economic activity are compared with the ritual cycle. Except for emergencies, the latter coincides almost without exception to the dry season, since during the rains the demands of agriculture are too exacting to allow for the proper execution of forms of worship.

The daily rhythm that continues irrespective of seasonal change dictates the allocation of time during a given day to the tasks immediately at hand. The day may be thought of as broken into segments delimiting the hours between rising and retiring. The limits of these segments are set by the time of the day at which meals are eaten. In West Africa, and to a degree over all the continent south of the Sahara, the breaks come at about ten in the morning and at midafternoon. At times the large meal is eaten late in the day, often shortly before going to sleep. It must be recalled that night falls early. The day comes without a prolonged dawn. There is no time for the preparation of a large meal at waking. At night, cooking in the dark is not favored. Thus, arising with the dawn, the African takes but a bite before occupying himself with his other concerns; at the other end of the day, when the principal meal is consumed, he rests.

The contrast between this seasonal and daily work rhythm and the work pattern of the industrial laborer will be at once apparent. Except in the case of large-scale agricultural under-takings, the seasonal factor does not enter. The routine of work in extractive and industrial enterprises moves around the calen-dar with a schedule of operations fixed not by natural conditions but through decisions reached far from any contact the worker may experience and as much beyond his control as are the sea-sons. He is thus caught up in a system that goes contrary to his prior experience. The variety of economic activities in which he engages under his own economic system is, furthermore, entirely lacking. His task remains the same from one day to the next and his time is apportioned for him, so that he is not free to vary the monotony of his work by moving from one aspect of a job to another. This is a commonplace for the industrial worker in a mechanized society. But in our Western economy a rhythm of life has been developed to afford some outlet to compensate for this monotony. The African sees no adequate reward in forms of his system of values to make this acceptable to him.

There is some tendency to define the industrial routine as disciplined, in contrast to an assumed carefree round held to characterize "primitive" man. Yet it takes but cursory analysis of the economic organization of nonindustrialized societies to recognize that, if we approach this from a human point of view, what we are really contrasting is different types of discipline that derive their validation from differing sources. It soon be-comes apparent that no question of the presence or absence of discipline, as such, enters in either type of economy. The disci-pline of the worker in nonindustrailized societies is self-imposed, while that of the industrial operative is imposed from outside. To the worker born in an industrial society, as well as to others who live in terms of the cultural orientations existing there, this outer source of discipline is taken for granted, as is any other culturally sanctioned mode of behavior. But to the worker who has been accustomed to different patterns, especially patterns under which the allocation of time and energy are self-deter-mined, and who is newly brought into an industrial scene, the problem of reorientation necessitates a far-reaching process of adjustment. The degree of social no less than of personal dis-organization that has resulted from many such attempts to make an adjustment of this sort needs only mention; when we consider how far-reaching it must be, we may take it as a measure of the plasticity of the human organism that the amount of demoralization is not greater.

Adjustment to the daily rhythm imposed by industrial work presents problems of an equivalent order of difficulty. Here it is not the question of a fixed as against a self-determined rou-tine but of a difference in the cultural patterning of primary, biological drives. One of the most severe adjustments that is required here arises from the operation of a factor in the daily life of all of us, so taken for granted that it would be suprising if it entered in planning and executing technical aid programs. This factor concerns the schedule of mealtimes, whose im-portance in setting the daily rhythm of native labor has been indicated.

Habits associated with food consumption reflect some of the deepest conditionings of the human organism. It is a truism among social scientists that, while hunger is a basic universal human drive, the foods which satisfy the drive and the times when hunger is appeased are cuturally determined variables. The applicability of this principle to the foods consumed is quite well recognized; but the imfcrt nce of the fact that hunger, a biological phenomenon, operates on a cultural timetable is not. Therefore, where workers in underdeveloped areas are furnished their native foodstuffs, as is almost always done today, only half the requirement for adaptation to the new situation is met. The time of eating is almost of equal importance and, when neg-lected, can entail acute discomfort for the worker and go far to shape his feeling-tone toward the new situation in which he finds himself. On the unconscious level many seeds of hostility and aggression are sown in the process of exacting this con-formity to the new reorientation in the timing of meals.

This is true not only in industrial enterprises but also of projects in other f.elds with which programs of development are concerned, such as education. As has been pointed out, persons from the industrially developed countries, like all others, take their mealtimes for granted. Where the controls are in their hands, therefore, they tend quite automatically to set their own schedules for others to follow. That is why, when queried about the matter, Africans who were educated in mission schools have given as one of the most vivid recollections of their early school years the fact that they were constantly hungry because they could not eat at their accustomed times. Other Africans, employed by European industrial concerns, have stated that one of their principal adjustments was to adapt their time of eating to the schedule of hours set by their employers. One need only contrast a schedule of meals eaten before going to work, at midday, and early in the evening, with the indigenous pattern of midmorning and midafternoon meals to make the point that it is in such humble, taken-for-granted aspects of life that some of the most serious problems of adjustment are to be sought.

The second problem that we will consider arises out of the changes that occur in the manner in which the labor force is mobilized when indigenous societies of underdeveloped areas are brought under the canons of employment prevailing in the industrial communities of Europe and America. While the generalization is not without exception, in the main it is true that the economy of the West differs strikingly from that of most other societies in that it is based on individual effort, whereas these other peoples are communally oriented. In terms of these canons, the worker in this country and in Europe acts as an individual, and, if he organizes trade-unions to protect his position, such organizations still remain aggregates of individuals. In the economies of nonindustrial societies, on the other hand, the individual acts primarily as the member of a group, whether this group is based on kinship or residence or both. In Africa the factor of co-operative effort well exemplifies this. The problem of cultivating considerable tracts of land in West Africa during the short period at the beginning of the rainy season is met quite effectively by group labor of this sort. The hoe, in the hands of one man, is not too efficient an instrument; but many hoes in the hands of many men will in a day ready a large field for planting. Or, again, in the eastern part of the continent and other cattle-keeping regions, where herds must be taken daily to pasture, it is the small boys of the village who together care for the animals belonging to all their elders.

Another aspect of this tradition of group labor has to do with the direction of work. Europeans and Americans who come to Africa soon discover how deeply the concept of the responsible leader lodges in the customary work patterns of the Africans. One who wishes a given task performed does not hire workers as individuals, or, if he is under the illusion that he does, he finds that he soon is negotiating the problems that arise with the head of the group, who may alone be held to account for the quality and amount of work done. To reprimand an individual worker invites diff.culties; it is the responsible head alone who must see to it that those in his group do their work, and it is he alone who may call his men to task.

Again, far-reaching adjustment is plainly required when a person coming from a society where patterns of this sort prevail moves into contact with a system oriented in terms of individual effort. In a very real sense, such a person is likely to be lost in the new situation. The social support which he has been accustomed to expect and receive is entirely lacking. It is not chance that in the New World the descendants of Africans, like many indigenous American Indian groups, deprived of their aboriginal setting of a clan structure, took over the *compadre*, or godparent tradition, from some of the individualistically oriented cultures of Europe as a compensating device. The degree to which this tradition has been elaborated in various parts of Central and South America and the Caribbean region is an index of the urgency of the need felt by members of these groups for social support in their daily contacts.

Gang labor has been one response to the recognition of the tradition of co-operative work among workers in underdeveloped areas by those charged with the operation of large-scale projects in industry or agriculture or mining. Yet, again, the perception of this institution of co-operative effort as something that can be built on in effectively utilizing labor power has proved to be only a half-measure, owing to the superficial nature of the percept. For in the African pattern the accountability of the leader of a work group is only secondarily to the employer and not as is the case in industry. His primary responsibility is to the members of the group he directs and of which he himself is a member. The system whereby a group of men working as individuals for a common employer is directed by a leader who is also hired as an individual by the same employer is the most casual of resemblances to the democratically controlled indigenous co-operative work group.

In short, then, the problem resolves itself into one in which the worker, who comes from a culture where the pattern is one of collective effort based on inner control, is to adapt himself to a system where individualism is the dominant motif. From the point of view of programs aiming at the development of under-developed areas, it constitutes an aspect of first importance, in terms not only of the impact of these programs on the worker himself, but also on the societies where they are instituted. It is not too much to say that these differences in approach to the problem of mobilizing labor is at the base of much of the social disorganization and individual demoralization that has too often been the concomitant of even the best-planned schemes of development.

Some attention has already been given to the third point to be considered—that of labor incentives. As may be gathered from the preceding discussion of it, this has been recognized as crucial by all those concerned with projects in the underdeveloped areas. Because it strikes to the very heart of the question of the impact of one economy on another, it is closely tied in with the two problems we have just sketched—the rhythm of work and the democratic pattern of co-operative labor—and can profitably be considered further.

One of the complaints most frequently heard in many of these operations, especially in Africa, is that when a native has become integrated into the system of Euro-American economic procedures, and his earnings, in terms of local standards become steady, his "family"—that is, the members of his wider kinship group—feel free to descend on him to share what he earns. In terms of accepted modes of conduct among these peoples, he must care for them or in other ways make his contributions to their joint undertakings. This not only holds true for the wage-worker. The small native shopkeeper and the European-trained professional man are similarly called on to conform to these traditional patterns. In cultural terms such a man as an earner works in accordance with the patterns of an economy based on individual initiative, but his consumption patterns are dictated by the traditions of a collective system. The conflicts that arise from this, as regards both the earner and the group out of which he has come, can be serious. Equally pertinent is the fact that individual initiative, essential to any success in an economy of free enterprise, is scarcely encouraged by the necessity of continuously meeting such obligations, made the more imperative by the fact that they arise out of some of the deepest ties that an individual can experience.

The factor of seasonal rhythm also impinges on this matter of incentives. Here a reinterpretation of preindustrial patterns often operates to cause the worker to leave his job. In the indigenous economic systems the dry season was the time of travel. Men left their homes to trade or to engage in hunting or to pay visits to relatives. The ceremonial round likewise often took them away from home for considerable periods of time. These changes in the established routine were welcome, and they remain even more welcome to the native wage-worker in an industrial enterprise or in a mine or on a plantation. It would seem that, on the basis of past experience, thought could profitably be given to developmental projects, at least where agricultural development is concerned, wherein the co-operative principle can be applied to organizing the productive efforts of individual or group owners of land and in which the routine would be close to the earlier organization of time given to the work to be done.

One of the most striking examples of an area that has brought this type of economic agriculture into the world economy, making its potential resources generally available and raising the standards of living of its inhabitants, is to be found in the history of the cacao-growing industry of the Gold Coast. Long antedating present-day developmental schemes, and initially quite without benefit of Western economic planning, it has in large measure achieved many of the ends envisaged in the technical aid programs of this and other countries and of the

United Nations agencies concerned with these matters. The native standard of living in the Gold Coast is the highest of any dependency in Africa; its political growth has been steady and today represents the closest approach to self-government of any African colony; its educational system has far wider ramifications into the villages than elsewhere on the continent. All this has been achieved not without stress and tensions, but in essence it represents the results of inner developments based on pre-existing patterns rather than development induced by the direct application of forces impinging from outside and cast in terms foreign to native practices.

Here there is no lack of incentive to expand production. Moreover, Africans, using the capital they accumulated through raising cacao, have moved into areas of commerce and minor industry with a minimum of dislocation of established institutions. There are no extremes of what has been termed "detribalization," but the claims of relatives have, in many cases, been resolved by opening opportunities rather than by merely sharing wages or profits with them. This is not unlike a situation found in eastern Nigeria, among the Ibo, where resources of large family groupings are being pooled to permit certain of their members to take advantage of opportunities that will accrue to the benefit of all. A promising young man is in this way aided to obtain the higher education that will allow him to function to the credit of his family unit in the changing economic and political scene. A good trader is helped to expand his operation and thus contribute to the resources of the group as a whole. This, as in the Gold Coast cacao industry, is an extension of pre-existing patterns to fit the new scene.

Admittedly, to move from this type of development, motivated from within, to planned programs brought from outside is not simple. Yet the African cultures, at least, are receptive to the modern scene, and, if the motivation exists, Africans show appreciable plasticity. In terms of existing orientations it is plain that it is less difficult to provide incentives in agricultural projects than in industrial developments. One successful plan of this kind is the Gezira scheme in the Anglo-Egyptian Sudan; another is in French West Africa, where native production of cotton and ground nuts, through uniting the work of individual farmers, has materially increased production. The published reservations to both these schemes are substantial, and it is apparent that special circumstances have been present to cause the Gezira project to function as it has. Whatever the reservations, however, one may with profit contemplate the difference between the successes obtained here and the failure, in human no less than in technological aspects, of the ill-fated ground-nut scheme in East Africa. Developmental projects, it is plain, must build on ways that make sense to the people involved in them if incentives to active participation are to result in the effective attainment of stated ends.

Factors such as these, which come into play to further or impede the success of projects looking toward the economic development of underdeveloped areas, constitute only a part of the whole problem. We have still to consider how what is brought to a people is integrated into their ways of living, as against the manner in which their established patterns of behavior are adapted to the requirements of a new economic and technological system. Here we are confronted with the question of the meaning of a way of life for those who live in accordance with it. This, in turn, can be understood only in the light of the findings of that phase of psychoethnography that has to do with the mechanisms of learning and conditioning which shape the characteristic motor habits, reaction patterns, and accepted modes of thinking of a people.

It may be useful at this point briefly to recall the nature of culture and the manner in which it functions. By general consensus, culture is defined as the learned, socially sanctioned behavior of a people. As something learned, its dynamic quality derives from a continuous process of relearning that results from the constant readjustment of individuals to stimuli arising both from within the group and from outside it. Culture fulfils a twofold function. It provides those born into a society with means to adapt effectively to their human and natural setting by training them in the forms of behavior recognized as valid by their group. More than this, however, it provides a background against which the creative aspects of the total human response pattern can be projected, a base from which exploration into new orientations in living can move. From the point of view of human personality development, culture is thus the medium through which adjustment is achieved, a point of particular importance when the maladjustments that result from contacts between peoples with disparate cultures are taken into account.

As individuals, we learn our cultures by a process termed "enculturation." This is subtle and all-pervading and so thoroughly absorbed that for the most part we live our lives in terms of reactions that lodge below the level of our consciousness. Only when some alternative is presented to us do we become aware of the assumptions which otherwise we take as given or of the overt forms of behavior that we manifest so spontaneously. Then we must consider, judge, evaluate, choose. We relearn the new alternative; or, in terms of cultural theory, we undergo a process of re-enculturation.

It is in the area of values that enculturation strikes to its greatest depths. Here we learn the sanctions that give meaning to behavior, the rationale for living. Evaluations of this character, in the last analysis, maximize the satisfactions that culture affords man. Hence, when we put into force programs aimed at changing the modes of living of peoples so that they may enjoy satisfactions outside the purview of the system of values of their culture, we are saying, in effect, that the ends we envisage are so superior to those already in force that their desirability is beyond challenge. It is thus assumed that, when these new values are presented to peoples having other traditionally approved ends, they must ultimately displace the values to which these people were originally encultured. But this is a proposition that calls for the closest testing in the light of our knowledge of cultural dynamics.

East Africa affords us an instance precisely in the field of those economic goals which are primarily under discussion here; that is, of the problems that arise when attempts to develop resources of underdeveloped areas involve the reconciliation of two different systems of evaluating ends. This instance has to do with the utilization of the rich possibilities presented by the high grassy plateaus of the area for the production of cattle for the world market. This region has long been noted for its excellence as pasture land. Here is where the great herds of wild animals roam, taking advantage of the same pasturage that has provided sustenance for the cattle owned by the natives.

One of the drawbacks to the utilization of this area for the purpose of producing beef for export has been the presence of the tsetse fly in various districts, since the sting of the tsetse is fatal to cattle. A few years ago the discovery of a vaccine against tsetse was announced. East Africa, it was stressed, now rid of its handicap, would become a new Argentina and would supply the meat-hungry parts of the world with beef. Potentially, all the favorable elements for development programs seemed to be present. An existing resource was to be utilized; an expansion of the pre-existing economy would raise indigenous standards of living by increasing cash income, while at the same time meeting a pressing world need; this could be accomplished without the evils consequent on detribalization and urbanization. Yet nothing seems to have happened.

We may leave to one side questions of a technical order that have been raised, such as the actual efficacy of the vaccine or whether the tsetse can be expected to breed a strain whose virulence will in effect nullify the immunization this new discovery was intended to provide. Here we will consider the problem of the value system of the indigenous peoples as it bears on the question of substituting new ends for those in existence. We may first describe the role of cattle in the indigenous cultures, in order to make clear the problems involved in attempts to utilize this resource as a profitable commercial venture.

In all East Africa wealth has traditionally taken the form of cattle. These animals, however, constitute a special kind of wealth, being essentially the depositaries of value in a system of prestige economics and not figuring appreciably in the subsistence economy, since only their milk is consumed. The subsistence economy, as a matter of fact, is simple. Each family is self-supporting to such a degree that, unlike many other parts of Africa, markets were found rarely, if at all, and, except for the ironworkers, there were no specialists. The subsistence economy, therefore, is taken for granted; it is an aspect of life to which a minimum of attention is paid.

Nothing could contrast more sharply to this than the attitude of these peoples toward cattle. Their herds literally give meaning and purpose to life. Ownership dictates social status; the passage of cattle alone validates marriage and gives children the stamp of legitimacy. Cattle, to the people of this area, have the sentimental value of our pets. They are thematic materials for poetry and songs. These animals are never slaughtered for food, so that beef is eaten only when a cow dies or when an ox is sacrified at the funeral of the owner of a herd. Some of the languages of the area have fifty or more words which we can only translate by the term "cow" plus a qualifying phrase. By the use of this rich and specialized descriptive vocabulary, color, size, shape of horns, even tempermental characteristics, can be denoted by a single term.

An incident that occurred during the visit of the United Nations Trusteeship Council Mission to Ruanda-Urundi may be cited to illustrate the way in which cattle are conceived as having individual personalities. A native veterinary assistant, clad in a white laboratory coat, was injecting the cows in the herds of his district with a preventive serum. As he finished with each animal, he made a mark in his book, then turned to the next. One member of the mission, curious, asked him how he knew which cows had been injected, since no animal was branded or marked in any other way. The native assistant, puzzled by the question, showed the visitor his book. "See," he replied, "I just make a mark after the name of each animal every time I inject it."

It is significant to observe that one value introduced from outside these cultures by those who exercise control over cattle-owning peoples meets with no resistance—the value laid on improving the quality of the breed and preventing disease in the animals. This means longer-lived and better cattle and, as an end result, more cattle. This in turn increases the wealth of an individual and the prestige that accrues to him. The fact that this improvement has raised serious problems involving over-grazing the restricted reserve areas allotted to the natives, and thus has intensified soil erosion as the area of white settlement spread, is here aside from the point. What concerns us in our present discussion is that the resulting increase of cattle yielded no marketable surplus. The end of raising cattle in the native mind being to have more and more of them, any program which necessitated disposing of animals, in terms of the established patterns of value, induced social disutility.

As far as can be determined, in one district only has any success attended efforts to persuade natives to sell their cattle. Here the political officers have instituted a campaign to convince the cattle owners that it is to their benefit, in the changed economy they now face, to dispose of a certain proportion of their animals in the market, so as to furnish meat for the various urban centers that have developed. They have painstakingly demonstrated that this can be done and still leave the owners enough cattle to permit pre-existing status patterns to be followed, to allow cattle to pass at marriage, and to continue the existing social orientations. There seems to be a growing response in the numbers of cattle offered for sale, but it is recognized by all concerned with promoting the project that this is a long process and must be developed at the local level on the basis of well-grounded personal relationships that engender mutual confidence.

Examples from Africa and the rest of the underdeveloped portions of the world could be multiplied to show how complex is the matrix of custom and sanction to be taken into account when the spread of technological knowledge and economic development to peoples living under differing conditions of life, and in terms of different goals, is contemplated. The fragmentation of knowledge in our society, as represented, for instance, by the specialized academic disciplines, has carried us so far that it is easy for us to forget that a culture is a functioning unit. We do not often take full cognizance of the fact that the aspects into which we divide custom for purposes of study are a fiction of science. By the same token, we overlook the principle that a change effected in any one of these aspects has repercussions over the total way of life on the culture as a whole.

This is as true for our own culture, despite its specialization, as for any other. Exclusive preoccupation with a single phase has been responsible for some of the more unrealistic approaches to various social, economic, and political programs that have been proposed in our society. The results of this overspecialization have become patent enough to give rise to the call for cross-disciplinary co-operation that is so marked a current in the intellectual stream of the present day. The introduction of new economic mechanisms based on technological innovations that increase production, even in our own society, has introduced far-reaching changes in social organization, the functioning of religion, and accepted standards of aesthetic perception. This, be it noted, has taken place as the result of the operation of internal impulses, something that has permitted a reasonable adjustment of sanctions as changes have occurred in the forms of institutions and in our re-enculturation to new modes of behavior. But this is quite different from a situation where changes of a fundamental nature are abruptly introduced from outside a society, changes which envisage the attainment of ends differing from those that previously had motivated conduct. In such a situation change lacks the elements of gradualness and measured infiltration by which internally induced cultural innovations are worked into pre-existing patterns.

Because our know-how has raised our standard of living and by extending the frontiers of our knowledge has given us benefits that we prize, we assume it can be applied in other societies with equal profit. We implement our good will with projects designed to bring our skills to those who do not possess them. As we move into the area of technical aid programs, however, we discover that even the know-how on which we pride ourselves is not always transferable or even applicable. The knowledge possessed by indigenous peoples concerning the utilization of their land is not scientifically derived, but it is the result of a long process of adaptation to their natural setting, and much of it meets the pragmatic test. Large-scale planting by the use of mechanical agricultural implements has been introduced in many parts of the tropical world. In some instances, however, the land, unprotected by the forest growth, is exposed to the rains that leech out its chemical content and render it less productive than when worked in small patches with the hoe. Benefits anticipated on the basis of the returns these methods yield in temperate climates did not materialize.

This, however, is only one of the more obvious aspects of the matter. At the outset of this discussion note was taken of the acceptance by social scientists of the aims of the exact and natural disciplines, prediction, and control. As was indicated, the difficulty of predicting the outcome of a given social development, even in our own culture, is reasonably well recognized. The fact that controls, on the scientific no less than the practical level, when applied cross-culturally take us into questions of value and purpose of the most fundamental character is, however, a lesson that must still be learned. The manipulation of inert matter or of biological organisms that do not have recourse to the symbolisms of language is one thing. Man, however—and this must never be forgotten—is the only animal who can talk back. When attempts are made to manipulate his behavior, to say nothing of his thinking, important philosophical problems remain to be examined. Man alone, with his gift of projecting experience through the symbolisms of language, has developed culture and the wide range of institutions that mark human societies over the world. Because of the nature of the enculturative experience, the expressions of value that supply the motivations for the behavior of any given people provide the primary points of reference in any judgment that is drawn. The emotional loading given the institutions and values to which an individual has been enculturated makes conclusions that are obvious to one group anything but obvious to another.

When the industralized people of the world bring their knowledge to those living in what we term "underdeveloped"—that is, nonindustralized—areas, the assumption is made that our ways are those which hold the answers to problems which have, in actuality, been answered in many ways. The fact that we speak of these peoples as "primitive," the territories they inhabit as "backward," or our continuous use of the word "progress" as a general over-all desideratum, when we really mean moving toward the attainment of goals we determine as good on the basis of our experience is an index of our attitude.

This has not escaped the attention of the growing numbers of those who, enculturated to the ways of the native societies from which they derive, through Western education have come to know the deficiencies as well as the good points of our culture. They read what we write about them and with time and repetition come to resent the implications of the inferiority of their cultures so often expressed in what they read. The growing nationalisms in the far parts of the world, in a very real sense, represent in no negligible measure a reaction that has as its driving force the refusal to accept our evaluations of their traditional way of life. Indeed, the student of culture cannot escape the conclusion that the movements called nativistic are highly keyed reaffirmations of the values in the cultures we term "backward." If we but take the example of China and Africa, where the cultures are deeply rooted in traditions of the continuity of ancestral generations, it is not difficult to see how the derogation of established ways, even by implication, can arouse both latent and manifest hostilities.

In a world where increasing rapidity of communication makes for increasingly close contact between peoples, programs of any sort that cut across cultures must take into account the intangibles of established custom if there is to be any positive, lasting gain. It must be recognized, first of all, that there is no single answer to the problems that are faced by mankind. What we term technological and economic "progress" cannot be achieved without integrating the new into the old; moreover, this integration can only be suggested, not forced. The peoples to whom technical aid is brought will, in the final analysis, decide what they will accept and what they will reject. Even where they do not control their own political destinies, the force of cultural inertia prevents their being manipulated like pawns on a chessboard. We know today too well that they are imponderables in the world scene, not pawns.

This is why it must be understood, above all, that the diffusion of ideas, and even of technology, is more than a unilateral process. If we keep firmly in mind the force of our own enculturation, we will be able to understand how the ways of others are similarly valued by those who live in terms of them.

We can learn as well as teach, and there is no more effective mode of convincing others of the worth of what we have to teach than by expressing a willingness to learn as well. Only when considerations of this nature enter into instituting and implementing technical aid programs can these projects unite rather than divide free men and women and leave the residue of friendship and co-operation that is their ultimate aim.

SOME SOURCES OF THE VULNERABILITY OF THE STRUCTURES OF RELATIVELY NON-INDUSTRIALIZED SOCIETIES TO THOSE OF HIGHLY INDUSTRIALIZED SOCIETIES

By Marion J. Levy

THE problem under discussion here is a particular problem in the field of social change. Some general remarks about the analysis of social change are in order prior to the discussion of the problem itself. In the first place the term "social change" as used here will refer to alterations in the social structure[1] of the system or unit spoken of as changed. In any given discussion of social change the analysis is limited to changes in the social structure of the unit on the level of generalization given by the definition, that is, on the most general level of structure of the unit concerned. The systematic study of change at lower levels of generalization requires the definition of units at lower levels.

In any particular instance of change three stages may be distinguished: the initial stage (i.e., the basis from which change takes place); the transitional stage (i.e., the state of affairs during the process of change that is being studied); and the resultant stage (i.e., the state of the structure of the unit at the end of the process). Obviously there is always an arbitrary decision in stating a problem of social change and hence of distinguishing three such stages, since, at least in terms of the passage of time, change in empirical phenomena is never observed as actually stopped. Like so many other concepts in science, these do not necessarily describe empirical phenomena but

---

1. The term "social structure" is here defined as observable uniformities in social action. "Social action" is defined residually as all operation (including in that term mere persistence) by individuals of a given species that (1) is explicable or analyzable in empirical terms and (2) cannot be adequately explained or analyzed for the purposes intended in terms of the factors of the heredity of that species and its environment exclusive of other members of that species. I have discussed these concepts more fully in my recent book, *The Structure of Society* (Princeton: Princeton University Press, 1952).

help us erect more or less useful models for understanding it. Any attempt to find "ultimate origins" is of course futile within the limits set by scientific analysis, since the search itself involves the metaphysical assumption of some unobserved ultimate starting point. It is possible by discovering the functional and then the structural requisites of a given social unit to determine its most general structures on the level under consideration. If we know these structures for any two of the three stages, we can systematically discover those of the third, if not exactly, at least within certain ranges of possibility.[2]

The strategic factors for change (i.e., the factors necessary and sufficient for a change given the initial stage) may be internal factors (i.e., factors produced by the operation of the unit without any new influences from other units), or external factors (i.e., factors newly introduced to the system from other units), or some combination of the two. We are concerned here primarily with cases of strategic external factors, although the original cases of development of highly industralized societies may be usefully studied in terms of models such that the strategic factors are internal ones. Whether one develops hypotheses about change in terms of internal or external factors, however, it is never possible to ignore some internal factors, even though they are not the strategic ones, since the initial basis from which change takes place is always relevant.

In these terms the scientific inadequacy of the Marxist theory of economic determinism or of any similar monistic theory emerges. In the first place, defense of the theory of economic determinism by citing an "economic" cause for any cause shown to be strategic within certain limits falls to the ground as a special case of "ultimate origin" hunting or at least leaves untouched the argument that the "economically" caused "non-economic" cause could be strategic. In other respects it is no less vulnerable. If the term "economic" is defined in Marxist terms, as it frequently seems to be, as any factor capable of causing change, then the theory is perfectly "true" (i.e., economic factors cause all changes); but it is also perfectly meaningless (i.e.,

2. There is not space to go into this matter in detail here. I have discussed these questions more fully in the book mentioned in n. 1.

the only factors capable of causing changes cause whatever changes there are). If the term "economic" is tied down to some more restricted referent (e.g., having to do with the allocation of goods and services), the theory is quite meaningful (i.e., one of all possible variables causes whatever change there is), but it is also false (i.e., cases can be found in which change takes place and economic factors do not vary on the level under consideration, or are not the strategic factors, or both). The Marxist and other general monistic theories are not the only sources of difficulty in these respects. The temptation, in the face of striking social changes like those of the late nineteenth and twentieth centuries, to focus on limited external factors and ignore the relevance of internal ones is striking. The internal ones are always relevant, even if not strategic, if only because they form the initial basis from which change takes place and hence as a minimum set limits on the possible range of change. Given the ordinary sense of the terms, one cannot make a silk purse out of a sow's ear, and the starting materials are more relevant in explaining this theory than any forces brought to bear on them. The starting conditions may be less limiting in other cases, but they are always limits of some sort.

The initial stage with which we are concerned here is that of relatively nonindustrialized societies. A society for present purposes will be considered more or less industrialized to the extent that in the allocation of goods and services (i.e., in their production, consumption, and distribution) the members of the society utilize (1) tools that multiply, in however complex a manner, the effects of their applications of energy and (2) inanimate sources of power (or energy). Given this definition, there are probably no societies totally devoid of industrial factors, since even the use of a sailboat or a waterwheel would constitute such a factor. However crudely it may be done, it is possible to distinguish very highly industrialized societies from relatively nonindustrialized ones in these terms. There are societies whose members use tools that multiply tremendously their own outputs of energy and of other energy applied by them and that utilize inanimate sources of power for the overwhelming proportions of energy consumed in the allocation of goods and services. The scale of variation in these respects may be continuous, or it may be radically discontinuous in certain portions of the scale, as I suspect it is. Nevertheless, a superficial examination of different systems (e.g., modern United States, modern England, Imperial, or even present-day, China, and the Trobriand Islands system) certainly reveals enormous differences in these respects. Furthermore, it would seem a plausible hypothesis, at least, that some of these units are very highly industrialized (e.g., modern United States and modern England) as compared with others (e.g., Imperial, or even present-day, China and the Trobriand Islands system). It would even seem that a further reasonable hypothesis can be made that, whatever the differences in these respects between the systems at one of the extremes on this scale, their differences from one another are not so great as the differences between systems taken from opposite extremes of the scale. My present interest is in the social implications of the introduction of the social structures common and/or necessary for the systems at one end of the scale into systems at the other, that is, the introduction of patterns of highly industrialized into relatively nonindustrialized systems. Empirically speaking, the specific problem of these meetings is not with the case of indigenous (or internal) development of these patterns but is rather with the introduction of these patterns into "underdeveloped" (i.e., little industrialized or nonindustrialized) systems.

In developing some hypotheses about these implications, we will focus our attention here on three types of variables concerned with three aspects of the patterns (or structures) of relationships among members of societies. These aspects have to do with the cognitive aspects, the memberships criteria aspects, and the substantive definition aspects of relationships. These variables are presented in pairs. Cognitively speaking, a relationship will be classified as rational or nonrational. The relationship as a whole will be considered more or less nearly rational or nonrational to the extent rationality is or is not institutionally expected of the action in terms of the relationship. Action is considered rational to the extent that the objective and subjective ends of action are united. For present purposes the intricacies of the distinction may be ignored,[3] and a relationship may be considered rational to the extent that it is institutionally expected that the members of it apply reasoning in terms of critical scientific standards, regardless of whether scientific knowledge as such is specifically distinguished from other sorts in the system or not. It may be considered nonrational to the extent that reasoning about action in terms of the relationship proceeds primarily in terms of what is justified by custom or transcendental powers regardless of the empirical effects of the application of such reasoning.

As regards membership criteria a relationship will be considered more or less nearly universalistic or more or less particularistic. It will be purely universalistic if its members are chosen in terms of criteria such that (1) no individual is institutionally barred from possessing or acquiring them and (2) they are germane to the purpose for which selection is made. The criteria will be termed more or less particularistic to the extent that any departure is made from either or both of these two conditions.[4] For present purposes relationships will be called predominantly universalistic to the extent that they stress what an individual can do that is germane to the purpose of choice. They will be considered predominantly particularistic to the extent that choice is made on the basis of who a person is regardless of whether that knowledge is germane to empirical performance.

As regards substantive definitions, a relationship will be regarded as more or less functionally specific or functionally diffuse.[5] A functionally specific relationship is defined as one in which the activities or considerations or rights and obligations covered by the relationship are precisely defined and delimited.

3. The definition of the terms "rational" and "nonrational" follows Pareto's logical-nonlogical distinction. There is not space here to go into the development of these concepts and their subcategories (e.g., irrational, methodologically arational, and ultimately arational). They are discussed in detail in the manuscript mentioned above and in my paper, "A Note on Pareto's Logical-Nonlogical Categories," *American Sociological Review*, XIII, No. 6 (December, 1948), 756–57.

4. These terms and the following two (functionally specific and functionally diffuse) represent applications with some modifications of these concepts as developed by Talcott Parsons. See his "The Professions and Social Structure," *Essays in Sociological Theory Pure and Applied* (Glencoe, Ill.: Free Press, 1950), pp. 185–99.

5. See n. 4.

A functionally diffuse relationship is defined as one in which the activities, rights, etc., are vaguely defined and delimited. The typical business-contract type of relationship is in theory at least functionally specific. In the event of a dispute over what is included in the relationship the burden of proof rests on the person claiming "something extra." The relationship of family members is typically a predominantly functionally diffuse one. In such relationships the burden of proof lies on the person refusing "something extra," and that proof in general involves the statement of some overriding obligation recognized by the parties of the dispute and not the statement that the claimant cannot prove that the "extra" factor is owed.

With respect to these three types of relationship patterns it would seem that a fairly sharp line can be drawn between highly industrialized and relatively nonindustrialized societies. Like the industrial distinction itself, this is not an all-or-none proposition. There is certainly no society in which rational action is nonexistent, and probably there is none completely lacking some predominantly universalistic and functionally specific relationships. Similarly no highly industrialized society is devoid of nonrational action or of some predominantly particularistic and functionally diffuse relationships. There is not space here to go into the matter, but a fairly tenable theoretical case can be made out for the impossibility of any society being an all-or-none proposition in these three respects. Nevertheless, particularly in the sphere of economic structure (i.e., patterns having to do with the allocation—including production, consumption, and distribution—of goods and services) the differences in degree between the two types of societies would seem to be radical. The argument is not going to fall into economic determinism at this point. The economic aspect of action is focused on for its heuristic value in these respects. Limitations of space again prevent detailed arguments as to why these differences can never be limited solely to the economic sphere, but that statement must be taken as a hypothesis at least for the present.

When one looks at the social structure of relatively nonindustrialized societies, with considerable uniformity one sees relationship patterns that emphasize traditional thinking, particularism, and functional diffuseness, and this would seem to be as marked with respect to the economic structure of those societies as with regard to others. While Marxist theory of social change is hardly to be taken seriously as a scientific theory, Marx contributed at least one major service to the development of social analysis. He made it virtually impossible to ignore the relevance of economic factors. One need not assume them the sole relevant factors, but they will always have some relevance, because the limits of possible variation of members of societies and of societies themselves are such that survival cannot take place in the absence of allocation of goods and services. Other factors are necessary for survival, too, but this one is never to be ignored.

It is another basic hypothesis of this paper that all societies in their operation produce dysfunctions—that no society operates without stresses and strains that focus on individuals who are members of those systems. It is also a hypothesis of this paper that in no society are the vast majority of members inherently masochistic, so that no motivation for escape or defiance of the system exists. But again and again we see cases of societies in which, though the stresses and strains seem to be enormous, revolts and escapes are not wholesale. In some cases the stability is so impressive (as in the case of Imperial China) that many scholars conclude that the stresses and strains cannot be great and give as evidence thereof the stability of the patterns. But this does not follow. The stresses and strains may, at least in theory, be enormous and still be contained, especially in societies emphasizing traditional thinking, highly particularistic criteria of employment, and functionally diffuse relationships. By revolt or escape in such societies an individual cuts himself off from the criteria that state who he is. Admission to functionally diffuse relationships is more risky than admission to functionally specific ones because of the vagueness of the obligations such admission may carry. Finally, the man who revolts and escapes violates traditional thinking. He at once becomes in some respects a critic where others are not with all the friction that this may imply. There are, no doubt, other reasons for stability in such systems. Socialization processes may minimize deviance, and other factors may operate. But, where motivation for deviance is not prevented from developing, deviance itself may still be prevented because of the extreme difficulty often experienced in the rebel's finding alternative economic roles that will permit him to live satisfactorily. The situation in which these patterns function to contain great stresses and strains is by no means the only possible one in relatively nonindustrialized societies. It is, however, one with socially explosive potentialities in the face of the introduction of the patterns of highly industrialized societies. In the late nineteenth and twentieth centuries we seem to have witnessed case after case in which indigenous social structures have disintegrated or begun to disintegrate, some after long periods of stability, in cases of both large-scale and relatively small-scale introduction of industrial factors. The explosive case may be an extreme one, but it may also teach us much about some of the factors of importance, though of less dramatic character, in less extreme cases.

The requirements of highly industrialized societies reverse the picture relative to these relationship aspects. Stresses and strains are no less a feature of these than of other societies, but the method of containment outlined above cannot operate so effectively. Emphases on rationality, universalism, and functional specificity are inescapable in these societies for fairly obvious reasons. The demands of a highly complex technology and of science that serves as a basis for further technological change[6] imply a high emphasis on critical rationality in these respects on the part of the members of the society. Furthermore, there is good reason to believe that it is virtually impossible to emphasize such patterns in a single sphere or aspect of action and confine them to that sphere. Here again one of the problems of stability in modern industrial societies arises.

The emphases on universalism and functional specificity are equally related to the requirements of industrialization. Advanced degrees of industrialization greatly accentuate the importance of differences in ability on the part of individuals. This

6. One of the most strategic factors in maintaining stability in these societies probably lies in the maintenance or increase of such a rate of change.

is true of even slight differences in ability. The accentuation is a function of the tremendous and complex multiples of effort that result from the machines and the inanimate sources of power. Slight differences in skill may be reflected in enormous differences in output under such circumstances. The difference between the amounts accomplished by an unskilled versus a skilled digger using hand tools may be great, but the difference in amounts that can be accomplished by machine-shovel operators with comparable differences in skill is enormously greater in both degree and absolute amounts. Furthermore, the differences in skill are strategic not only in terms of output; they are also strategic in a negative sense. The difference in damage that can be done by the relatively less skilled in highly industrialized situations as opposed to relatively nonindustrialized ones is also enormous. A craftworker who drops a tool or a piece of material may ruin relatively little. A mass-production worker may ruin or delay tremendous amounts of capital and work. Even the simplification of jobs by technological advances does not lessen this emphasis on differences in skill. It may, of course, lessen the importance of absolute amounts of skill. Assuming the possibility of comparable measurement, an automobile worker who merely presses a start-and-stop button on a machine may have far less "skill" than a carriage worker in the late nineteenth century. But a split second's difference in reaction time on the part of one such automobile worker and another may have implications running into hundreds of thousands of dollars, whereas this was never the case (even given adjustments for changing price levels) for such differences in carriagemakers. Highly industrialized production may not increase the importance of absolute amounts of skill, but the increased emphasis it places on the significance of relative differences in skill would seem undeniable.

The high emphasis placed on functional specificity in highly industrialized systems is related to the practicable scale of operations in such systems. These scales are large with regard to both units of production and output of goods. Under such circumstances the accounting problem alone would make highly functionally diffuse relationships impossible both in terms of employment for production of goods and services and in terms of disposition of output. The "old family retainer" type of employer-employee relationship is possible with regard to very limited jobs in highly industrialized systems. These jobs would seem to be limited to those of very restricted numbers and those emphasizing craftsmanship. The production of material goods and services is so inordinately large that disposal of these goods on the basis of personalized contacts is out of the question from the point of view of most of the producing units. An automobile manufacturer could not possibly maintain such relationships with the consumers of automobiles, and even retail outlets for such goods cannot operate with the necessary efficiency on such terms. The disposal of such quantities as hundreds of thousands of automobiles or millions of bottles of cold drinks per month simply could not be accomplished except on the basis of highly specific and delimited relationships.

The argument here has in general stressed these patterns one by one and in the field of economic allocation. Their strategic position in such systems is increased when one considers two facts about them. First, certain distinct clusterings of these variables are indicated. Second, it is impossible to confine these patterns rigidly to the economic aspect of action. With regard to the first the argument may be briefly developed as follows. Let us say that, for whatever reasons, it is eufunctional (i.e., makes for the maintenance of a system) for a given system to place a high emphasis on universalistic criteria of employment. Then the probability is high that great emphasis must be placed on both rationality and functional specificity. If the relationship is not functionally specific, it becomes to that degree impossible to determine what are germane criteria of employment. If rationality is not emphasized, the continuation of the relationship cannot be maintained on the basis of germane criteria, and indeed no objective decision as to what is germane can be made. Nor can the relationship be specifically delimited because of the introduction of nonempirical factors. Arguments for the clustering of the nonrational, particularistic, and functionally diffuse patterns are in part the obverse of these and in part have other bases.

The second consideration mentioned is equally relevant because it focuses attention on the apparent tendency of these patterns to become generalized widely through a social system if that system is to maintain its adjustment to its setting. The allocation of goods and services is only analytically separable from the allocation of power and responsibility. Highly universalistic relations in the economic aspects of action are functionally incompatible with highly particularistic ones in the political (i.e., allocation of power and responsibility) aspects of action.[7] It is because of such functional interrelationships among different spheres and aspects of action that these clusters of patterns seem on the whole to appear widely diffused in social systems rather than narrowly confined. When they are narrowly confined, they would seem to be either highly unstable or else most carefully insulated against influences from other parts or aspects of the system. Thus, in a society like the United States predominantly universalistic relationships are widely institutionalized in the economic, political, educational, and recreational spheres, to mention only a few. They even assume an unusually prominent role (e.g., in the treatment of children) in the stronghold of particularistic relations, the family system. In Imperial China, on the other hand, such relationships were institutionalized almost nowhere save in the Imperial bureaucracy, and here the dynastic cycle (and the breakdown and renovation of the Imperial bureaucracy) had as one of its most notable aspects the constant intrusion and elimination of particularistic factors.

Leaving aside the introduction by military means of these patterns associated with highly industrialized societies, the sources of stress and strain in nonindustrial societies, whether they be those of economic want or desire to escape an unpleasant situation in other respects, account for the motivation for participation in action in terms of the new patterns. The

7. Study of the prospects for long-run stability of highly industrialized systems of economic allocation combined with highly authoritarian systems of political allocation turns up extremely interesting hypotheses. They are hypotheses that, if tenable, are extremely pessimistic for long-run stability of such systems, though they do not obviate the possibility of such systems eliminating alternative types prior to their own dissolution.

low labor costs and relatively untapped markets and resources associated with relatively nonindustrialized societies motivate the introduction of the activities by the members of highly industrialized ones. In case after case neither group seems to stop "trying" in these respects, and quite often the taste of the new motivates the indigenous attempts of persons in relatively nonindustrialized societies to try their own hand at industrialization. Japan presents a dramatic case of this attempt.

Whatever the motivation, the two sets of patterns are mutually subversive. In almost every case of contact, however, the motivation (or force in the case of military activity) to attempt the new has seemed to outweigh the subversive effects of the old. In the potentially explosive case the effects may be dramatic. China, after a two-thousand-year history of decay and renovation of a relatively nonindustrialized system that has in most major respects withstood repeated invasions of nonindustrial patterns, now shows signs of genuinely revolutionary changes in social structure. This holds despite the fact that industrialization itself has barely touched that system if its contact is to be judged by absolute amounts of modern industry. Japan changed less radically in some respects but much more swiftly and dramatically, having in terms of her social structure the possibility of withstanding the spread of these patterns into some areas of the system while maximizing their spread in others. China lacked, relatively, such possibilities of controlled change.

The introduction of new patterns from one relatively nonindustrialized society to another can frequently be absorbed with relatively slight changes. They represent a transfer of nonrational, particularistic, functionally diffuse patterns from one purpose to another or at most from one type to another. The highly industrialized patterns break this mold and as a minimum afford an alternative economic base for deviance not otherwise provided. In case after case the initial patterns of family organization, of production units, and of authority and responsibility have broken down. In the sphere of family patterns tendencies in the direction of multilineal conjugal patterns, the "emancipation" of youth, "romantic love" as a basis for marriage, etc., have been noted again and again. Furthermore, it would seem that no known case has yet started such a trend and reversed it. Present models of totalitarianism and the complementary growth in effectiveness of the technology of weapons may reverse this picture, for they may conceivably destroy the material and social necessities for industrialization, but they have not yet done so.

The mutual incompatibility of these alternative types of patterns is too obvious to require elaboration here. The net balance of subversiveness would seem to be a function of the motivation or pressures to attempt the new patterns. Here the process would seem to be a one-way process because the attempt to introduce the nonindustrial patterns to highly industrial cases would, as one result, motivate maintenance of the prevailing patterns because of the drastic implications for standards of living, among other things. In many, if not most, cases not only material hardships would result but even widespread decimation might well occur. Contemplate if you will the implications of a halving of the efficiency of the transportation system of the United States. On the other hand, the process once started in the other direction may create stresses and strains that motivate further abandonments of the old, if only because of presentation of a functioning alternative to serve as a standard of judgment.

The relevance of these three types of patterns to the question of the vulnerability of the structures of relatively nonindustrialized societies to those of relatively industrialized ones is by no means the only explanation of that seeming vulnerability. A detailed comparison of the structural requisites of the two types of society would no doubt reveal many other structural differences at least as significant as these in explaining such phenomena. The hypotheses presented here about the relevance of these extremely specific variables, if tenable, do not constitute an answer to this problem but merely a plea for its more general systematic analysis in structural terms.

THE PROBLEM OF SELECTIVE
CULTURE CHANGE

By MORRIS E. OPLER

THE topic of this paper is complex and formidable and one that could lead through many bypaths of development and theory. Given the general theme of this Institute, however, I shall limit myself to a consideration of those decisions involving change in underdeveloped countries which have as their purpose economic growth and have as their means the utilization of technical aid.

Struck, as the representative of Western culture usually is, by need and poverty in the underdeveloped regions of the world, it is easy for him to expect that all energies should be bent to the kind of selective culture change that has been mentioned, namely, that which has as its purpose economic growth and as its means modern technological aids. It must be realized, however, that much of the purposeful and planned culture change now going on in the underdeveloped regions of the world, and especially in nations which have lately come to independence and a new self-consciousness, is not primarily concerned with economic growth or the employment of the fruits of Western technology.

I might use examples from various localities, but, since I have lately given considerable attention to culture change in India and to the impact of Western technology upon that country, Indian examples come readily to mind. Recently an animated debate over language ended in India, and it was decided that Hindi, a language derived from Sanskrit which is primarily spoken in north-central India, would replace English as the lingua franca of the nation and as the language of instruction for higher education throughout the land. As a result, people of parts of India in which Hindi was never spoken will now have to learn Hindi, a scientific terminology in Hindi will have to be devised, and basic Hindi textbooks in dozens of different subjects will have to be written.

As far as efficiency and making good use of technical aid from abroad go, they will probably suffer during the transition period. Trained men who have not learned Hindi sufficiently well will labor under a handicap. Indian students, who have made a relatively easy adjustment to English and American technical schools because of their knowledge of English, will lose this advantage. English and American technicians will not find, as is the case now, that the entire well-educated and technically trained group can converse with them in their mother-tongue.

Some Indians and many foreigners have deplored the raising of the linguistic issue at a time when increased food supply and enhanced general production seem the all-important issues. But this change that has been decided upon and which is registered in the supreme law of the land is a response in part to patriotism and sentiment and has been taken in the ultimate interests of internal unity. By their decision the Indians seek to develop a common tongue, rooted in their own background and acceptable to the mass of the people. They seek to eliminate the linguistic distinction which has marked off the educated class from the rest of the people. They intend to subordinate a language which was imposed upon their educational system by the conqueror. Without attempting an exhaustive analysis of the background and psychology of the linguistic issue in India, we may view this as one sample of the kind of selective culture change going on apace in underdeveloped countries—a type of change only indirectly related to economic growth and unconcerned about our technology.

This point might seem too obvious to emphasize, but in my talks about India with students and with the general citizenry, I have found that almost everyone knows that India has an economic problem about which something has to be done, but very few indeed know that India has a linguistic problem about which it has been felt that something has to be done. Just as ignorant, on the whole, is the American public about the choices India has made for changes in her legal, domestic, religious, and class institutions. This ignorance of an insensitivity to change which is not obviously economic in character, or spearheaded by the kind of technology with which we are familiar, is likely to give us the impression that less is happening than is really the case and may lead to an impatience, not wholly reasonable and certainly not helpful, with developments in far places.

The illustration of the choice of Hindi as the national language of India is illuminating in another way. The decision topples English from its high estate in India and relegates it to the status of a foreign language, taught in the schools as an optional subject. A decreasing number of Indians will probably elect it, and a linguistic chasm between India and the English-speaking world will form and grow wider. This need not be an unbridgeable chasm, but it will prove a troublesome one for those who have hoped for closer relations between the nations concerned. The interesting thing is that this linguistic separation and barrier to communication is growing up during the very period of American technical aid to India. This is worth while underscoring because it challenges the notion held by so many that, if we extend technical aid to a people and help their economy grow along lines similar to ours, they become like us in outlook and interests, and we inevitably gain an ally and confederate. The truth is that the solutions and decisions of a foreign nation in respect to its problems are, to an extent not ordinarily appreciated, a function of the dynamic of its own peculiar history, and the use of similar tractors or seed will not necessarily erase the influence of differing backgrounds and traditions. Thus, in the constitution of India, adopted late in 1949, one of the directive principles of state policy is the prohibition of the slaughter of milch and draft cattle. There is in our thinking about underdeveloped areas a mischievous undeclared assumption that economic means and aspirations completely condition all social forms and thought, an assumption reflected in the expectations of those who vigorously reject economic determinism as a doctrine.

Actually, in respect to matters in which modern Western scientific techniques and aids seem imperative and even unavoidable in view of the goals, historic roots, pride, and political considerations may combine to give a quite unexpected result. Thus, the improvement of health and medical facilities is a declared aim of the central and state governments in India. But nationalism aroused during the independence movement and pride in independence have given impetus to a search for ancient Indian roots and characteristics for modern programs. As a result there has been a revival of interest in the Ayurvedic and Unani systems of medicine and increased government support for them, though a modern Western medical practitioner would regard them as a slight cut above magic. The United Provinces Panchayat Raj Act of 1947, for instance, specifically lists the establishment and maintenance of Ayurvedic and Unani hospitals and dispensaries as a duty and function of the newly constituted village legislative bodies.

In short, it must not be assumed that decisions concerning the means to be used toward achieving common goals will be based on logic and science and will result in the unquestioned acceptance of the particular technical aids which we have to offer. Tradition, sentiment, and familiarity count for something, and sometimes for a great deal, and those who represent our technical aid programs abroad must not be surprised or discouraged to find themselves in competition with officially sponsored indigenous rivals.

One thing which will have to be kept in mind is that the underdeveloped regions of the world are coming to nationhood, independence, and prominence and have to make selections and decisions at a time of much confusion, contrary counsel, and political division in the world. Voices are raised advocating a concentration of industry for the sake of efficiency and a well-trained labor force; contrary voices advise decentralization to avoid congestion and slums and as a safeguard against atomic weapons. It is claimed that large-scale industry is needed for maximum production, and it is also argued that home and local industries are required to prevent man from becoming an automaton and to forestall the eclipse of creativity. Those who have the responsibility for guiding the new or renascent nations are assured from one direction of the advantages of collectivism and from the other of the excellence of individual enterprise.

And the international tension and search for friends and allies is so acute today that few astute people accept that much of any advice is given in a wholly detached and uncalculating spirit. My judgment is that this state of affairs has encouraged a resistance to extravagant claims and single solutions from abroad in the minds of the educated and the leaders of underdeveloped countries. They are in an experimental mood; they are not committed to any one view; the debates and conflicting claims have created division and uncertainties in their own ranks, and they wil accept the techniques and methods of any one country, our own included, warily and only to a limited degree.

I think it is important to point out that people in other parts of the world are often preoccupied with considerations of social change, political change, and religious change as well as with economic change, because some of us tend so completely to pin our hopes for progress in these lands on economic growth stimulated by technical aids. Only the other day a prominent American politician again made headlines by advocating in a commencement address that the woes of the world be remedied by a flow of American technicians and materials on a grand scale to underdeveloped countries.

Yet, in the eyes of responsible persons in these regions, the solving of internal problems of a different order often is considered of primary importance and is believed to be the necessary foundation for growth and progress of any kind. When Indian leaders are asked what they consider the prime achievement of India since independence to be, they almost always cite the political integration of hundreds of princely states into the union and not the progress on the Damodar Valley Project. We may suppose, then, that to be properly timed and to have the maximum likelihood of success, technical aid programs must take into consideration the general cultural developments in the recipient country and must be understood and desired by the populations of those countries.

But whether or not technical aid programs are likely to be as potent a force as some expect and whether they are the first step or the second in the programs of underdeveloped countries, the fact remains that they are desired and requested and are increasingly being put into practice. It is important, therefore, to consider some of the problems that this type of selective culture change faces.

One of the very broad problems which will have to be kept in mind is the *purpose* for which the changes are being made or the programs are being inaugurated. We often read or hear that one of the greatest, if not the greatest, achievements of British rule in India was the building of the railway trunk lines. Yet the Indian intellectual will tell you that the building of these same lines has been one of the most serious impediments to the economic growth of his nation. He will point out that these tracks run to the seaports from which England took Indian raw materials for her factories and to which she sent her manufactured articles. Thus, in spite of the thousands of miles of track that were laid and the feats of engineering which were accomplished, the Indian charges that the transportation system was geared to England's economy and market needs and that, because of the policy, internal communications, which would have stimulated industry and made for self-sufficiency, languished.

I shall not try to settle the merits of these claims and counterclaims, but I do wish to point out that, even when the general efficiency of a technical change program may be undisputed, its objective may be called into question.

It is difficult, of course, to keep our own practical problems divorced from our activities and prescriptions, but we shall have to keep in mind that, if what we propose and what we do serves our own political or military aims rather than the general welfare of the country to which we go, we shall be open to repercussions of this kind.

After we have decided whether the objective is really to benefit the receiving rather than the donor nation, there arises the question of who, specifically, is benefited in the country where selective culture change takes place. It requires a very well-rounded program to assure that many are aided and few are penalized in a program of culture change.

I have been interested in reports of greater efficiency and yield in agriculture attributed in part to American technical advice and methods in a region of North India. The landowning farmers are undoubtedly being helped by this turn of affairs, but there is in this area a large group of landless day laborers whose handwork in the fields is curtailed by the employment of more efficient implements. On the basis of increased cereal production figures the project is hailed as an example of what technical programs can accomplish, but not long ago, when I asked the chief American consultant to the project what was in store for the hard-pressed landless laborer, and whether more problems might not be created than are being solved, he could only say that he, too, was worried about the final outcome.

In this instance, to my mind, too little attention has been paid to seeing that wages for farm work advance with agricultural income, that retraining of farm labor for other callings is attempted, and that subsidiary industries are established in the region. The honest assessment of the results of planned change demands that we not only take into account those shifts which we desire and approve but also related fluctuations, whether they are welcome or not. And in the end success is likely to be judged, not solely in terms of reaching the initial target, but also in dealing wisely and constructively with the by-products of the target effort.

Another problem that should be mentioned is the illusion, experienced mainly by officials during certain technical aid programs, that something is changing, when in reality it is not. Not long ago I made a study of a number of village rehabilitation projects of India which came and went through the years without leaving any enduring mark on the villages where they were attempted. Yet during the time when they were being carried on the progress reports were optimistic and encouraging. I suspect that this evanescence is large because they were too literally technical *aid* programs and not nearly enough attempts to enlist the *participation* of the people involved.

On one occasion I brought an Indian villager to a medical dispensary established by American missionaries. The American doctor in charge diagnosed the case as malaria and prescribed a course of atabrine tablets as treatment. The only directions to the patient had to do with when to take the pills.

On talking the matter over with this villager, I learned that he had no idea that mosquitoes had anything to do with malaria.

He owned a mosquito net but used it only when the mosquitoes became too annoying and not out of fear of contracting disease. This man was certainly "aided" by the services at this American clinic; in fact, he was cured temporarily by the treatment. But few will hold that this kind of technical aid is enough. The person helped remained unconscious of his problem and unable to prevent a repetition of his sickness. Needless to say, he could communicate nothing useful about the matter to others. Yet this man was very intelligent, quite receptive to new ideas, and a leader in his caste and village. It is obvious that malaria and this kind of treatment could exist side by side for hundreds of years, and yet I have heard this kind of performance described as "bringing modern medical practice to the villager." This is, to be sure, an extreme example of unwise direction from the top, and, of course, there is a wide range of practice in this regard. But it cannot be overemphasized that the problem of continuity is one of involving the people to be helped as much as possible in the conduct and perpetuation of the program. This requires some respect for their intelligence and educability and some clear picture of what they can grasp, how information and opportunity for participation are to be offered, and what they can be trained to handle technically. It will be a temptation in the future, as it has been in the past, for experts to want to direct and be obeyed without question and without the necessity for long explanations; but it is a temptation which will have to be resisted unless we are to have enough trained personnel to serve for a long time at the local level in underdeveloped countries.

There is one more problem of selective culture change which I feel should not go unmentioned. I find in many quarters in discussions of technological aid and culture change an assumption that substantial technological change in underdeveloped countries is bound to result in sweeping alterations in their social institutions and in their value patterns and that economic growth can only result in the sloughing-off of older instrumentalities of social control and interaction. And this is usually accepted not only as inevitable but as fitting.

Now this conception of economic growth as total cultural replacement is, to my mind, quite unrealistic. No culture, whatever its new experiences and acquisitions, is likely to become so discontinuous that its present and future will be uninfluenced by its past. Not only is it very unlikely that underdeveloped countries will break with the social, ethical, intellectual, and aesthetic forms of the past upon industrialization but it also arouses resistance to technical programs to give the impression that this is sure to be the case. Much of the talk about the dangers to Eastern civilization of Western materialism has this loose talk and thinking at its root.

My own feeling is that to combat such fears, to aid stability during a transition period, and to prevent unnecessary dislocation, existing institutions and structures should be used in advancing programs of technical aid wherever possible. There is no reason why, in many instances, this may not result in the retention, revitalization, and reinforcement of social institutions long existent rather than in their elimination. One of the most successful technical aid ventures in India of which I know has made good use of the *panches* or traditional Indian arbiters and leaders. By bringing them together in camps and giving them special opportunities to obtain information about the project and to observe its workings, the program enhanced the prestige of these leaders and gained for itself spokesmen and powerful champions in the villages.

A lesson in this respect is also taught us by the Indian state of Uttar Pradesh. The ancient village assemblies or *panchayats* of the state had long been in competition with the British courts and had suffered badly in influence and prestige. After independence, in 1947, by the United Provinces Panchayat Raj Act, they were given legal status, encouragement, and considerable authority over local matters. Today the United Provinces government is making these *Gaon Panchayats* the center of its effort to introduce modern programs in improved agriculture and education. It is too early still to predict how effective these ancient village legislatures will be in promoting the new techniques, though there is strong evidence that many of them have already proved valuable for this purpose. But I have a strong feeling that they would have been quite effective in opposing technical innovations had they been ignored and consigned to political oblivion as outworn symbols of the past.

THE INTERRELATIONS BETWEEN CULTURAL FACTORS AND THE ACQUISITION OF NEW TECHNICAL SKILLS

By WALTER R. GOLDSCHMIDT

I HAVE taken my task to be to view the problem before this Institute from the farther side, as it were; to seek those reasons why a culture might naturally or logically reject the proffered assistance for increasing its productive capacity or developing those amenities which we consider the better life. In taking the part of the people of backward areas, I will inevitably appear critical of European patterns.

The data from this discussion will come largely from the studies of acculturation in the anthropological literature, so that the examples will have reference to the more primitive peoples. They will also have reference to societies that have to a considerable degree already been altered by European influence.

The task has both a scientific and a moral side, and to address the subject at all is to face the moral connotations. My position can be summarized briefly and should be made explicit at the outset. I do not believe that all cultures are equally good, nor do I believe that ours—in any of its variations—is necessarily the best. I consider that culture good which (1) satisfies the physical needs of its population; (2) is so organized that it will be able to continue indefinitely to satisfy such needs; and (3) offers its members the satisfactions necessary to a personality adjustment within the context of its own system of values so long as it does not exploit physically or psychologically some other population or segment of the population. I do not evaluate a culture in terms of its means of achieving these ends (with the exception indicated) or in terms of the cultural expectations in our own society.

While I view change to be inherent in all cultural systems and inevitable in a contact situation, the moral obligations of the culture-bearer are to bring about the alteration with a minimum of social disruption. In terms of practice, this means neither the eager transformance of the culture into a pale image of our own nor the blind assumption that the culture will and should remain unaltered. It means rather a careful examination of cultural assumptions on our part and of cultural consequences on the part of the backward areas affected.

today.

One theoretical point must also be introduced in these prefatory remarks; namely, that the culture of a human group is no mere congeries of behavioral traits, knowledge, and ideas but is an interlocking and systematic whole. This means that a change at any one point of culture will have repercussions on other parts, and, since the concept of culture is a broad one, this implies a systematization of factors which transcend the normal rubrics in social science. That is, there is a relationship between economic production, political system, religious belief, social life, and even those subtle underlying orientations and ethical attitudes that receive only indirect expression.

For our purposes this means that cultures are never going to meet at a single point; rather, they meet as systems. It means that we can neither introduce changes in technology stripped of our own cultural baggage nor expect the technical innovations to leave other aspects of the society unaffected. Concerning the latter of these two involvements we will have much to say, but perhaps we should illustrate briefly the former with a matter close at hand.

The Point IV program was based upon the assumption of the inherent value of progress. In the President's words, the people of backward areas could "realize their aspirations for a better life" if we bring them "the benefits of our store of technical knowledge."[1] This is an affirmation of a faith, deeply intrenched in our cultural order, that progress is in itself good; that material gain leads directly to the better life. Though we all in greater or lesser degree accept this notion, a moment's reflection makes us realize that this is a cultural assumption which much of our experience in fact belies. The bringers of the culture—and I mean here the specific persons whose job it is to

1. Harry S. Truman, "Inaugural Address, January 20, 1949," *Congressional Record* (Washington, D.C.: Government Printing Office, 1949), XCV, 477–78.

introduce the changes—do in fact make this cultural assumption. Reports to the home office are replete with the refrain that the people fail to appreciate what is being done for them, for not all people assume the value of "progress" or the virtue in material gain, even discounting the disruptions that may attend the processes of cultural acquisition.

It will be our task to learn why peoples reject the assistance that our technological knowledge can supply. This rejection takes two related but different forms. In the first place, innovations cause disruption of the existing social order, create difficulties and hardships, and make life difficult for the members of society. Such problems may not even be recognized, but in the long run they exact their toll. In the second place, cultural innovations may run counter to established practices of the people and meet with established attitudes and prejudices which lead to rejection. Thus even well-intended and helpful changes may be rejected for reasons lying deep in the culture of the native society.

I will deal with the rejection of cultural innovation in terms of four general areas within the total spectrum of culture as follows: (*a*) the ecological or relation of man to his resources; (*b*) the sociological or structural relationships between members of the culture; (*c*) the ideological or established system of values, goals, and sanctions; and (*d*) the psychological or culturally patterned life orientations.

THE ECOLOGICAL AREA

Every culture must come to grips with its environment. This means that the population is limited to the carrying capacity of the environment with the technical means at its disposal. The manner in which populations are restricted may, of course, be extremely harsh such as infanticide, geronticide, or warfare. The disruption of this adjustment between man and his environment may make for hardships even more severe.

The Navaho Indians of our own Southwest present a case of extreme hardship derived from the introduction of technological improvement into their economy. With the introduction of sheep-herding as a means of livelihood, the tribe increased from an estimated 9,000 in 1868 to a present population of well over 60,000.[2] A concomitant of this expansion was extremes of poverty a full twenty years ago, and the circumstances of these Indians have received much public attention in the past few years. Not only has there been a problem of present poverty, but the cumulative effects of overgrazing have reduced the carrying capacity of the range. Stock reduction programs have helped materially but do nothing to alleviate the existing overcrowded condition.

Here, then, is a disruption of the relation between man and his environment based directly upon the introduction of a new technological skill. Though this was not a conscious effort, such as Point IV envisages, yet it was an introduction of a technological skill.

Monica Hunter has reported an almost identical problem with respect to cattle in South Africa.[3] The Europeans systematized the dipping of native cattle, with the result that disease was reduced and the stock multiplied. The overgrazing has caused serious damage to the range, and reduction has been necessary. To a people whose measure of status is in terms of numbers rather than quality of livestock, reduction is not readily accepted.

The involvement may be far more subtle. Thus a detailed study of Mexican dietary habits suggests extreme caution with respect to any attempt to change food patterns of a native population.[4] The analysis of the food habits suggests that "it may be possible to nourish the Mexican people without the use of dairy and meat products. These results indicate that the food pattern of Mexico is quite different from that in the United States. Thus it would be inadvisable to base the Mexican nutrition program on the United States."

2. U.S. Government, Department of the Interior, *The Navajo: A Report of the Commissioner of Indian Affairs* (Washington, D.C., March, 1948); Clyde Kluckhohn and Dorothea Leighton, *The Navaho* (Cambridge: Harvard University Press, 1946), discuss the economic problems and resources in detail.

3. *Reaction to Conquest* (New York: Oxford University Press, 1936).

4. René Cravioto B., Ernest E. Lockhart, Richmond K. Anderson, Francisco deP. Miranda, and Robert S. Harris, "Composition of Typical Mexican Foods," *Journal of Nutrition*, Vol. XXIX, No. 5 (May, 1945).

Significant among the important sources of nutrition are items like malva, an abundant wild plant of the Mexican plateau similar to spinach in appearance and sufficiently rich in calcium, iron, carotene, and ascorbic acid so that one portion of malva supplies from half to more than all the daily needs of these elements for an adult. Or, again, there is the native pulque, a maguey cactus beer, which, I understand, well-meaning people would like to see eliminated from the diet because of its alcoholic effects and its general unsanitary and unpalatable character from our standards. Yet it furnishes significant quantities of minerals and vitamins, especially ascorbic acid.

It is unlikely that the ecological problem will be either recognized or felt by a native people, and we have thus far been discussing disruptive effects. If technical change is rejected, it will be in terms other than these ultimate and unforeseen consequences. Appeal to habits in practice, to tastes in food, and to established routines of daily life are far more likely to act as the immediate deterrents. And these illogicalities, even if they have their ultimate verity, are lightly brushed aside by a "rationalized" and "efficient" administrative agent.

THE SOCIOLOGICAL AREA

Every society is an organized entity. This means that there are established, permanent groups designed to perform some task necessary to the maintenance of the culture and the well-being of its members. It means that there are positions of authority held by persons who act as leaders in such activities. Without such structure there would be no society, only a mélange of individuals. New technological practices are disruptive to such entities and threaten the position of the leadership of the existing system.

The impact of Western civilization upon native cultures may be generalized in the following terms: A money economy and an individualized social system impinge upon some type of familistic order with a pattern of group responsibility and sharing.[5] That is to say, most primitive and peasant societies

5. This is the central burden of Karl Polanyi, *The Great Transformation* (New York: Farrar & Rinehart, 1944).

organize life-activities about some larger familistic unit within which work is toward a mutual end, and family ties predominate. In such a system the members share both material and emotional sustenance.

Such an organization of economic enterprise is not out of keeping with money as such, but it does conflict with the commercial nature of Western civilization, where human relationships are overwhelmingly translated into pecuniary terms. In the era of the "white-man's burden" and the bland assumption of European superiority, direct efforts were made to destroy the inhibiting effects of familistic social orders. Such a philosophy was behind the Glen Gray Act in South Africa and the United States Indian Service's allotment system, two efforts to place ownership in individual hands rather than maintain larger co-operative entities.

The cynical may assert that such action made possible the easier exploitation of native labor and the acquisition of lands by Europeans, and undoubtedly the philosophy and policy did serve such cupidity. But the fact is that there is a functional antagonism between the two organizing principles which creates problems quite aside from any selfish motives.

Schapera describes the influence of money economy upon the family system of the Kgatla, a Bantu people of Bechuanaland.[6] Here a system of mutual obligations surrounds the marriage, not merely between the partners but between the families, and families acted as the economic production unit. Hence, the marriage was arranged by the elders. But with urban employment the sons were released from economic dependence upon the father, they were given physical separation from the cultural system, and their marriages were perforce delayed. All three factors combined to make the youth act independently in seeking a marriage partner, to undermine the authority of the parental generation, and to lessen materially the unity of the family as a system of interdependence.

The disruptive effects in this instance are not hidden but are clear to at least some of the persons of the native community, and, insofar as they are, there will be considerable resistance to

6. I. Schapera, *Married Life in an African Tribe* (New York: Sheridan House, 1941)

accepting the changes involved. Thus the old people who are deprived of satisfactions will be loath to see the young people act disrespectfully, flaunt their socially expected roles, and run counter to strong religious sentiments.

In addition, the principals involved will lose the psychological supports of family backing and the economic cushioning effect of sharing. Examples could as readily have been drawn from other African peoples, from Melanesia, or from the Indians of the United States. For instance, the Hopi, whose system of matrilineal clans is perhaps as closely woven as any known to the literature of anthropology, are beginning to feel the effects of monetary employment. Where this has taken place, the men tend to take over family leadership and establish their own herds and farms on an individual conjugal unit basis. The imperative dictates of the extremely sparse environment may well not permit of the changes that follow from such pecuniary organization; that is, they will result in abandonment or impoverishment and complete dependency. Significantly, the Hopi rejected efforts to create an allotment system in 1911.[7]

The individuated pattern of social action does not rest entirely upon industrialization. The introduction of dairying into the New Zealand Maori economy has had an almost identical effect on the old patterns of mutual assistance and the satisfactions of social life.[8] In his analysis of this situation, Hawthorn writes:

> The emergence of the individual family is related to changes in the methods of earning a living. This economic unit is well-suited to dairy-farming with its demands for a small but well-organized working team and its need of firm authority to maintain the dull routine. On the other hand, the family is less suited to fishing and gardening, which were more efficiently carried out by the traditional cooperative techniques.[9]

Dairying has demanded for its successful operation a change in every aspect of village economics. It has demanded a regular-

7. A most important contribution to the problem of cultural change and administrative problems is presented by Laura Thompson, *Culture in Crisis* (New York: Harper & Bros., 1950). Additional data have been supplied by Mr. Edward Dozier, who is currently engaged in research on the Hopi.

8. H. B. Hawthorn, *The Maori: A Study in Acculturation* ("Memoirs of the American Anthropological Association," Vol. LXIV [New York, 1944]).

9. *Ibid.*, pp. 57–58.

ity of routine greater than in any other pursuit, a smaller grouping of workers for continuous co-operation, and an organization of the whole village for occasional co-operation. It requires further a learning of many new principles of animal husbandry and a tightening of authority and its perpetual maintenance to fit this routine. It is rewarded by money alone through an automatic and impersonal system of marketing. "Much of this was strange to those who began dairying . . . twenty years ago, and, except the final result, distasteful."[10] These distasteful qualities are the narrowing of leisure, the curtailment of visits, and the interruption of celebrations and serious meetings.

Under the heading of sociological factors we must also include the problem of leadership and authority in the community, for every social system involves the delegation of powers to make decisions and lead activities. The alienation of a population from its leadership is disruptive of the whole tenor of life and is not infrequently a factor in general dissolution of the culture.

This is true not only because decisions are requisite for the continued operation of the society but because the elite embodies the value system of the culture and hence acts as a concrete referent in goal-directed activity of the rank and file. Furthermore, the elite in any society will tend to act in such ways as to preserve the native culture against external influences which are often threats to their personal position in the social system and to the native values in which they have a vested interest. Hence, one of the most important impediments to technological innovation may be the quite reasonable opposition of the native leadership.

The alienation of leadership was painfully obvious among Athabascan villagers of the Alaskan interior with whom I spent a few days in 1946. This extremely simple society had long benefited by certain technological innovations, but the full impact of Western culture came only with the completion of the Alcan Highway. Leadership traditionally rested with the older men, skilled in hunting and trapping through years of experience. But the younger men were less impressed by these qualities than

10. *Ibid.*, p. 84.

by the superior position of the whites. As a result, they turned to immediate satisfactions rather than the long-term interests which might have better served the continued existence in this harsh environment. This was not merely a matter of women and liquor but such purely economic considerations as co-operative arrangements and avoiding the depletion of fur-bearing animals. The hopelessness of the old men in this situation was not something easily forgotten.

The British policy of indirect rule has been a conscientious effort to avoid this problem and utilize the elite in the administration of native people, a policy described as "find the chief."[11] The solution is far from simple, however, for the leadership will either be recalcitrant and hence dangerous to imperial interests or docile and then no longer real leadership.[12]

A study of the Blood of the Canadian Plains demonstrates the role of the elite in the acceptance and rejection of technological innovations.[13] The Blackfoot had a social system in which elite status was dependent upon war honors and measured largely in horses. With European domination and the elimination of warfare, a closed class system came into being which materially altered the organizational principles of the society. The early effort by the Canadian government to turn the attention of the Blood to agriculture and dairying met with no success. This failure stemmed partly from habit patterns such as unaccustomedness to constant responsibility and uninterrupted effort and the viewpoint that such physical work was degrading.

But an important factor was the attitude of the elite who did not find such pursuits to their advantage. Their status rested upon an outmoded but nevertheless culturally real basis of large herds. Furthermore, patterns of generosity and food-sharing

11. Sir F. D. Lugard, *The Dual Mandate in British Tropical Africa* (London: Blackwood, 1929).

12. The governmentally appointed chieftains in Uganda have the qualities of the "bureaucratic personality." See Lucy P. Mair, *An African People of the Twentieth Century* (London: Routledge, 1934).

13. Esther S. Goldfrank, *Changing Configurations of the Social Organization of a Blackfoot Tribe during the Reserve Period* ("Monographs of the American Ethnological Society" [New York, 1945]).

made it impossible for the diligent to accumulate any wealth and thereby translate their efforts into status. After nearly twenty years, only three hundred acres were farmed by the fourteen hundred members of the Blood tribe.

In 1894 the Canadian government traded cattle for horses on a head-for-head basis. This enabled the wealthy to maintain their relative standing, and it is not surprising that the rich men readily accepted this arrangement. In twelve years the total stock reached 7,500 head.

About 1910 the second effort to introduce farming, this time on a cash-crop rather than self-sustaining basis, was successful. New techniques and the development of red fife wheat made the work less onerous and more rewarding. Yet it is significant that "the new farming program received its strongest support from those individuals who had the smallest stake in their society"; that is, the poor and formerly dispossessed. Success came at the cost of certain institutions—the pattern of generosity, the system of societies by which position was validated, and the organized channels of authority within the tribal community.

A democratic system might have arisen had not the vagaries of climate and our business cycle effectively returned the Blackfoot to penury. Large landholdings formed the material basis for a new elite that emerged at the close of the 1930's, an elite which did not continue the older obligations of leadership.

The sociological effects of technological change and acculturation are to break down the ties of group solidarity and to undermine the native system of authority. They tend to substitute an individuated pattern for the former and an external Western authoritarian system for the latter. Resistance to such changes varies with circumstances of the cultural situation, but the new pattern often fails to meet certain felt needs, especially certain sources of personal security. We shall return to this later.

THE IDEOLOGICAL AREA

The third element in our discussion is the established value system of the culture—the pattern of behavior, the definition of circumstances—which acts as goals for the members of the community. These are generally given concrete form in some symbolic items which we would call wealth. Both the symbols and the underlying qualities of the persons are given elaborate support by myth, ritual, and moral teaching. The introduction of change offers a threat to this value system, even when none is intended, and the people will cleave to their intrenched ideology.

Innumerable exemplifications can be found of the threat of external cultural influences to the value system, of efforts of native peoples to cling to their system of values, and of the unanticipated consequences of the destruction of such values. We have already suggested the importance of livestock to the Navaho, the Blood, and the Bantu. In each case value rested in sheer numbers rather than in production efficiency or quality and thus was at odds with Western values. Since the native values were not conducive to the maintenance of the social system, they may be considered inferior; yet, in each case, there has been evidence of an extreme reluctance to give up the established value patterns.

The disruptive influence of the alienation of a population from its values and the compulsive endeavor to return to old values or to seek a new normative system are both illustrated by the repeated occurrence of nativistic movements.[14] In America, Africa, and Oceania religious movements appeared shortly after the full impact of Western civilization. In general, they express either the insistent return to the "old ways" or the old ways as they are misremembered or the fervent expectation of "pie in the sky."[15] They are the public expression for the yearning for a set of values which have meaning in terms of the background of the people and which at the same time are attainable by them. The nonrealistic character of the expressed values makes such movements die of their own weight or be transformed into substitutive meaningful action. The disillusion that frequently follows such frenetic movements often leaves an ethical inani-

14. Ralph Linton, "Nativistic Movements," *American Anthropologist*, Vol. XLV (April, 1943). Monographic reports on such religious movements are by now quite substantial.

15. For this latter, and as an example of a most recent occurrence, I cite Hugo Pos "The Revolt of 'Manseren,'" *American Anthropologist*, Vol. LII (October, 1950).

tion which further devitalizes the population and makes the development of positive values yet more difficult.

Alteration of the value systems and the ideological sanctions has the effect of altering the position of authority. This has already been discussed in the preceding section in our treatment of leadership. I want to return to the matter here in discussing some elements of the modern situation in Uganda.[16] It is an exceptionally informative case, in part because it is well reported but very largely because the British made it the primary experiment for a most enlightened set of policies. Thus it shows the limitations of good will (and I believe it is true that there was an exceptional amount of good will) when it is uninformed.

In native theory the king had been owner of all lands, but this was relatively meaningless, since the peasants had free access to sufficient productive resources. The British, however, gave title to the lands to neither the king nor the peasantry but to 3,700 intermediate officials. At the same time they introduced cotton production, a cash crop by means of which the landowner could reap rewards in money and hence in unlimited amounts. The immediate result was the creation of an owning class without restraints to its power and a completely dependent laboring class. The large size of the land units rendered it virtually impossible for the peasant to rise in the economic and social hierarchy, while the owning group consolidated its power.

This was further implemented by the preservation of the bureaucracy but with a new basis in sanctions. Formerly the lesser officials were appointed by the king from the general population; they owed allegiance to him and were controlled by custom and the freedom of the peasantry to take up residence elsewhere. Now, however, the sanctions of their power lay enentirely outside the native social system with the British government and fixed by the introduction of Western concepts of landownership. As a result, the population at large has been

16. The Baganda were described by Burton Roscoe (*The Baganda* [London: Macmillan & Co., 1911]) and their present situation by Lucy P. Mair (*op. cit.* and elsewhere) and R. L. Buell (*The Native Problem in Africa* [New York: Macmillan Co., 1928]).

deprived of freedom, of rights in land, of power, and of opportunity for social advancement.

The destruction of sanctions to a social order is disruptive not only to that aspect of the culture but to the whole fabric of the society. Modern sociologists speak of alienation and of anomie as descriptive of this situation. Perhaps it should be made explicit that a social order suffering anomie is readily subject to the vagrant winds of political nostrums, a condition conducive neither to the health of the native society nor to the maintenance of an imposed social order.

THE PSYCHOLOGICAL AREA

The fourth and last segment of culture that must be given consideration has to do with those underlying orientations to which the individual is committed through the subtler involvements of culture. The reality that lay behind the quite erroneous race psychology of an earlier generation has been re-examined and found to be most significant. In its various aspects this area of consideration has been called "unconscious motivation," "patterns," "basic personality structure," "world view," "themes," and "covert culture."[17] These abstract terms refer to the fact that the personnel in any sociocultural system will share a generic orientation to the world and to their fellow-men, will have certain basic predispositions to act in particular ways, will make certain assumptions about the nature of the universe, and will exhibit certain norms of behavior. Because these qualities lie so deep in the makeup of the individual, they appear to be in the nature of man; and, when variations are found to exist, the lay observer assumes that these differences are bio-

17. Edward Sapir, "The Unconscious Patterning of Behavior in Society," in *Selected Writings of Edward Sapir*, ed. David G. Mandelbaum (Berkeley: University of California Press, 1949); Ruth Benedict, *Patterns of Culture* (Boston: Houghton Mifflin Co., 1934); Abram Kardiner, *The Individual and His Society* (New York: Columbia University Press, 1939); Erik Erickson, *A Study of the Yurok: Childhood and World View* ("University of California Publications in American Archaeology and Ethnology," Vol. XXXV [Berkeley, 1943]); M. E. Opler, "Themes as Dynamic Forces in Culture," *American Journal of Sociology*, Vol. LI (November, 1945); Clyde Kluckhohn, "Covert Culture and Administrative Problems," *American Anthropologist*, Vol. XLV (April, 1943). There are important differences in the specific meaning of each concept, but each deals with this aspect of human behavior.

logical. The very depth of these characteristics, together with this lack of self-conscious formulation, suggests immediately that they represent real blocks to cultural reorientation.

The classic example of the importance of these underlying patterns is taken from studies of Hopi and Zuni Indians, where the culture demands a personal self-effacement and subordination to the group and denies individuated and competitive activity. As a consequence, it is extremely difficult to get native leadership outside the normal channels of clan and ceremonial organization. Sports must be noncompetitive, the individual should not be singled out for praise or blame, competition cannot be used to secure better performance, and it is difficult to get a foreman for a job.[18]

It seems obvious that this orientation toward the world would make difficult the acquisition of those patterns necessary for competition in Western society. As has already been pointed out, these attitudes are closely related to ecological necessities in the area. Personality structure does not only vary in kind but varies as well in degree of integration or healthiness. The studies of Hallowell among the Ojibwa Indians have shown the breakdown of personality under progressive culture contact and acculturation.[19] Here again is a disruption which is not manifested to the individual in the acculturative situation but is, nevertheless, a real consequence of culture change. It seems not at all unlikely that the persons turn to the nativistic movements already described in an unconscious endeavor to seek a means of personal integration.

SUMMARY

The discussion has shown that cultural innovation raises problems of two kinds in various areas of the total cultural spectrum: it is disruptive to the social and personal integration of the existing system and it meets a resistance to change by members of the community anxious to avoid such disruptions in their

18. Thompson, *op. cit.*

19. A. Irving Hallowell, "Acculturation Processes and Personality Changes, as Indicated by the Rorschach Technic," *Rorschach Research Exchange*, Vol. VI (April, 1942); "Ojibwa Personality and Acculturation," in *Acculturation in the Americas*, ed. Sol Tax (Chicago: University of Chicago Press, 1951); "Values, Acculturation and Mental Health," *American Journal of Orthopsychiatry*, Vol. XX (April, 1950).

habit patterns, attitudes, and established modes of thought and action. The presentation appears therefore to have a negative orientation, suggesting a general disapproval of a program for the advancement of backward areas.

Such a conclusion is not, however, justified. At the very outset we made two things clear: change is inevitable, and culture contact has already been initiated. A third factor must also be made explicit, namely, that a native culture is itself not necessarily ideal even for those people who are committed to it. A reading of ethnological literature does not support Rousseau's concept of the happy savage any more than it supports the opposite one of degenerate mankind. Thus, for instance, we have examined certain unfortunate consequences of British policy in Uganda, yet, if Roscoe is right in his description of that land, the old form left even more to be desired.

A Pueblo Indian student made this point with reference to the Indianismo policies recently fostered by the United States Indian Service. He quoted with great irony Collier's poetic responses to seeing a Pueblo ceremonial and its evidence of a spiritual oneness among these Indians.[20] Our student was all too aware how much of that unity was effected by the browbeating tactics of the ceremonial leaders and how unwilling was the spirit of many of the participants. From our point of view it makes little difference whether the student's attitude would have been found under precontact conditions; it is found today.

The real question is not, therefore, whether action should be taken but what the course of action should be. And because of the diversity of cultures to which technological advancement is proffered, the rules must be laid down in exceedingly general terms. Let me conclude by listing a few principles that may guide us to success in bringing our technology to peoples, together with "the better life."

1. The introduction of technological developments must be in terms of the needs of the native society—either felt needs or those which can be demonstrated to exist—and should not be introduced because they appear to be necessitous to us. Here

20. Some of this is expressed in *Indians of the Americas* (New York: Mentor Books), chap. i.

we may be reminded of well-meaning efforts to induce changes in the Mexican diet in terms of American standards.

2. Any technological improvement must be analyzed in terms of its consequences and involvements both physical and social and adequate safeguards established to prevent the deleterious effects which may follow. Here we may recall the ecological consequences of sheep-raising and cattle dipping and recognize that this does not mean that the practice should not have been introduced but only that the consequences be anticipated and averted.

3. The newer techniques should be fitted into the organizational principles of the native society. The introduction of new production methods to a people whose life is oriented in terms of family solidarity should be done so as to support rather than destroy familism, even at the cost of certain elements of efficiency. It would have been possible, I believe, to introduce dairying into New Zealand native economy without destroying the community solidarity if the importance of the latter had been appreciated.

4. This principle must be followed with its converse, however. It is entirely possible for overzealousness toward the native culture to lead to a crystallization and rigidity in organization which is in itself dangerous. We must never forget that all social systems are dynamic and flexible and that malleability is essential to its healthy continuation.

5. Both of the preceding rules must be applied also to the native system of values. The destruction of native goals for action leads only to anomie and not to the automatic acquisition of Western values. This in turn leads to unrealistic values, the orientation of behavior to unrealizable goals, and patterns of hostility and dependency. At the same time there are value judgments to be made of values, and a blind insistence upon preservation of old values may be equally destructive.

It is important to realize that the Bantu and Navaho values in size of herds are destructive to the continued welfare of the society and must be shifted (as they are being in the Southwest) to other stock-raising considerations.

6. It is necessary also to remember that healthy social sys-

tems make possible the achievement of values by the rank and file of the society. It is therefore important to preserve the channels for advancement in the social sphere and the satisfaction of culturally induced expectations. Here again we refer to the Baganda situation, where the fixing of power has closed off the means for achieving personal success.

The research of a student of mine, examining the personality changes among the Wisconsin Menominee, builds upon the work of Hallowell already referred to. His investigations show that the availability of a channel for successful goal realization in terms of Western values—made possible by the native operation of a large sawmill—has allowed the development of an integrated personality structure at the acculturated end of the scale.

7. Finally, if these precepts are to be met, it is obviously necessary to have a detailed understanding of both the cultural system of the society to which change is being brought and of the possible consequences, physical and social, of the innovations that are contemplated.

THE APPEAL OF COMMUNISM TO THE UNDERDEVELOPED PEOPLES

By Morris Watnick

I F TIME is a power dimension in any political strategy, the odds facing the West in the underdeveloped areas of the world today are heavily weighted against it. The effort to capture the imagination and loyalties of the populations of these areas did not begin with the West in President Truman's plea for a "bold new program" of technical aid to backward areas. It began more than a generation earlier when the Communist International at its second world congress in 1920 flung out the challenge of revolution to the peoples of colonial and dependent countries and proceeded to chart a course of action calculated to hasten the end of Western overlordship. We thus start with an initial time handicap, and it is a moot question whether we can overcome the disadvantage by acquiring the radically new appreciation of the human stakes involved necessary to meet the challenge of the Communist appeal to the peoples of these areas.

Fortunately, there is no need to trace out the tortuous course of the careers of the various Communist parties in the backward areas of the world in order to gain some appreciation of the extent and intensity of their indigenous appeal. For purposes of this discussion we can confine ourselves to China, India, and the area of Southeast Asia, where they have had their greatest successes to date. Despite the blunders and ineptitudes which marked their initial grand play in China in 1924–27, ending in almost complete disaster for their most promising single party organization in these areas, they have emerged today as a political magnitude of the first order, boasting a seasoned leadership, a core of trained cadres, and a mass following recruited mainly from the peasant masses of the region. It is the purpose of the remarks which follow to indicate the nature of the Communist appeal to the peoples of these areas and to suggest some of the sociological factors which have made that appeal so effective.

It was once the wont of certain Continental writers, preoccupied with the problem of imperialism, to refer to the peoples who form the subject of our deliberations as the "history-less" peoples. Better than the Europacentric term, "underdeveloped peoples," it delineates in bold relief all the distinctive features which went to make up the scheme of their social existence: their parochial isolation, the fixity of their social structure, their tradition-bound resistance to change, their static subsistence economies, and the essential repetitiveness and uneventfulness of their self-contained cycle of collective activities. With a prescience which has not always received its due, these theorists of imperialism also called the right tune in predicting that the isolated careers of these archaic societies would rapidly draw to a close under the impact of economic and social forces set in motion by industrial capitalism and that these history-less peoples would before long be thrust onto the arena of world politics, impelled by a nascent nationalism born of contact with the West and nurtured by a swelling resentment against the exactions of its imperialism.[1]

The final result of this process is unfolding today with a disconcerting force and speed in almost all the backward regions of the world. We can see its culmination most clearly among the classic exemplaries of history-less peoples in China, India, and the regions of Southeast Asia where the political and economic predominance of western Europe is being successfully challenged by forces unmistakably traceable to the forced absorption of these societies into the stream of world history. Their internal cohesiveness, largely centered on self-sufficient village economies, has been disrupted by enforced contact with the West, giving way to a network of commercialized money transactions in which the strategic incidence of economic activity has shifted from subsistence agriculture to plantation production of raw materials and foodstuffs for the world market.

---

1. For typical discussions see Otto Bauer, *Die Nationalitätenfrage und die Social-demokratie* (Vienna, 1907), pp. 494–97 *et passim;* Rudolf Hilferding, *Das Finanzkapital* (Vienna, 1910; Berlin, 1947), p. 441.

Their economies thus took on a distorted character which rendered the material well-being of the native populations peculiarly subject to the cyclical fluctuations of the world market. All this, coupled with rapid population increases which the existing state of primitive technique, available area of cultivation, and customary allocation of soil could not adjust to the requirements of maximum output, has conspired to create widespread rural indebtedness, abuses of plantation and tenant labor, and other excrescences traditionally associated with the prevalence of a raw commercial and financial capitalism superimposed on a predominantly agricultural economy.[2]

Given the fact that the new economic dispensation in these regions was fashioned under the aegis if not active encouragement of the Western imperialisms, it should occasion no surprise that these regions, particularly Southeast Asia, have seen the efflorescence of a distinctive type of nationalism, especially after the debacle of Western rule during the second World War, differing in many crucial respects from the historical evolution of nationalism as experienced by western Europe. Indeed, the employment of a term like "nationalism" with all its peculiarly Western connotations to describe what is going on in Southeast Asia today is in a sense deceptive precisely because it diverts our attention from some of the distinctive attributes of native sentiment which set it apart from the nineteenth-century manifestations of nationalism in Europe. It is, moreover, a particularly inappropriate characterization because it inhibits a full appreciation of the potency of the Communist appeal among the populations of these regions. Historically, nationalism in western Europe has flourished with the burgeoning of an industrial technology, the urbanization of the population, the growth of a self-conscious middle class and an industrial proletariat, the spread of literacy, and the multiplication of media of mass communication. Now it is one of the distinctive features of the movements of revolt in Southeast Asia today that they lack any of these marks of Western nationalism. The indigenous "nationalism" of Southeast Asia today, lacking any of these props, never-

2. For an excellent analysis of the economic impact of the West on the rural economies of Southeast Asia, where the results are most clearly apparent today, see Erich Jacoby, *Agrarian Unrest in Southeast Asia* (New York, 1949).

theless derives its peculiar potency from a universal reaction of personalized resentment against the economic exploitation of foreign powers. Whether all the economic and social dislocations of this region are directly attributable in refined analytic terms to Western rule is quite beside the point. The simple and crucial datum which we must take as the point of orientation in all our thinking is that to the mind of the masses of indigenous peoples they do stem from this common source. The Indo-Chinese peasant victimized by usurers, the plantation worker in Malaya periodically deprived of his income by a drop in world price of rubber, the Indonesian intellectual debarred from a higher post in the government service, the Burmese stevedore underpaid by the *maistry* system of contract labor—all tend to attribute the source of their grievances to the systems of government and economy imposed on them from without. The distinctive and novel aspect of the native movements of Southeast Asia, then, is that they represent a mass collective gesture of rejection of a system of imposed economic and social controls which is compelled by historic circumstances to take the form of a nationalist movement of liberation from foreign rule.[3]

It is this distinctive coalescence of two sources of resentment which offers the Communist parties the opportunities they lack elsewhere to any comparable degree. The two-dimensional direction of native resentment lends itself ideally to Communist appeal and manipulation for the simple reason that Communists can successfully portray Soviet Russia both as a symbol of resistance to political imperialism imposed from without as well as a model of self-directed and rapid industrialization undertaken from within.[4] This twin appeal gains added strength from the multinational composition of the U.S.S.R., which

3. Bauer (*op. cit.*, pp. 262–63) has given the classic formulation of this relationship in his analysis of the problem of national conflicts in the old Austro-Hungarian Empire which showed some formal resemblance to the situation in the backward regions today. The resemblance was superficial, however, since the lines of conflict were far less clearly drawn in Austria-Hungary, especially as regards professional and intellectual groups.

4. It is noteworthy that variations of both types of Communist propaganda have also been attempted in western Europe in the last three years. The Marshall Plan, for example, has been presented to Europeans as an attempt on the part of the United States to impose its political rule over the Continent and to throttle its industries, without, however, carrying the conviction it enjoys in Asia.

enables indigenous Communists of Southeast Asia to confront their audience with the glaring disparity between the possibilities of ethnic equality and the actualities of Western arrogance and discrimination. Communist propaganda has accordingly exploited this theme in almost all important policy pronouncements directed to the people of Asia.[5]

With the victory of the Chinese Communists, the incidence of these appeals has perceptibly shifted the symbolism of successful resistance and internal reconstruction from Russia to China, which is now being held up as a model for emulation by the other areas of Southeast Asia.[6] The shift is not without its tactical and propaganda value, since the adjacent region of Southeast Asia is now regarded as the "main battle-front of the world democratic camp against the forces of reaction and imperialism."[7] Success in this case carries its own rewards beyond the frontiers of China itself, for it is altogether probable that Mao Tse-tung will take his place alongside Lenin and Stalin as a font of revolutionary sagacity for these movements in India and Southeast Asia.[8]

Unfortunately, recent discussions of the Communist movement in Asia have done more to obscure than to clarify the nature and direction of its appeal to the indigenous populations. All too frequently, the tendency has been too fall back on the blanket formula that Communists have sought to identify

5. See the report of L. Soloviev at the Congress of Asian and Australasian Trade Unions at Peking, November 19, 1949, in *World Trade Union Movement* (organ of the WFTU), No. 8 (December, 1949), pp. 25–27. Also cf. "Manifesto to All Working People of Asia and Australasia," *ibid.*, pp. 43–46.

6. "Mighty Advance of National Liberation Movements in Colonial and Dependent Countries," *For a Lasting Peace, for a People's Democracy!* (organ of the Cominform), January 27, 1950; cf. speech by Liu Shao-chi at the Trade Union Conference of Asian and Australasian countries, Peking, 1949, *World Trade Union Movement*, No. 8 (December, 1949), pp. 12–15.

7. R. Palme Dutt, "Right Wing Social Democrats in the Service of Imperialism," *For a Lasting Peace, for a People's Democracy!* November 1, 1948, p. 6.

8. See statement of Ho Chi Minh's newly constituted Laodong party, which "pledges itself to follow the heroic example of the Communist party of China, to learn the Mao Tse-tung concept which has been leading the peoples of China and Asia on the road to independence and democracy" (Viet-Nam News Agency, English Morse to Southeast Asia, March 21, 1951). Likewise, the ruling body of the Indian Communist party fell into line with the general trend by declaring its adherence to Mao's strategy (*Crossroads* [Bombay], March 10, 1950).

themselves with local nationalism and demands for agrarian reform. We have already seen that their identification with nascent nationalism, if such it must be called, derives its peculiar strength from certain of its unique qualities. It is no less important to an appreciation of the problem to recognize that the Communist appeal does not by mere virtue of this process of identification acquire the same uniform access to all sectors of the population. Indeed, the most striking and disconcerting feature of much of the propaganda appeal emanating both from Moscow, Peking, and other centers is that it is not, and in the nature of the case cannot be, designed for peasant or worker consumption. The appeal of communism as such in these areas is first and foremost an appeal which finds lodgment with indigenous professional and intellectual groups. Its identification with native nationalism and demands for land reform turns out to be, when carefully scrutinized, not so much a direct appeal to specific peasant grievances, powerful though its actual results may be, as it is an identification with the more generalized, highly conscious, and sharply oriented outlook of the native intelligentsia.[9]

Given the entire range of sociological and economic forces at work in these areas, the very logic and terms of the Communist appeal must of necessity filter through to the peasant masses by first becoming the stock in trade of the intellectual and professional groups. To revert to the terminology suggested at the outset of this paper, we may say that, by and large, it is the old history-less style of social existence which still claims the loyalty and outlook of the bulk of the indigenous populations. It is still the old village community which serves as the center of peasant and worker aspirations, and, if they have taken to arms, it is

9. Failure to appreciate the true direction of the Communist appeal in these areas frequently causes some observers to commit the mistake of minimizing its effectiveness. Thus, Mr. Richard Deverall, the AF of L representative in these areas and an otherwise very perceptive student of the subject, ventures the opinion that Communist propaganda in these areas is mere "rubbish" because it is for the most part couched in terms which hold no interest for the masses, having meaning only for intellectuals (see his "Helping Asia's Workers," *American Federationist*, September, 1951, p. 16). Mr. Deverall's account of the nature of Communist propaganda is quite accurate, but, if the thesis presented above is a valid estimate of the current situation in Asia, he has not drawn the conclusion which follows from the evidence.

because European rule has destroyed the old securities and values without replacing them by new ones.[10] Without leadership and organization, their unrest would be without direction and certainly without much chance for success, quickly dissipating itself in spontaneous outbursts against individual landowners and achieving no lasting goals. Whatever else it may be that we are facing in Southeast Asia today, it certainly does not resemble the classic uprisings of peasant *Jacquerie* but a highly organized and well-integrated movement, with a leadership that has transcended the immediate urgencies of its mass following and can plan ahead in terms of long-range perspectives.

That leadership is supplied by the new indigenous intelligentsia. It is from this group that native Communist and non-Communist movements alike recruit their top leadership as well as the intermediate layers of cadres, for, of all the groups which make up the populations of these areas, it is the intelligentsia alone (taking the term in its broadest sense) that boasts an ideological horizon which transcends the history-less values of the bulk of the population and makes it the logical recruiting ground for the leadership of political movements. For this, it can thank the formal schooling and intellectual stimulus provided by the West, which not only brought such a group into existence but also—and this is crucial—condemned large sections of that intelligentsia to a form of *déclassé* existence from the very beginnings of its career. The new intelligentsia was in large measure consigned by the imperial system to hover uneasily between a native social base which could not find accommodation for its skills and ambitions and the superimposed imperial structure which reserved the best places for aliens. There were, of course, considerable variations and differences in the various areas of Southeast Asia—India, for example, did succeed in

10. In most backward areas the tie to the countryside is still apparent in the tendency of laborers engaged in industry and mining periodically to drift back to the village (W. E. Moore, "Primitives and Peasants in Industry," *Social Research*, XV, No. 1 [March, 1948], 49–63). See also the observations of Soetan Sjahrir in his *Out of Exile*, trans. C. Wolf (New York, 1949), pp. 74–75, concerning the mental outlook of the masses in these regions. This fact was not lost on the leaders of the Communist movement. In the 1928 resolution on colonial strategy the Sixth Comintern Congress noted that the proletariat "still have one foot in the village," a fact which it recognized as a barrier to the development of proletarian class consciousness (see *International Press Correspondence* [Vienna], VIII, No. 88 [December 12, 1928], 1670).

absorbing a good many of its professionally trained native sons —but, by and large, the picture is one of a rootless intellectual proletariat possessing no real economic base in an independent native middle class. The tendency in all these areas, moreover, has been to train technicians, lawyers, and other groups of professional workers in numbers far out of proportion to the absorptive capacity of the social structures of the home areas, even if more of the higher posts in industry and administration were thrown open to native talent. In any case, those who did find such employment were frozen in minor posts, the most coveted positions going to Europeans.[11]

But if these groups could not be integrated into the social structure of these dependent areas, the same does not hold true of their acclimatization to the cross-currents of political doctrine. Western education exposed many of them to the various schools of social thought contending for influence in Europe, and from these they distilled the lessons which seemed to offer the best hope for their native communities. Western capitalism was necessarily excluded from their range of choices if for no other reason than that its linkage with imperialist rule over their own societies debarred it from their hierarchy of values. The anticapitalist animus is common to the intellecual spokesmen of these areas, whatever their specific political allegiance or orientation may be.[12] Nor does it appear that any populist variety of Gandhiism, with its strong attachment to the values of a static subsistence economy, has won any considerable following among these intellectual groups. Soetan Sjahrir voiced a common sentiment when he wrote:

11. Some interesting data on this score for Indonesia are offered by J. M. van der Kroef's "Economic Origins of Indonesian Nationalism," in *South Asia in the World Today*, ed. Phillips Talbot (Chicago, 1950), pp. 188–93, and his "Social Conflicts and Minority Aspirations in Indonesia," *American Journal of Sociology*, March, 1950, pp. 453–56. Cf. L. Mills (ed.), *New World of Southeast Asia* (Minneapolis, 1949), pp. 293–95.

12. For a typical rejection of the capitalist solution coming from anti-Communist sources see D. R. Gadgil, "Economic Prospect for India," *Pacific Affairs*, XXII (June, 1949), 115–29; Sjahrir, *op. cit.*, pp. 161–62; and the remarks of H. Shastri, of the Indian Trade Union Congress at the Asian Regional Conference of the International Labor Office, Ceylon, January 16–27, 1950, *Record of Proceedings* (Geneva, 1951), p. 112. Cf. van der Kroef's article, "Social Conflicts and Minority Aspirations in Indonesia," *op. cit.*, pp. 455–56, and J. F. Normano, *Asia between Two World Wars* (New York, 1944), pp. 83–87.

We intellectuals here are much closer to Europe or America than we are to the Boroboedoer or Mahabrata or to the primitive Islamic culture of Java or Sumatra. . . . For me, the West signifies forceful, dynamic and active life. I admire, and am convinced that only by a utilization of this dynamism of the West can the East be released from its slavery and subjugation.[13]

The sole possibility, then, which appeared acceptable to them was one or another of the forms of state-sponsored reconstruction and industrialization, for which liberation from the rule of European states was naturally considered to be a prerequisite. Liberation and internal reconstruction thus came to be two inseparable operations, intimately tied together as they seldom have been before.

We can now appreciate the enormous initial advantage which was thus offered the Communist movements in these backward areas. The Russian Revolution of 1917 and the subsequent course of planned industrialization could not but fail to impress native intellectuals as offering a model pattern of action by which they could retrieve their communities from precapitalist isolation and backwardness without paying the price of continued foreign exploitation. There is doubtless a large measure of self-revelation in Mao's reaction to the Russian experience in his statement:

There is much in common or similar between the situation in China and prerevolutionary Russia. Feudal oppression was the same. Economic and cultural backwardness was common to both countries. Both were backward. China more so than Russia. The progressives waged a bitter struggle in search of revolutionary truth so as to attain national rehabilitation; this was common to both countries. . . . The October Revolution helped the progressive elements of the world, and of China as well, to apply the proletarian world outlook in determining the fate of the country. . . . The conclusion was reached that we must advance along the path taken by the Russians.[14]

It should also be noted, in passing, that the Comintern lost no time in launching a large number of international front organizations such as the Red International of Trade Unions, International League against Imperialism, International of Seamen and Dockers, International Red Aid, etc.—all of which fur-

13. Sjahrir, *op. cit.*, pp. 67 and 144.

14. Mao Tse-tung, *On People's Democratic Rule* (New York: New Century Publishers, 1950), pp. 2–4. For the same reaction of M. N. Roy, one of the earlier leaders of the Indian Communists who later broke with the Comintern, see his *Revolution and Counter-revolution in China* (Calcutta, 1946), p. 522.

nished the necessary organizational scaffolding and support for facilitating the dissemination of propaganda. Finally, as will be noted presently, the Comintern provided a rallying point for their aspirations by outlining a program of revolutionary action in the colonies and dependent areas which was ideally calculated to provide them with a mass peasant following.

The result, though viewed with some misgivings by the leadership of the Comintern, was merely what might have been expected under the circumstances. The Communist parties of these underdeveloped areas of Asia were from their very beginnings initiated, led by, and predominantly recruited from (prior to their conversion into mass organizations as has been the case in China after 1949) native intellectual groups. Though this vital sociological clue to the nature of the Communist appeal in the colonial areas has not received the recognition it deserves, amid the general preoccupation with the theme of Communist appeals to the peasantry, its implication was perfectly plain to the leaders of the Comintern. One of the most revealing (and to date largely unnoticed) admissions on this score is contained in the Sixth Comintern Congress in 1928 in its resolution on strategic policy in the colonies and semicolonies in which the point is very clearly made that

experience has shown that, in the majority of colonial and semi-colonial countries, an important if not a predominant part of the Party ranks in the first stage of the movement is recruited from the petty bourgeoisie, and in particular, from the revolutionary inclined intelligentsia, very frequently students. It not uncommonly happens that these elements enter the Party because they see in it the most decisive enemy of imperialism, at the same time not sufficiently understanding that the Communist Party is not only the Party of struggle against imperialist exploitation ... but struggle against all kinds of exploitation and expropriation. Many of these adherents of the Party, in the course of the revolutionary struggle will reach a proletarian class point of view; another part will find it more difficult to free themselves to the end, from the moods, waverings and half-hearted ideology of the petty bourgeoisie.[16]

The fact that this did not accord with the *idée fixe* of this and all other Comintern pronouncements that leadership of colonial

15. "The Revolutionary Movement in the Colonies and Semi-colonies; Resolution of the Sixth World Congress of the Communist International" (adopted September 1, 1928), *International Press Correspondence*, VIII, No. 88 (December 12, 1928), 1670.

revolutionary movements is properly a function of the industrial urban workers should in no way blind us to the fact which Comintern leadership was realistic enough to acknowledge, namely, that membership of these Communist parties is heavily weighted in favor of the intelligentsia. One may, in fact, go one step further and say that, in accepting the predominance of the "colonial" intelligentsia, the Comintern was closer to the genus of Leninist doctrine than were any of its indorsements of the leadership role of the urban proletariat. No other group in these areas but the intelligentsia could be expected to undertake the transformation of the social structure under forced draft and in a predetermined direction and thus fulfil the main self-assigned historical mission of Leninism.[16]

If we bear this key factor in mind, it throws a new light on the nature of the grip which Communists exercise on the political movements of these areas. The usual formulation of the character of these movements is that they stem from mass discontent with the prevailing system of land distribution, with the labor practices in force, with the overt or indirect political control of these areas by foreign governments, etc. These are perfectly valid empirical descriptions of the necessary conditions for the rise of liberation movements in these areas. But they obviously fail to take notice of the specific social groups that give these movements their *élan*, direction, and whatever measure of success they have had thus far. As matters stand today, the intellectuals are the sole group in these areas which can infuse these raw social materials of agrarian discontent, etc., with the organization and leadership necessary for their success. And it is largely this group which has acted as the marriage broker between the international Communist movement and the manifestations of indigenous revolt.

Enough empirical material exists to warrant the conclusion that the "colonial" Communist parties of Asia today, as in the 1920's, are the handiwork of native intellectuals. Since 1940,

16. Though cognizant of the role of the intellectuals in the Chinese party, Benjamin Schwartz's illuminating study, *Chinese Communism and the Rise of Mao* (Cambridge, 1951), falls short of an appreciation of its significance by focusing attention on a purely strategic problem—Mao's peasant-oriented movement—and concluding from this that Mao's ideology represents a radical break with classical Leninism.

they have, of course, greatly expanded their mass following and membership, but their leadership is still drawn overwhelmingly from the intelligentsia. As regards China, this elite character of Communist party leadership was expressly recognized by Mao Tse-tung in 1939,[17] and the entire history of the party from its founding by Li Ta-chao and Ch'en Tu-hsu to Mao Tse-tung and Liu Shao-chi is virtually an unbroken record of a party controlled by intellectuals.[18] India illustrates the same trend. Its earliest Communist leadership is exemplified in M. N. Roy (who later broke with the movement), a high-caste Brahmin of considerable intellectual attainments. Also indicative of the predominance of intellectuals in the leadership of the Indian Communist party is the fact that, at its first All-Indian Congress in 1943, 86 of a total attendance of 139 delegates were members of professional and intellectual groups.[19] And in the postwar period the leading position of this social group in the affairs of the Indian Communist party finds expression in men like Joshi, Ranadive, and Dange.[20] The same pattern also holds good for the Communist parties of Indochina, Thailand, Burma, Malaya, and Indonesia, all of which show a heavy preponderance of journalists, lawyers, and teachers among the top leadership.[21] The Burmese Communists afford an especially pointed illustration in this respect, since the parent-organization, the Thakens, originated in the early 1930's among university students who today comprise the leadership of both rival Communist factions.[22] If any doubt exists as to the extent to which the leadership of these movements is dominated by intellectual

17. Mao Tse-tung, *The Chinese Revolution and the Communist Party of China* (New York: Committee for a Democratic Far Eastern Policy, n.d.), pp. 13–14.

18. Mao Tse-tung's excursion into an instrumentalist approach to Marxian philosophy is one manifestation (see his "On Practice," *Political Affairs* [organ of the United States Communist party], April, 1951, pp. 28–42).

19. *People's War* (organ of the CPI) (Bombay), June 13, 1943.

20. See a review of Dange's *India, from Primitive Communism to Slavery* (Bombay, 1949), in *The Communist* (organ of the CPI) (Bombay), III, No. 4 (October–November, 1950), 78–91. Cf. M. R. Masani, "The Communist Party in India," *Pacific Affairs*, March, 1951, pp. 31–33.

21. See, e.g., biographic data in V. Thompson and R. Adloff, *The Left Wing in South East Asia* (New York, 1950), pp. 231–86.

22. *Ibid.*, pp. 80–82.

groups, it is quickly dispelled by an examination of the top echelons of trade-unions, as instanced, for example, by the names of those attending the WFTU-sponsored Congress of Asian and Australasian Unions in Peking in 1949. Here, at least, we can appreciate the full impact of the trend by noting that, while European trade-union leadership (in contrast to the leadership of parties) has been largely recruited from within membership ranks, the reverse is true in Southeast Asia. The trade-union movement in that region is largely a newborn post-war phenomenon, and the various bodies (whether Communist-dominated or controlled by other political groups) have been fashioned and directed by professionals with no direct experience in the occupations concerned.[23]

This, in its larger perspectives, is the structure of leadership for both the Communist and the non-Communist groups in the entire region. More detailed research might serve to throw some light on the sociological factors which determine the distribution of these professional groups among Communist and anti-Communist movements. But, even if a completely detailed analysis is still lacking, enough is already known of the larger trends to indicate that these sections of the native populations constitute the key operational factor in the Communist appeal. It is they who spearhead the propaganda drive, organize the unions, youth groups, and other organizations, plan the tactics of their parties, etc.

As matters stand, then, the organization and leadership of Communist parties in colonial areas do not accord with their accepted doctrinal precepts. For over a generation now it has been a standard item of doctrine, reiterated again and again, that the leadership of these parties must rest with the industrial working class.[24] The realities of the situation in these areas have

23. *New York Times*, May 21, 1950; see also Institute of Pacific Relations, *Problems of Labor and Social Welfare in South and Southeast Asia* ("Secretariat Paper No. 1 Prepared by Members of the ILO" [New York, 1950]), p. 20. Cf. statements of delegates from India and Ceylon to Asian Regional Conference of the ILO, Ceylon, January 16–27, 1950, *Record of Proceedings*, pp. 98, 113.

24. See, e.g., "The Revolutionary Movement in Colonies and Semi-colonies; Resolution of the Sixth Congress of the Communist International" (adopted September 1, 1928), *International Press Correspondence*, VIII (1928), 1670–72 *et passim;* and Mao's pamphlet, *The Chinese Revolution and the Communist Party of China*, pp. 15–16.

not been very obliging to this formula, though it still occupies its customary niche in all their pronouncements. From the standpoint of their own strategic imperatives and long-term objective, however, the Communist parties of these areas have not hesitated to draw the necessary practical conclusions. They have acquiesced in the primacy of the intellectuals in the movement because the acceptance of any alternative leadership coming from the ranks of the peasantry or the industrial workers (assuming the possibility of such leadership) would entail the sacrifice of the prime objectives of the party—viz., the seizure of power and the launching of a long-range plan for internal planning and reconstruction. Gradual and piecemeal reforms and certainly basic reforms designed to bring immediate economic relief to the masses (for instance, in the credit structure of an area) undertaken by non-Communist regimes would be welcomed by the mass of the peasantry because they are in accord with their immediate and most pressing interests.[25] A program of seizing political power followed by prolonged industrialization, economic planning, recasting of the social structure, realignment of a country's international position in favor of the U.S.S.R.—these are considerations of the type which can attract intellectuals only.[26]

Accordingly, if the main appeal of communism per se, in underdeveloped areas, has been to the native intelligentsia, a transgression has apparently been committed against an expendable item of party dogma, but the fundamental spirit of the Leninist position with regard to the relation between leadership and the masses has actually been preserved in its pristine form. There is no need to labor this point, since there is enough evidence to indicate that the leadership of Communist parties in underdeveloped areas is acutely aware of the conflict between its own long-range objectives and the "interests" of its mass

25. This is all the more true of large sections of Southeast Asia, where the land problem is not identical with the structure of ownership distribution and where no direct correlation prevails between tenancy and poverty. In large sections of this region the problem arises largely from the primitive credit and marketing facilities rather than from concentration of land titles.

26. Communist leaders are not loath to recognize that this cleavage exists between the immediate interests of the masses and the party's long range perspectives (see Liu Shao-chi, "On the Party," *Political Affairs*, October, 1950, p. 88).

following, as well as of the conclusions to be drawn for the practical guidance of their parties' activities. Thus a recent party document issued by the Malaya Communist party to cope with internal criticism of its leadership and policies contains this cogent passage:

> Regarding these masses, our responsibility is not to lower the Party's policy and to accede to the selfish demands of small sections of the backward elements, but to bring out a proper plan to unite and direct them courageously to carry out the various forms of struggle against the British. If this course is not followed we will retard the progress of the national revolutionary war, and will lose the support of the masses. The proper masses route is not only to mix up with them [mingle with them(?)—M.W.] but to resolutely and systematically lead them to march forward to execute the Party's policy and programme. By overlooking the latter point, we will not be able to discharge the historical duty of a revolutionary Party.[27]

If we discern the central driving force of communism in the underdeveloped areas to be its appeal to a considerable number of the indigenous intelligentsia, we are also in a position to reassess the meaning and changes of its mass appeal, most notably its program of land redistribution. To no inconsiderable extent, much of the confusion which attends thinking and discourse on the subject in this country can be traced to a widespread impression still current that the Communist movement in underdeveloped areas owes its success to the fact that it is finely attuned to the most urgent and insistent "land hunger" of millions of the poorest peasants living on a submarginal level of existence. There is just enough historical truth in this impression to make it a plausible explanation of Communist strength. It is unquestionably true that the mass base of the Communist parties in Southeast Asia can be accounted for by the almost universal prevalence of local agrarian unrest which thus constitutes the necessary precondition for the activities of

27. The document from which this passage is taken is contained in a Malaya Communist party publication titled *How To Look After the Interests of the Masses* ("Emancipation Series," No. 5), published secretly by the Freedom Press in Malaya, December 15, 1949, and made public after its seizure by the local authorities. Another document titled "Resolution To Strengthen Party Character" reaffirms the doctrine of democratic centralism against the more "extremist democratic" demands of some of the members. For an expression of the same standpoint regarding the relation between the party and the masses from a Chinese source see Liu Shao-chi, "On the Party," *op. cit.*, p. 78.

the Communists. But if—as is not infrequently done—this is offered as the crucially strategic element in the complex of circumstances which have served the cause of the Communist parties, we are once again confronted with the old confusion of necessary with sufficient causes.[28] For there is no intrinsic reason which compels the ground swell of agrarian discontent to favor the fortunes of the Communist parties—unless that discontent can be channeled and directed in predetermined fashion by the intervention of a native social group capable of giving organized shape to its various amorphous and diffused manifestations. If the foregoing analysis has any merit, the balance of the sociological picture in these areas will have to be redressed in our thinking to give greater weight to the Communist-oriented intelligentsia and to its role as the prime mover of the native Communist movements.

A more balanced picture of the sociological roots of the Communist movement in the underdeveloped areas would also serve to throw some light on the shift which has recently taken place in their agrarian reform program and therefore, too, in the direction of their appeal.

In its original form the agrarian program of the Comintern was an outright bid for the support of the poorest and therefore the numerically preponderant sections of the peasantry. At the Second Congress of the Comintern in 1920, Lenin placed the question of agrarian reform at the very center of the Communist appeal and dismissed as utopian any notion that a Communist movement in these areas was even conceivable without an appeal to the masses of peasantry.[29] The resolution adopted by that congress repudiated any attempt to solve the agrarian problem along Communist lines and instead accepted the inevitable fact that, in its initial stages, the agrarian revolution in these areas would have to be achieved by a "petty bourgeois" program of land distribution, directed "against the landlords, against large landownership, against all survivals of feudal-

28. An otherwise excellent discussion by Miss Barbara Ward verges on this error, especially in its opening remarks. See her article in the *New York Times Magazine*, March 25, 1951.

29. For the text of Lenin's remarks see *Selected Works*, X, 239–40.

ism."[30] Eight years later the Sixth Congress of the Comintern was more specific. Its resolution on the strategy of the Communist movement in colonial areas called attention to the presence of a "hierarchy of many stages, consisting of landlords and sublandlords, parasitic intermediate links between the laboring cultivator and the big landowner or the state" who were destroying the basis of the peasant's livelihood. More particularly, "the peasantry . . . no longer represents a homogeneous mass. In the villages of China and India . . . it is already possible to find exploiting elements derived from the peasantry who exploit the peasants and village laborers through usury, trade, employment of hired labor, the sale or letting out of land." While the Comintern was willing to collaborate with the entire peasantry during the first period of the liberation movement, the upper strata of the peasantry was expected to turn counterrevolutionary as the movement gained momentum. When the chips were down, therefore, the program would have to shift to "a revolutionary settlement of the agrarian question."[31]

The "revolutionary settlement of the agrarian question" was never accomplished, save in the case of Korea. Wherever the Communists have achieved power in these areas, the program of agrarian revolution, stipulated in the resolution of the Sixth Comintern Congress, soon became a dead letter.[32] Except for North Korea, where its application was dictated by the previous expropriation of native lands in favor of the Japanese, its place was taken by a series of moderate reforms designed to mollify the poorer sections of the peasantry without alienating the "parasitic intermediate links" or impairing the productive capacity of agriculture. During the period when the Chinese Communists held sway in the border regions, for example, steps

30. "Theses on National and Colonial Questions," *ibid.*, pp. 231–38. See also the speech of Zinoviev at the Congress of Eastern Peoples held in Baku, 1920 (*I. S'zed Narodov Vostoka September 1–8, 1920, Baku, Stenograf</i>cheskii Otchety* [Petrograd, 1920]).

31. "The Revolutionary Movement in the Colonies and Semi-colonies; Resolution of the Sixth Congress of the Communist International" (adopted September 1, 1928), *International Press Correspondence*, VIII (1928), 1663–67.

32. Except in Kiangsi and Fukien in the late 1920's and later discontinued. Similarly, the radical confiscatory program of 1946–49 was abandoned with the Communist's final accession to power.

were taken to alleviate the lot of the poorer peasantry in such matters as rentals and interest rates; but wholesale confiscation and redistribution were not attempted to any great extent. Similarly, under the present regime in China, the revolutionary formula has been virtually dismissed as a propaganda appeal, once useful for enlisting the support of the poorer peasantry in the period before the Communist accession to power, but having no relevance to the problems of agriculture today. In fact, the propaganda appeal is now designed to reconcile the middle and wealthier sections of the Chinese peasantry to the new regime in political terms and to promote increased output and land improvements as prerequisites to a program of industrialization.[33] Without the active intervention of a Communist-oriented intelligentsia, a large-scale peasant movement in China as well as in the region of Southeast Asia, if successful, would not go beyond agrarian reform pure and simple. The end goal would be Sun Yat-sen's and Stambulisky's rather than Lenin's, given the essentially static and conservative temper of the bulk of the peasant populations. As matters stand now, however, the schedule of agrarian reform under Communist sponsorship has definitely been subordinated to the long-range perspectives of industrialization with a program of collectivization in store for the future when conditions are more favorable to its success.[34] Accordingly, the imperatives of the "New Democracy" require a shift in the main incidence of Communist appeal to secure for the regime a base of support more in accord with its long-range plans.

The shift is equally apparent in the industrial field, where attempts are being made to enlist the support of the "national burgeoisie" during an indefinite transition period pending the introduction of "genuine" socialism. The present program envisions a form of limited state-sponsored and state-regulated

33. Liu Shao-chi, "On Agrarian Reform in China," *For a Lasting Peace, for a People's Democracy!* July 21, 1950, pp. 3–4; see also Teh Kao, "Peasants in the New China," *For a Lasting Peace, for a People's Democracy!* October 13, 1950, p. 2. For a summary of the history of the Communist agrarian program see F. C. Lee, "Land Redistribution in Communist China," *Pacific Affairs*, March, 1948, pp. 20–32.

34. Mao Tse-tung, *On the Present Situation and Our Tasks* (East China Liberation Publishers, 1946); see also remarks of Liu Shao-chi in *People's China*, July 16, 1950.

capitalist enterprise to promote the process of industrializations,[35] and the attractions now being employed to enlist entrepreneurial co-operation are strangely reminiscent of the "infant-industry" argument so familiar in "imperialist" countries.[36]

An identical transposition of appeal may also be detected in the program of Ho Chi-minh's newly organized Laodong (Worker's) party in Viet-Nam.[37] Its program proclaims it the leader of a national united front comprising *all* classes, parties, and races, and its leading motif is the need to oust the French oppressors who are charged not only with exploiting Viet-Namese workers but also native landlords and capitalists who must pay a tribute to the French in the form of high prices for imports and the sale of their own products at depressed prices.[38] The socialist regime is indefinitely postponed until such time as the country is ready for it, and in the meantime

the national bourgeoisie must be encouraged, assisted and guided in their undertakings, so as to contribute to the development of the national economy. The right of the patriotic landlords to collect rent in accordance with the law must be guaranteed.

Our agrarian policy mainly aims at present in carrying out the reduction of land rent and interest . . . regulation of the leasehold system, provisional allocation of land formerly owned by imperialists to poorer peasants, redistribution of communal lands, rational use of land belonging to absentee landlords.[39]

To say, then, that the Communist program in the underdeveloped areas of Asia is designed purely and simply as an appeal to the poorest and landless sections of the peasant population is to indulge in an oversimplification of the facts. The

35. See, e.g., Mao Tse-tung, *On People's Democratic Rule*, p. 12, and the text of the "Common Program of the People's Political Consultative Conference of 1949" included as an appendix to Mao's speech, esp. p. 19.

36. Wu Min, "Industry of People's China Grows," *For a Lasting Peace, for a People's Democracy!* November 17, 1950, p. 4. This outright nationalistic appeal to the interests of domestic business groups is also plainly apparent in the latest draft program of the Indian Communist party (see *For a Lasting Peace, for a People's Democracy!* May 11, 1951, p. 3).

37. Actually a revival of the Communist party dissolved in 1945.

38. Viet-Nam News Agency in English Morse to Southeast Asia, April 12, 1951.

39. Viet-Nam News Agency in English Morse to Southeast Asia, March 18 and April 10, 1951.

Communist appeal is rather a complicated function of the total interplay of political forces in these areas and has therefore tended to shift both in direction and in content with the degree of influence and political power exercised by the Communist parties. The only constant element among all these changes has been the abiding appeal of the Communist system to certain sections of the intelligentsia. Whether the new dispensation of the appeal can be expected to evoke the same degree of sympathetic response from the "national bourgeoisie" and the more prosperous peasantry as the discarded slogan of outright land confiscation had for the impoverished peasants is open to considerable doubt. The avowed transitional character of the program of the "People's Democracy" is alone sufficient to rob these appeals of any sustained response. It does not require any high degree of political sophistication on the part of the "national bourgeoisie," for example, to realize that a full measure of co-operation with a Communist-controlled regime would only serve to hasten its own extinction. How seriously such a withdrawal of support would affect the fortunes of a Communist regime would depend to a crucial extent on the speed with which it could find a substitute support in newly evolved social groups with a vested stake in its continued existence. Some indication of how the problem is visualized by the leaders of the Communist regime in China may be gleaned from the following remarks made by Liu Shao-chi in a speech to Chinese businessmen last year:

As Communists we consider that you are exploiting your workers; but we realize that, at the present stage of China's economic development, such exploitation is unavoidable and even socially useful. What we want is for you to go ahead and develop production as fast as possible and we will do what we can to help you. You may be afraid of what will happen to you and your families when we develop from New Democracy to Socialism. But you need not really be afraid. If you do a really good job in developing your business, and train your children to be first-class technical experts, you will be the obvious people to put in charge of the nationalized enterprise and you may find that you earn more as managers of a socialized enterprise than as owners.[40]

40. Quoted by M. Lindsay in *New China*, ed. O. van der Sprenkel (London, 1950), p. 139.

For the time being the challenge which confronts the West in its efforts to deny the underdeveloped areas of Southeast Asia to the Communist appeal is therefore compounded of two distinct elements. The more obvious of these is, of course, the problem of depriving the Communists of their actual and potential "mass base" by an adequate program of technical aid and economic reform designed to remove the blight of poverty and exploitation from the scheme of things heretofore in force in these areas. The other and more imponderable aspect of this twofold challenge requires the development of an ethos and system of values which can compete successfully with the attraction exercised by communism for those sections of the native intelligentsia which have been the source and mainstay of its leadership. To date, there is little evidence that the West is prepared to meet either of these challenges on terms commensurate with their gravity.

PART III

PROBLEMS OF ECONOMIC POLICY

AMERICA'S AIMS AND THE PROGRESS OF UNDERDEVELOPED COUNTRIES

By Jacob Viner

IT IS my assignment to speak of American interests in the question of the economic development of so-called under-developed countries. The first interest with which I will deal, and the one, I believe, which is going to be given major weight as long as the present international tension continues, will be the security interests of the United States.

We are seeking willing and strong allies. We are seeking the maintenance and the development of overseas sources of strategically important raw materials. We probably also are seeking to strengthen our own internal morale by offering evidence of a willingness to deal generously out of our riches with less-well-endowed peoples.

The second set of interests which underlie our national policy are economic in nature. It is the belief of our government, in its Executive Branch at least, and the belief of many Americans, that other countries which play a role in the international economic network of which we are a part contribute positively by their prosperity to our own prosperity. They give us growing and profitable markets for our exports. They give us good sources of supply for the goods which we desire to import. They feed us with ideas, designs, and technical innovations, as we feed them in turn. While prosperity is not, perhaps, as some enthusiasts have held, indivisible, it tends at least to be contagious, and we are more likely to prosper if the outside world is also prospering than if it is declining or remaining stagnant. Even under the freest of trade conditions there is economic rivalry as well as economic co-operation between nations; but it is a fundamental assumption of our current economic policy that, in general, our mutuality of economic interests with the outside world far surpasses our conflict of interest therewith.

There is also, I am convinced, a genuine humanitarian interest on the part of the American people in the welfare of the masses of people elsewhere who are living in a state which seems to us, and increasingly to them, one of distressful misery. The floor of Congress is not ordinarily the platform from which the more generous impulses of the American nation receive their most outspoken and vigorous expression. The Administration, which lives closer to Congress and has to respond to its views more fully than do those whose operations are confined to the academic lecture hall or the pulpit, has to be guarded in revealing any feelings of generosity to other peoples, lest Congress charge it with giving away the substance of the American people to gratify a soft-minded humanitarianism. It is not easy, therefore, to prove to foreign skeptics that a genuine sympathy on the part of large sections of the American people for the economic plight of low-income peoples is influencing American policy. I believe it nevertheless to be a fact—one which a properly concluded public opinion poll would verify and which we could verify for ourselves if we were to examine our own motives.

We have, I insist, interests in the welfare of foreign peoples going beyond our own national security and commercial prosperity. We want them also to have some participation in the good material things of this life which we enjoy and perhaps in some cases overvalue and are overboastful about. We want the common man and his wife and his children to have not only Coca-Cola and chewing gum and ice cream, not only modern plumbing, automobiles, refrigerators, and electric lighting, but also good health and good diet, good education and good prospects of betterment in life. We would like others also to enjoy the benefits and the virtues, as we see them, of political democracy, of social security, and of freedom from degradation of human dignity and from overarduous, overlong, or servile toil. These, and other things, we want other people to enjoy in fuller measure than they do now and in fuller measure even than some of our own underprivileged do as yet.

American philanthropy abroad is not a seedling of recent planting. It is an unexpected tribute to our national modesty that there seems to be no American history of our record in this connection and that the only account I have found reference to was published in Hitler Germany. Americans in times of calamity abroad have generally given aid on a commendable scale, individually and through private or official agencies. Much more important has been the systematic contribution of American religious organizations and of American missionaries to poor relief, to education, and to health in underdeveloped countries. I should also mention as an item in our record the contributions of our charitable foundations, and especially the Rockefeller Foundation, in pioneering the way for aid in public health work such as, in connection with Point IV, our government is now engaged in learning how to do on an official basis.

Humanitarian activities on a large scale and directed toward foreign countries grew to significant proportions only as the Western world accumulated economic surplus and only as it became psychologically possible to extend aid to the foreign needy without its being too obvious that there was unmet need at home. Charity has always begun at home, and it was late in modern history before it ceased to end there also. International philanthropy was a by-product of modern capitalism, of its development of a prosperous middle class with religious and moral awareness of obligations extending beyond national boundaries. Its early American manifestations were an offshoot largely of those of Europe. It has grown since World War I to new dimensions; it is now largely conducted under governmental auspices and from governmental financial resources; and the American share therein has become by far the largest. Peoples in need are now more vocal about their needs than they used to be, and we are now better informed about conditions elsewhere than formerly. The growth of relevant statistical information has made the disparity between our levels of living and those of other peoples more conspicuous than hitherto, and it is probably also greater in fact. Two world wars and widespread strife have spread ruin and hunger over wide stretches of the earth. Our participation in the two wars was shorter than that of our enemies, or our allies, and the actual fighting did not touch our home territory. For all these reasons, and, no doubt, others as well, our contributions in recent years to relief of need abroad have been on a much larger scale, have been directed toward a much greater area, and have been much more systematic in plan and execution than there is parallel for in our own past history or in the past or present experience of other countries.

While I would insist that our foreign-aid activities have been in some degree of a genuinely humanitarian character, it is, of course, undeniable that the American interest in the needs of other peoples has been stimulated, and the scale of American response to such needs has been permitted to grow to its recent dimensions, largely from considerations which, while thoroughly respectable, were not primarily philanthropic in character. It is with these considerations that I now propose to deal.

First, there have been economic considerations, some of which have been clearly rational and others, I think, misguided. It was genuinely enlightened self-interest on our part, for instance, to aid in the recovery of the economic health, which war had undermined, of those countries which had been in the past and could again be profitable economic partners for us. Not so easy to defend has been the argument repeatedly invoked by the government and in Congress that foreign aid was needed to maintain our current or future exports, even if this meant that directly or indirectly the exports would in effect be given away. In the first place, during most of the postwar period our exports have been embarrassingly large instead of distressfully small, as far as the availability of domestic markets for them and their impact on inflation and employment at home were concerned. In the second place, the predictions at the end of the war of the imminence of mass unemployment which only extraordinary measures, like foreign aid, involving huge federal budgetary deficits, could avert were an inexcusable aberration of my profession, or of a part of it, for which due penance is still to be exacted. Third, a reasonably well-managed economy should never get into such a state that government spending unjustified by its immediate object becomes an acceptable means, as compared to other available alternatives, of restoring or maintaining balance in a national economy. Finally, there was in some of the advocacy of foreign aid at least a hint that the mercantilist delusion that exports, aside from benevolent sentiments toward their recipients or interest in the imports by which at once or later they would be repaid, were a national good in themselves. In any case, economic considerations, wise and foolish, were important supports for our program of foreign aid.

Undoubtedly of most importance, however, in the Administration, in public opinion, and above all in Congress, in obtaining support for a series of large-scale programs of foreign aid, was the strategic consideration, the consideration of national security. Throughout most of our history our people has not felt that its national security faced any formidable external threat. We have therefore been too much disposed to regard with disdain and to apply disparaging terms to the foreign policies of other countries which did not consider themselves to be so fortunately situated. Even Woodrow Wilson and Franklin D. Roosevelt, each for a time, refused to distinguish between policies designed to carry out wilful aggression and policies designed for defense against aggression and applied to both aggressive policies and defensive policies, with undiscriminating opprobrium, the label of "power politics." Today, we are ourselves deeply enmeshed, if not in "power politics," then in "security politics," and it is now the role of other countries to irritate us by refusing to make fine distinctions between plans of aggression and plans of defense.

In any case, hostilities were barely over before we became convinced—somewhat belatedly, I can say, without undue benefit of hindsight—that our national security faced a major external menace from expansionist communism. Given this menace, we came to believe that aid to needy potential allies and to needy countries in general which were not yet caught in the Soviet net could make a valuable and even vital contribution to our national security, now and hereafter.

When Congress approved the Anglo-American loan, someone commented that Molotov was Britain's most successful foreign minister. Let us recall the circumstances at the time. The loan was large; the terms of repayment and of interest were, on past standards, very generous; then, as always, there was considerable anti-English feeling in this country; taxes were high; and neither Congress nor the public had received clear warning in advance that aid to England was contemplated after Lend-Lease had terminated. Nevertheless, Congress approved the loan. Russian diplomacy, in its timing, if not in its general direction, seems to be beyond the understanding of non-Communists. In any case, Soviet Russia had chosen just this critical moment to deal with us and to speak of us unkindly, and the *Congressional Record* is there as demonstration that Molotov speeded the loan through Congress and as evidence at least that without his aid it would have failed of passage. The hostility and the apparent menace to us of Russia are continuing to operate to make us more responsive to programs of foreign aid than we otherwise would be, which is another supporting instance for the maxim that it is an ill wind that blows no one any good.

It seems that we no longer have a monopoly of the atom bomb. We do, however, have a monopoly of the resources available for economic aid on a large scale to other countries. Russia is fully aware of this and apparently attaches considerable weight to it, for she is engaging in counterpropaganda which asserts, not only that recipient countries will have to pay dearly, in sacrifice of their independence, for such aid, but also that aid received from abroad yields no lasting benefit and that the only economic progress which is genuine and durable is that which is accomplished by one's own effort and resources. I can conceive this sour-grapes propaganda as being successful with their own people, but it should find hard going in countries to which American aid has actually been extended.

Using calendar-year 1950 data, the United States government gave in outright grants to Europe and its colonial dependencies, to the Far East, to Latin America, to the Near East, to United Nations activities, and in contributions to international philanthropic agencies, about 4.5 billion dollars, of which about 80 per cent went to Europe. Private charitable remittances abroad amounted to about 500 million dollars. Government external loans, net, were only about 150 million dollars, and private investments abroad were around 1 billion dollars. This makes a grand total of about 6 billion dollars, net, of grants and loans, public and private, of which about five-sixths were grants and about three-fourths were public.

These are substantial figures. But this new term "foreign aid" includes ambiguously loans on a nearly commercial basis, loans on special terms, and grants. If all of it is to be regarded as philanthropy, then we should remember, as we can be sure that the recipients do, that a minor but significant fraction of it is philanthropy at 3 per cent or more per annum. Also, if loans and grants are treated alike, and private investment is included, the scale on which foreign aid is being extended is not out of line with past experience. Before World War I, England, which was then the leading international lender, was investing abroad at an annual net rate of about 8 per cent of its national income and about 50 per cent of its annual savings. If we were to match such rates today, our foreign aid in the form of private and public loans and of grants would have to exceed their actual current rates several fold.

There are important differences in character, of course, between American foreign aid today and the British export of capital before World War I. We are in the main making outright grants. Our governmental loans are at low interest rates, with the interest subject in some cases to cancellation, and the terms of repayment are flexible and otherwise moderate. Except for the American private investment, moreover, none of the American loans is being made on a strictly commercial basis in the expectation of remunerative interest or dividend returns. The British export of capital before World War I, on the other hand, was all strictly private and was all governed exclusively by the expectation of greater profit to the investors than would be derivable from investment at home.

There are still other differences. The British lending was at high contractual rates of interest. While the actual yields on the earlier lending, after defaults and conversions, were not very different from the rates on loans we now are charging, the lenders then were unconcerned as to the productivity of the investments for the borrowing countries except as this might affect the prospects of repayment, and they accepted high contractual rates of interest as adequate compensation for poor prospects of productive investment and mediocre prospects of repayment according to schedule. The American government, on the contrary, is very much concerned with the productive use of the grants and loans it makes and is probably only mildly concerned with the interest yield or even with ultimate repayment of principal.

Before 1914 a large part of international investment consisted of direct investment in private enterprises and in loans to private firms. Later on, the doctrine evolved that these loans had been the means of economic exploitation of, and imperialistic domination over, the debtor countries. There was some basis for this interpretation. The record is clear, however, that the great bulk of the capital which went to underdeveloped countries carried with it no real threat to the independence of the debtor countries and that, when there was wasteful or exploitative investment, the shortcomings of local governments were at least as much responsible as the malice or cupidity or indifference to local interests of the foreign investors. Today, in any case, the governments of debtor countries are more alert to such dangers and perhaps also better qualified to cope with them, and the danger in particular of creditor-country designs against their territorial sovereignty, to whose realization their state of indebtedness may contribute, can be taken as nil.

Americans in particular must not be too disdainful of the benefits which flowed to debtor countries from foreign investment before World War I. European capital investment greatly speeded up the rate of economic development of this country and made it a much less painful process as far as pressure on the current standard of living was concerned. American debtors, moreover, like other debtors, did not always pay their debts.

Economists in the underdeveloped countries have additional criticisms to make of the past record of international investments. They assert that these investments, insofar as they were not loans to wasteful and corrupt governments, went largely to the development of sources of supply of foodstuffs and raw materials for the investing countries and thus helped to fasten on the undeveloped countries an agricultural and raw-material pattern of production, labeled by them a "colonial" pattern, which added to instead of removing the obstacles to the industrialization which they now generally regard as essential to true economic progress. They claim also that the European capital went largely to the countries least in need of it, to countries which already had relatively high per capita incomes and capital resources. They cite the United States, Canada, Australia, and New Zealand as illustrations of this. They point out that even capital-exporting countries which had large colonial empires, England and France, did not make large investments in their own low-income colonies but permitted their surplus capital to flow in the main to less needy areas.

This is a fairly accurate transcript of the record. International investment in the past was largely unplanned and was conducted by private interests in pursuit of their own advantage. Neither benefit to the countries to which the capital went nor benefit to the countries from which it came was of direct concern to the investors. Such benefit did result, but it came as an incidental by-product, not as a major objective, of the investment.

One exception, however, needs to be pointed out, namely, the instances where governments, mainly French and German, steered foreign investment in certain directions for reasons of national political and strategic interest. The most notable case was the great flow of French capital to Russia from the early 1890's to 1914, mostly in the form of loans to the Russian government. These loans were an important factor in the formation and maintenance of the Franco-Russian alliance, and French private investors were induced to place their savings in them by the combined efforts of the French government, of the large French banks, and of the French press in promoting their sale, and by the exclusion from the Paris money market, through government regulation and informal pressure, of competing foreign investment outlets for French savings. Russia borrowed largely for railroad construction purposes. While these railroads made a contribution to Russian economic development, they were largely designed and located with strategic considerations in the foreground. The French loans to Russia thus bore a close resemblance to the program of military aid to western Europe which we are now embarking on. One important difference, however, is that our present program takes the form exclusively of intergovernmental grants and loans, whereas the French aid to Russia involved the necessity of persuading individual French investors that Russian government bonds were good investments.

It is more generally an important difference between the international finance of pre–World War I and of the interwar period, on the one hand, and of the present time, on the other, that the relative importance of private investment has greatly shrunk. Heavy taxation and wartime impairment of capital have greatly reduced the amounts of private capital available for foreign investment. Capital export controls in the lending countries and new hazards to the investor in the capital-poor countries in the form of, among other things, political unrest, fear of confiscation and expropriation, discriminatory taxation and regulation, and a widespread hostility to the foreign capitalist are operating as formidable obstacles to international private investment. The United States is now the only important net exporter of capital. American private investment abroad is of small dimensions. What there is, is largely concentrated in mining investments, notably in the petroleum field, where extraordinarily high short-run profit prospects offset the also extraordinarily high appraisals of the political and other risks. If there are excluded a few favored spots, such as Canada and some of the Caribbean countries, it is probably substantially true that in the absence of very special circumstances no American private capital will now venture abroad unless the prospects are good that, aside from political risks, the returns will amortize the investments within five years or so.

Great as is the contribution to economic development which international investment has made in the past and can make in the future, there is sometimes a tendency to exaggerate its importance as compared to other types of international economic co-operation. Much of the contribution of international investment itself has been indirect, through acting as carrier for the transmission of technology and of administrative capacity and through the migration to sparsely settled areas which it has facilitated. But the most important form of international economic co-operation has been and will continue to be ordinary and routine foreign trade. England in the nineteenth century and the United States at its recent peak of foreign financial aid made a much greater contribution to the economic growth and prosperity of other countries by their ordinary trade with them than by foreign investment or foreign grants. We should not move into the establishment of foreign aid as a permanent institution which merely provides other countries on a loan or grant basis with dollars which, were it not for our trade barriers, they could earn by export to us. We should not use foreign aid as conscience-money payments for our tariff.

I turn now to the question of the nature and functions of economic development itself. What manner or kind of economic development are the underdeveloped countries seeking? And what kind have we good reason, whether in terms of our national economic interest or on humanitarian grounds, to wish to promote? Even we are not so rich that we could respond to all the requests for aid which would come from other countries if they were free to choose whatever form of economic development seemed most attractive to them and to call upon us to meet by unconditional loans or grants any consequent deficits in their international balances of payments. But I will leave aside the economic limitations which exist on our capacity to render foreign aid.

In the literature on economic development, both the immensity of which in the last decade and the scarcity of which earlier are almost beyond belief, the term is used with great ambiguity of meaning. Often it is used so as not necessarily to mean more than growth in national indexes of aggregate production or income. Such growth could come solely or mainly as a result of mere growth of population, with no improvement and even with impairment of average income or average output. For countries other than the one directly in question, the nature of the economic growth may not be, from the strictly economic point of view, a matter of much concern. It is even conceivable that, for some other countries for which it is an important export market or source of supply of essential foodstuffs or raw materials, the economic growth of a particular country which is mainly the consequence of growth in its population and involves no major change in its standards of living or in its allocation of productive resources may be the most beneficial type of growth. But why should any country want growth of this kind for itself, especially where it means chiefly that more persons are there to endure a substandard level of existence?

One might just as well ask why Chicago wants to be a still bigger city than it is already or why an overgrown university wants still further growth. Welfare rests on prestige, and prestige goes with size for many minds. To the native of India, it is likely to seem a self-evidently good thing that there should be as many Indians as possible, even if they be wretchedly poor and sick and illiterate. Earthly misery may be regarded as an unimportant prelude to eternal paradise in a later life. Numbers are widely supposed to bring military strength of themselves, and military arithmetic, rightly or wrongly, in comparing the power of different countries, turns first to a merely quantitative comparison of their populations.

Economic growth which is merely the result of growth of a population which was and remains miserably poor, ill fed, ill housed, ill governed, unwashed, untutored, and unhealthy seems to me a menace to be avoided rather than an objective ardently to be pursued. That many do not share this view, however, is only too apparent. Take a look at even the sophisticated literature on economic development, as issued by the United Nations, by governments (including our own), and by learned men from the universities, and see how much of it neither presents nor seeks statistical evidence or criteria of desirable economic development which could not be fully met by a country swarming with ever more crowded and ever more miserable population, provided only its national indexes of total production or aggregate income, or total exports, continued to rise. There have been important state papers in which mere growth in this sense, without explicit qualification or reservation, has been treated as a matter for congratulation if it has occurred and as a goal to be striven for in the future.

A second kind of growth, a more attractive one, would be growth in per capita output and per capita income, whether or not accompanied by growth in population or in aggregate production or income. But even such growth, if associated with an increasing inequality in the distribution of income, is consistent with an increase both in the absolute numbers and in the percentage of the total population which is living in squalid and diseased poverty. If associated with mass immigration, this kind of growth is even consistent with no one being better off than his parents were at the same age.

It would be a superior kind of growth, to my taste at least, if it involved, in addition to an increase in the average income, an improvement in the standard of living of the majority of the people. It would be better still if there was not associated with it the impairment in the standard of living of any class, and especially of any low-income class, of the population. Economic growth which met even these tests, however, would be consistent, if population were simultaneously growing, with a growth in the absolute number of those living in a state of economic misery.

I would suggest, therefore, that we accept no program of economic development as a fully satisfactory one, entitled to our support and aid, unless it is designed to promote, among other improvements, an absolute decrease in the numbers of those living at less than some minimum level of income.

It may be objected that this would mean setting a utopian standard, which perhaps not even the United States has met. I am, indeed, not at all sure that the number of persons in the United States now living in a state of crushing and degrading poverty is not greater than the number so living in, say, 1900. If so, then in this important respect at least ours is also an "underdeveloped" country. In any case, it is healthy for us to realize that many of the evils of "underdevelopment" which appeal to our consciences when we see them in less-privileged countries are present also, though in less degree, in our own country, and that those who suffer from them here have even more obvious claims on us to promote their removal.

There are differences, of course, in the causes and the appropriate remedies for extreme poverty as between a rich country and a country in which poverty is general. I do not pretend to be well informed in this field, but I would suppose that the major factors responsible for the persistence of large clusters of extreme poverty in this country are race discrimination, the incomplete assimilation of our immigrant population, and the impoverishment and social deterioration which have occurred or persisted in "distressed areas" which have not enjoyed the full impact of American economic progress in general. In some cases, perhaps, these areas should be given back to the Indians or to the wilderness, and their present inhabitants should be attracted to locations where an acceptable standard of living is attainable. If our foreign-aid program is to have any of the characteristics of a global attack on poverty, it will be rational, and it will make the program more acceptable at home, if as part of it or parallel with it we systematically attack our domestic manifestations of "underdevelopment."

Corresponding somewhat to these different concepts of economic development are two radically different approaches to the planning of economic development. The distinction between the two approaches is rarely clearly perceived, and I have never encountered a systematic discussion of it. It lies only half-concealed, however, in much of the literature, and it is implicit in much of governmental planning. I label the two approaches as, first, the "humanitarian," or, perhaps, the "sentimental," and, second, the "aristocratic." These, I concede, are not altogether satisfactory labels, and I adopt them only for lack of better ones.

The humanitarian approach calls for investing directly in the amelioration of the poverty of the lowest-income groups of a country a large fraction of the surplus resources above meager subsistence available from domestic resources or obtainable by loan or otherwise from abroad. This means applying available capital resources to improvement of the health and diet of the poorest classes, to extension of the facilities available for their general and technical education, and, where they are self-employed, to financing their acquisition of more and better tools and more and improved land.

To this approach, three kinds of objections are raised in the underdeveloped countries themselves or are implicit in the character of the development programs which they actually adopt.

First is the argument that in most underdeveloped countries the available capital resources are such that, if they were applied to the direct amelioration of the living and working conditions of the masses of the poor, they would have to be spread so thinly that they would be absorbed in a negligible improvement of their current standard of living, or in costs of administration, without any permanent betterment resulting.

Second, it is argued that a modest addition to the income of the poor would have as its chief short-run result a reduction in mortality rates and/or an increase in marriage and birth rates, with the only lasting result an increase absolutely and relatively in the numbers of miserably poor.

Finally, it is argued that such procedure would weaken the forces leading to the domestic capital formation on which long-run improvement must largely depend on transferring ownership and command of income from those who would apply it to building up the material productive capital of the country to those who would use it up in current consumption without productive aftermath.

These arguments perhaps suffice to indicate the nature of what I have called the "aristocratic approach." Stated positively, it runs along the following lines:

Available resources that can be wrested from current unproductive consumption should be invested in large part not only in the most productive forms of physical capital equipment but in those capital facilities whose returns will go where they will be used for further investment, so as to contribute indefinitely to the process of capital formation. Insofar as there results currently any increase in current income available for current consumption, it should as far as practicable be directed toward those sections of the population, whether class, racial, religious, or regional groups, which can be most relied upon to use the increased income not in relief of current misery or in the support of larger families but in strengthening their long-run productive capacity by better education, by increased savings, and by providing themselves with more abundant or more efficient productive equipment. Exponents of this approach would deny lack of any sympathy with the economic distress of the miserably poor, but they would insist that, given the shortage of resources, the only way lastingly to ameliorate their position is first to help those who will thereby add to the economic strength and the capacity for progress of the country as a whole, and only when large enclaves of economic health and strength have thus been built up to invest resources in the gradual extension of their prosperity to the masses below.

The aristocratic approach could have been termed a "Malthusian" approach, because it rests on a belief in the existence of a Malthusian tendency for populations with low standards of living to absorb any increments of income in mere increase of numbers instead of improvement of living standards and because the remedy it proposes is one of the two remedies which Malthus proposed, although not the one which he most emphasized and which is most associated with his name.

Whether or not the issue is ever seen as sharply as it has here been presented, or faced as frankly, everywhere in poor countries choices are being made, more or less knowingly, as between these two approaches. Let me give you some concrete illustrations which could be extended almost indefinitely.

Shall a poor country put any additional resources available for expansion of its educational facilities into extending and raising the quality of its secondary education and its colleges or into a campaign against the illiteracy of the masses?

Shall a poor country distribute its tax burden so as to hit lightly margins of income which if left untaxed would be likely to be saved, or shall it tax them relatively heavily because they represent superior "ability" to bear taxes?

Shall national policy in general favor the relatively more prosperous small landlords, small-scale manufacturers, and the professional classes or low-income farm and urban labor?

Shall urban populations be favored over rural, even if the

former have higher real incomes on the average, because urban dwellers are likely to have smaller families, and in greater degree to use increased income to accumulate capital and to raise their standard of living, than are rural families?

There is here a basic problem, calling for difficult decisions, which poor countries must either deliberately face or deal with by indirection, compromise, or blundering improvisation. It is a problem which our country must also face if it is to proceed with large-scale promotion of economic development abroad and if its programs are to have clear-cut and well-considered objectives. It will be difficult, here and abroad, perhaps as much here as abroad, to face the issue frankly and to indicate frankly the choices that are being made, for, whatever the choice, it will have unpleasant associations. There will be a tendency—there is a tendency—here and abroad, to flinch from the issue or to fudge it.

The aristocratic approach clashes with our humanitarian impulses. In many countries it may no longer be politically practicable. It presents a vulnerable point of attack for Communist propaganda. It makes the paper solutions of communism seem more attractive to many. Communism promises aid to the depressed classes while denying that under communism the problem of excess population can arise and insisting that only under communism can disposable income be effectively mobilized, by forced saving, for long-run economic development. The humanitarian approach, on the other hand, in the absence of Communist ruthlessness and discipline, may lead to a race between technological progress and population growth, which is liable to be won by the latter and to culminate in universal misery, the recurrent threat of famine, and cultural and moral stagnation or even deterioration.

I yield to others, for the time being at least, the answer to this question. I venture only to insist that it is a most serious question and that there probably is no easy answer to it; but ignoring it, or refusing to acknowledge its existence and to examine its significance, is liable to result in its being answered by the course of history in a manner which no one would welcome in advance.

I turn now to another question which is a matter of lively concern, and of some debate, in a number of underdeveloped countries. Shall they, in programming and planning their economic development, make their primary objective industrialization and urbanization, or shall they concentrate their investment in agricultural improvement and development? This is not by any means an issue wholly independent of the one which I have just been discussing, but I must leave their interrelations for you to explore on your own.

In many quarters it is claimed, often on the basis of reasoning and evidence of incredibly low quality, that industrialization automatically and necessarily leads to improvement in average income. Sometimes argument, good or bad, is dispensed with, and industrialization is tacitly, or by arbitrary definition, taken as synonymous with improvement in per capita income. Let me give you an illustration from an American economist who, I am sure, knows better: "Industrialization, as defined in this paper, comprehends the sum total of the factors that have made and will continue to make for increase in net output per worker and/or per capita."

Many complex and troublesome questions could be neatly and decisively settled if this mode of defining terms were to be generally followed. For instance: "Industrialization can be defined as the growth in urban manufacturing which results when taxes are laid on agriculture, or on rural industries in general, to provide the subsidies to keep non-self-supporting urban industry going, with all-round lowering of per capita real income as a consequence."

Underdeveloped countries do want industrialization. They frequently also want that industrialization to be largely in heavy industry and in large-scale units. It is now a stereotype that industrialization means urbanization, that cities are synonymous with progress, and that urban populations everywhere are more prosperous than the surrounding rural ones. To what extent urban per capita *real* incomes are genuinely higher than agricultural ones and, to the extent to which they are higher, whether the industrialization and urbanization are the cause or the effect of higher national per capita incomes are questions which have rarely if ever been competently and objectively examined.

The actual facts are, I am convinced, much less simple and one-directional than are the current dogmas. It is conspicuously apparent that in some underdeveloped countries the scanty capital resources have by subsidization or direct government action been directed into premature or misdirected industrialization projects and that much of the urban industry which is allegedly high-income-yielding in such countries is really a parasitic growth supported by direct and indirect levies on rural industry which, while it may be returning only low incomes to those engaged in it, at least is earning those incomes.

On the ancient debate as to the relative virtues of urban and rural life, I will make only three comments. First, it is apparently a universal phenomenon that predominantly agricultural countries take a romantic view of cities and that industrialized countries look at the countryside through rose-colored glasses. Second, there is a general tendency to exaggerate the extent to which industrialization necessarily involves urbanization. In many countries, I am sure, the economically most promising opportunities for industrialization, at least in its earlier stages, lie outside the large cities and even in the open countryside— such activities, for example, as cotton gins, seed-crushing plants, sawmills, tile and brick kilns, hydroelectric plants, fruit-sorting and fruit-packing plants, fertilizer plants, cement mills, mining, and light cottage industry in general. Third, granted that cities are needed as civilizing and educative centers, they rise in adequate degree for these purposes in even predominantly agricultural countries, as governmental, educational, professional service, and marketing and transportation centers, provided the rural population is prosperous enough to need and want urban services in substantial proportions.

The one wrong way to attack the problem of urban industrialization versus development of primary industries is to adopt a dogma that one is inherently superior to the other and then to promote the expansion of the favored one by subsidizing it as the cost of the one which is out of favor. The one correct general principle, or so at least it seems to me, is to make decisions in terms of projects or related groups of projects rather than of wholesale categories and to base these decisions on careful estimating of prospective long-run returns to what is to be invested, always with reference to what types of resources, material and human, are needed for different types of development and what types of resources are relatively abundant in the country in question. In some underdeveloped countries such investigation would no doubt lead correctly to programs of industrialization, including heavy-industry, large-scale plants and rapid urbanization. In many of them, however, probably in most of them, it is highly likely that it would lead, at least for decades or even generations to come, to the concentration of the available resources for development on primary industry, on agriculture, on village industries, on transportation and power facilities, and on improvement of education and health.

Land reform is often one of the most urgent needs. What constitutes land reform, however, is often not a simple matter. It always is used to mean a system of land tenure different from the one which prevails, but sometimes it means larger units, or collectivization, as in the Communist countries; and sometimes it means the breaking-up of large estates into small holdings. That the substitution of peasant-proprietorship for large holdings can sometimes constitute a great reform from the points of view both of productivity and of social peace and progress, Ireland offers a conspicuous example. I suspect, however, that we take too readily for granted, even with respect to American conditions, that small-scale owner operation is necessarily superior economically to tenancy. Whether it is or is not, I would suppose, depends on many circumstances: the quality and efficiency of the landlord class, the ability of small proprietors to finance the equipment of their farms with adequate productive facilities, their ability to apply without supervision advanced methods of cultivation and soil conservation and to assemble farms of adequate size to permit efficient operation. Here, again, sound policy must operate on the basis of careful examination of the local circumstances, cultural and political, as well as economic, rather than on maxims and arbitrary dogmas.

I can say only a few words on a matter which is of great

importance in the realm of economic development but which in the present-day uncritical enthusiasm is often given little consideration until it forces itself directly upon the attention by quickly reducing to obvious failure overambitious or overimpatient or otherwise ill-designed or ill-managed programs—that is, the host of obstacles to economic development in the form of poor natural and human resources, of cultural patterns resistant to change, of deficient government, and of scarcity of capital. Rapid economic progress has come only to few countries and usually only for limited periods of time. Except for temperate-climate countries richly endowed by nature and originally empty of population or nearly so, it has never come to regions with high birth rates. We have presumably learned from past experience how to avoid earlier mistakes, and the great accumulation of technological knowledge gives modern peoples a much greater degree of power of control over their physical environment; but we still do not know how to work miracles. What may be the equivalent of a miracle, however, is the present possibility that countries which have gained an advanced stage of economic prosperity and accumulated great capital resources, and especially the United States, will make available on generous terms their knowledge, their personnel, and their capital to aid the less-advanced countries in the difficult process of escaping from mass poverty.

I will turn now, as my last topic, to a consideration of what we can reasonably be expected to do for underdeveloped countries, as well as what they must be left to do for themselves.

We can, of course, make free grants to them, and we can lend them capital on moderate terms of interest and repayment, working out with them ways by which this can be done on an adequate scale on fair and safe conditions for both creditors and debtors. I do not believe that, where the winning of allies in a tense situation of great-power conflict is not an important and durable factor, outright grants will or should play an important role. International sharing is even a less practicable procedure politically than voluntary domestic sharing and is less likely to work smoothly and without breeding tensions and animosities than programs which frankly demand mutuality of interest and benefit for both those who give and those who receive the aid. There is no historical experience which supports the view that national benevolence on a global scale, without expectation or prospect of a counterflow of readily visible and material benefit, is a sturdy plant which can thrive for a protracted period of time.

We can give valuable assistance to underdeveloped countries by making capital available to them on generous terms and also by sharing with them our store of technical knowledge and lending them our skilled personnel, which, incidentally, when done under government auspices, is apparently an extremely expensive operation per expert capita. I believe, however, that the most important single means available to us of rendering mutually beneficial aid consists in proceeding further in the reform of our commercial policy which began in 1934. A reduction of our trade barriers, which after fifteen years of being whittled away still remain formidable, can be of greater benefit to other countries than all the much-advertised grants, loans, and technical aid. It is probably true, however, that it is even more difficult to get really significant cuts in the American tariff through Congress than to persuade it to give money away.

Given the level of our trade barriers, we buy much more from other countries, and pay better prices for our imports, when we are prosperous than when we are having one of our periodic, though not inevitable, depressions. Other countries have been insisting, unilaterally and through the United Nations, that we owe it to the rest of the world, as well as to ourselves, to stabilize our economy. Our boom-and-bust record is one of the most effective elements in the psychological warfare which Soviet Russia is conducting against us.

The great depression of the 1930's, in its intensity and duration, was a phenomenon without excuse and unlikely to be repeated. We have ample knowledge of ways in which, without weakening and even with strengthening of the free-enterprise foundations of our national way of life, we can prevent depression from being severe or protracted. If we should fail to act accordingly should the occasion arise, it will be because of a cultural lag comparable to but less excusable on our part than the stubborn resistance to change of the Hopi Indians and of other primitive peoples which, in our more private conferences, the anthropologists have been emphasizing, if I understood them—which is not to be taken for granted—as invulnerable barriers to the acceptance of even the most urgent and the most rewarding economic reforms.

Sophisticated public opinion in other non-Communist countries shares—and indeed surpasses—my confidence that we do not have to submit to the recurrence of major depressions. Much of it, however, would not agree with me that we can escape the cycle without largely abandoning our free-enterprise system and is, in any case, without confidence that we will, in fact, conquer our instability. Many foreign observers, especially if they are socialists, regard us as in this respect a backward people, clinging stubbornly to the obsolete social patterns of behavior which, they believe, darken our economic prospects and threaten ruin to themselves if they should become too closely involved with us. This does not make them reluctant to accept outright grants from us if there are no unpalatable conditions attached to them, but it does lessen their eagerness to borrow from us even on what on past experience would appear to be very generous terms. It also contributes to their unwillingness to plan for their future development along lines which involve a large measure of dependence on exports, and especially on exports to us, and leads them to press us for guaranties, of a kin which it seems unlikely that we will ever be willing to concede, that we will not permit our annual supply of dollars to the outside world to fall below stated minimums.

This lack of confidence in us as an economic partner may wear off in time, as year after year depression fails to make its much-heralded appearance. Let us suppose, however, that we will no longer have major depressions; that we will continue to lower our trade barriers; that we will give and lend abroad, both publicly and privately, on a large scale and on generous terms; and that international tension will subside so that our aid will go to genuine economic development rather than to rearmament. Even then, what we can contribute to the economic progress of underdeveloped countries will be of minor importance as compared to what they must do for themselves.

Countries do not achieve economic progress by default. If they attain it at all, they do so by fashioning their government policies and their social patterns so as to foster economic development rather than to hinder it. They must steer their educational programs so as to provide the needed skills and attitudes. As incomes rise, they must divert increased proportions of them from current consumption to capital formation. They must develop reasonably efficient government and good credit facilities and must provide for their middle class incentives to enterprise and for their working classes incentives to productive effort. They must succeed in providing the masses of their peoples at least the minimum standards of health, of education, and of social security that are essential prerequisites of genuine economic progress and in arousing in their upper classes the public spirit and the leadership without which domestic effort and foreign aid will come to naught.

What this amounts to, if we consider the advantages enjoyed by us and the handicaps which they must carry, is that, to make real progress, perhaps even to hold their own, the underdeveloped countries must marshal greater effort, must husband their resources more carefully, and must practice greater social discipline than, aside from strategic considerations, we will be urgently called upon to do. Most of these countries are living in a vicious circle of low productivity, poor health, inadequate education, and meager equipment with capital. In the worst cases the circle may not be breakable without both heroic effort and discipline and substantial external aid.

In addition to all this, if there is to be real hope of genuine betterment of economic conditions in those underdeveloped countries which already have a high ratio of population to natural resources, they must find some solution of the population problem which will prevent all the product of more abundant capital equipment and of improved methods of production from being sunk in the support of increased numbers on a bare subsistence level.

It seems certain that most of the underdeveloped countries will rely heavily on government planning and government initiative to achieve the economic progress they aspire to, and I feel fairly certain that most of them will go further in this direction than will be to their long-run advantage. But what the proper division is between government initiative and private enterprise must depend largely on the extent to which the general public is able and disposed to exercise the needed initiative, enterprise, and skill. In some countries the masses of the people are probably too poor, too ignorant, and too bound by old patterns of behavior to do much for themselves; and, if there is to be progress, it must be initiated and, for a time at least, largely conducted from above. In some cases, government itself will not be able to recruit sufficient talent for these purposes from domestic sources, and there will be need for importation of skilled personnel from abroad.

There will be cases where governments will waste scarce resources on grandiose projects; there will be corruption and graft; many projects will be failures; some projects will fail despite the most honest and intelligent planning. There are few of the underdeveloped countries whose prospects of rapid economic development, if objectively appraised on the basis of present circumstances, warrant a high degree of optimism, whatever degree of help, within the limits of reasonable expectations, they may get from outside sources. Most countries, if their peoples are to be satisfied with their rate of progress, will have to move forward at a much more rapid rate than did in the past century those countries which are now the most advanced; and many of these countries have disadvantages of poor natural resources, unfavorable climates, and populations already dense, which neither western Europe, the British Dominions, nor the United States, had to face. At best, the attainment by the now underdeveloped countries of satisfactory standards of living for the bulk at least of their peoples will be a slow, painful climb up a very arduous path. Foreign aid cannot reasonably be expected to do much more than to make the climb somewhat less arduous.

We should be sympathetic, therefore, if their first efforts do not immediately yield spectacular results. We should make our advice and counsel readily available, but we should not press it upon them. We should not, in complacent satisfaction with our own prosperity, take for granted that we will always be able to give them better solutions for their problems than those they would find for themselves. We should especially beware of assuming that what has worked well with us, whether it be forms of government, tax systems, factory design, or agricultural technique, is necessarily suitable for them.

There will inevitably be a strong temptation on our part to make acceptance of our advice and supervision a condition of our extension of aid. We must exercise great self-restraint in this connection. We cannot, of course, be unconcerned if our aid is patently misapplied or misappropriated. We must, however, avoid patterns of aid which involve us in detailed interference with the internal affairs of other peoples. In that direction lies only frustration, friction, and failure. Once we have approved of a claimant as deserving of aid and as having an acceptable plan for its use, we must then, as a general rule, leave it to its own devices, hope for the best, and not expect too much. That, after all, is very much how our people deal with our own governments, federal and local, how our federal government deals with Congress, and how the federal government and Congress deal with us. We must leave it to other peoples to initiate their own social revolutions, to do their own purging of the inefficiency, extravagance, and corruption of their governments, and to find their own ways of adapting ancient cultural patterns to the requirements of modern economic progress. They may make a mess of it, but that is a risk they must be permitted to take. It is a lesser risk, in any case, probably for them, and certainly for us, than would be involved if we undertook to manage their affairs for them, a role in which we have had no experience and in which no country has had highly successful experience.

There is one more issue on which something should be said, although to attempt an adequate consideration of it would unduly protract this paper, and this is the question as to the extent to which we should administer our foreign aid ourselves or intrust it to United Nations organizations. We are now doing both, but the bulk of our aid is granted by us directly to the recipient countries. There is no doubt that most countries would strongly prefer receiving aid via the United Nations. It must not be taken for granted, however, that the United Nations would attach less stringent conditions or administer grants more laxly and more generously than we do. We are very sensitive to the charge of "imperialism," to which the United Nations, as a multinational institution, is scarcely susceptible. The United Nations might in many cases be more disposed to encroach on national autonomy, and its encroachments might more readily be tolerated, than would be the case if it were a single great power which was interfering. There is not much actual evidence as yet to aid judgment, but it is possible that recipient countries might take contractual obligations to a multinational agency more seriously, and treat them as less susceptible to unilateral deviation, than obligations to a single government which might have political and other reasons for refraining from pressing vigorously for adherence to pledges. It is probably an open question as to whether we, or the United Nations, would be a more efficient or more economical administrator of foreign aid, although it is already evident, if we may judge by prevailing salary scales and scales of staffing, that both will be expensive on the domestic standards either of this country or of the recipient countries.

There are at least two important reasons, however, why we must, for the time being at least, reserve to ourselves the control over the allocation and the use of the bulk of our foreign aid. As long as we are the donors of an overwhelming proportion of the foreign aid being granted, the United Nations will in the main reflect the views and attitudes of claimant countries rather than of donor countries. As long as strategic and military considerations continue to be important, we cannot surrender to the United Nations, which includes the Iron Curtain countries, "neutralist" countries, and border-line countries, in which regional and other species of log-rolling have already attained a high level of efficiency, and in which Soviet Russia has veto power, the decision as to how and for what purposes our aid is to be allotted.

Should, however, the international tension subside, and should a return to world prosperity make less unbalanced the ratio of donor to recipient countries, it would become desirable on many counts, some of which I have here suggested, that international aid should be made, exclusively or predominantly, a function of multinational agencies.

PERSONALITY AND CULTURE PROBLEMS
OF POINT IV

By Samuel P. Hayes, Jr.

FROM the first announcement of the Point IV program in President Truman's Inaugural Address in January, 1949, we who have been concerned with the program have been advised from all sides to utilize social science in planning and administering this program. (By "all sides" I mean inside as well as outside, for there are a number of social scientists in the Point IV central organization and in the various government agencies co-operating in and financed by Point IV.) We have been cautioned: "Beware of changes that conflict with religious beliefs or practices"; "The personality structure of other peoples must be understood by all field technicians"; "Don't assume that material values necessarily outweigh the other values people find in their lives"; "Don't apply the economic syllogisms of a highly developed market exchange economy to the large nonpecuniary economic activities of underdeveloped areas."

This is good advice, but most of it is precautionary, even negative. We are told to beware, to find out before we rush in, to recognize and respect other people's value systems. This is a healthy attitude, especially for the many of us who have never worked abroad or among people with markedly different backgrounds and values. It sensitizes us to the problems we may meet. It helps prevent us from simply transferring American methods without adapting those methods to new conditions.

In this connection I might mention that we have contracted with the Association of Applied Anthropology to provide us with a "cross-cultural" manual to be used in training our Point IV personnel, and the main purpose of this manual and the training that will utilize it may be said to be the sensitizing of technicians to the problems likely to be encountered in working with people of different personality structures, cultures, and economic systems.

We need more than this, however. We need information and analyses that tell us in positive and concrete terms what we *should* do, not just what we should *not* do. It takes too long for every agricultural technician, sensitive though he may be to differences in psychological, cultural, and economic conditions, to work out for himself how to get people to use green manure. It takes too long (and it may be beyond its professional competence) for each Point IV mission abroad to work out with another government the likely impact which different kinds of potential development may have on the society and the economy. Anything that social scientists can do to provide positive and concrete guidance for administrators, telling them what methods to utilize in promoting what kinds of economic development, in particular areas at particular times, would be of the greatest value in facilitating the administration of the Point IV program.[1]

In the main, we are working in this program with independent peoples, people who have pretty definite ideas about what kinds of development they want, and how fast; and who make their own decisions in these fields (within the limits of the feasible, of course).

It is not at all a matter of our imposing our ideas upon other governments. Certainly, we do make suggestions! We do sit down with the officials of other governments and circulate ideas around the table. Some of the ideas that are finally acted upon possibly have their source in that kind of friendly interchange; but there are very severe limits on the extent to which one government can appropriately make suggestions to another. The only kinds of suggestions that are going to be effective, the only kinds of programs that will get anywhere, are those that have the real support of the peoples that are involved directly

1. I use the term "Point IV" in a general sense here to cover all activities carried on by relatively industrialized countries to promote the economic development of relatively underdeveloped countries. Social science guidance is needed by government agencies (of the United States and other countries), by international organizations, by business concerns, and by private nonprofit agencies, and it is needed in capital investment and business activities as well as in technical co-operation activities.

in them. That is basic to all our operations. We do not undertake abroad anything for which we have not had a formal request from the other government and which the other government does not make clear it wants us to undertake in their country.

The direction of economic development, then, is set by the nature of the goals chosen by the people concerned. This may be a choice consciously and explicitly made by the whole people or by particular groups having political or economic power, or it may be a choice drifted into as a consequence of many minor decisions. Whatever the process of decision about direction and pace of desired economic development, it is obvious that a powerful additional impetus to development can be given by forces outside a nation, and that those forces may impinge upon any of the many aspects of a society involved in the development process.

Economic development includes capital formation *and* the international flow of capital. It includes technological change *and* the international transfer of technical knowledge and skills. It includes changes in production and consumption *and* changes in the volume and composition of international trade. It includes the growth of population and changes in its age and occupational composition, partly arising from international migration. It includes changes in social, economic, and political institutions and in the relative power of different groups, both domestically and internationally.

The variety of interests in relationships involved in the process of economic development may be indicated by listing the main kinds of persons who participate in that process and who need to be studied by various social science techniques:

A. In the underdeveloped countries themselves
   1. Farmers and businessmen, who must decide whether or not to change their production methods, to invest new capital, to change their volume of production and their selling prices, to modify their marketing arrangements, to reveal their know-how, etc.[2]
   2. Other persons with capital to invest, who must decide among different types of investment (including hoarding).
   3. Consumers, who must decide between consumption and saving and

2. Cf. Samuel P. Hayes, Jr., "Some Psychological Problems of Economics," *Psychological Bulletin*, XLVII (1950), 289–330.

among different types of consumption and whose decisions about the size of their families partly determine total levels of consumption.

4. Employees, who must decide whether or not to work for wages, how long and how hard to work, where and for whom to work, whether or not to learn new skills and to adjust to new equipment and work organization, etc.

5. Local leaders and government representatives, without whose active support and participation few projects can actually reach the great majority of the people who are rural village dwellers.

6. Government officials (including ministers and whole bureaucracies), who must administer many development projects, determine many policies, and carry out governmental activities (tax collection, economic controls, etc.) which greatly influence economic development.

7. Legislators, who must approve the carrying-out of governmental projects and the general policies influencing various kinds of economic development.

8. The voters, or perhaps more strictly the participants in the political process, who must support the policies and programs submitted to legislators.

B. In the relatively industrialized countries

1. Private businessmen who undertake direct equity investment abroad, who manage operations abroad (perhaps with no equity investment), who permit access to and the use of their own technology, and who provide training to foreign nationals both in their own country and abroad.

2. Private investors in foreign securities, to be held as portfolio investments, but who are not engaged in direct equity investment.

3. Government officials and experts who administer programs of loans, grants, or technical co-operation, or who participate in such programs as officials or experts abroad.

4. Private individuals and experts, usually officials or employees of non-profit organizations, who engage in educational activities (either at home or abroad) and in health, agricultural, and other demonstration and training activities abroad.

5. Legislators, who must approve the carrying-out of governmental projects and the general policies influencing economic development abroad.

6. The voters, who must support the policies and programs submitted to legislators.

For all these people, particularly those in the underdeveloped areas but not limited to them, economic development means change—changed methods of doing things, changed equipment and other resources with which to work, changed habits of consumption, saving, and investment, changed relationships to other people, changed availabilities of goods and services, and often changed attitudes, motivations, and ways of life.

The extent and rate of change that take place are heavily dependent on such economic factors as the nature and accessibility of resources, prices, and demands in world markets and rates at home and in capital-exporting countries. The extent and rate of change are even more heavily dependent, however, on the personality and culture characteristics of the society seeking development. Changes must be accepted. New habits and attitudes must be learned. New relationships to people must be established. If personality and culture are unfavorable to such changes, economic development may take place only slowly, if at all.

A paragraph from Bacon in his essay on innovations is pertinent here:

> It is true, that what is settled by custom, though it be not good, yet at least it is fit, and those things which have long gone together, are, as it were, confederate within themselves; whereas new things piece not so well; but, though they help by their utility, yet they trouble by their inconformity: besides, they are like strangers, more admired, and less favored.[3]

The central questions which we need help in answering are these:

1. What groups in particular areas are most influential in promoting or retarding economic change and development and what are the personality and culture traits of these groups that are favorable (or unfavorable) to particular changes required for economic development?

2. If there are psychological or cultural barriers impeding desired types of development, what ways can be found to eliminate or surmount these barriers?

3. How can those local leaders be identified and those local organizations be utilized (if they exist or brought into being if they do not already exist), without which popular support and participation cannot be secured and maintained?

These are among the most important questions that social scientists might help program administrators to answer. Expenditure of time and money to answer them might pay for itself many times over in heightened effectiveness of programs to promote the economic development of underdeveloped areas.

3. Francis Bacon, Essay No. 24, "Of Innovations," *The Works of Francis Bacon* (Philadelphia: Parry & McMillan, 1855), I, 32.

Psychological and cultural traits vary in their significance for the individual and in their resistance to or their support for particular changes that affect them. It is highly probable that changes in attitudes or ways of doing things will meet great resistance if they contravene the folklore, religion, superstitions, magic, or other beliefs (projective systems) which serve in ordinary living to release the anxiety feelings of the individual, for conflicts with such beliefs threaten the security of the individual.

Resistance will also be encountered if changes are proposed that run counter to learned attitudes, habits, customs, and institutions in which basic drives (sex, ego gratification, etc.) are involved. Obviously, the medicine man will resist hospitals or clinics that have no place for him and tend to drive him out of business. So also will the landlord resist changes in land tenure, and the feudal aristocracy will resist the rise of a new commercial and industrial class.

Less resistant to change are learned attitudes, habits, customs, and institutions that do not involve basic drives, although it must be remembered that any change is likely to be somewhat uncomfortable. Most favorable to change are "pure empirical reality systems," best exemplified by the objectivity of experimental science.[4]

If this or any other differentiation among traits has validity, it points up very emphatically one major need of program administrators that social scientists can help meet. The traits of particular groups in each area must be identified and described; they must be analyzed and their significance determined. Exactly what beliefs are bound up with the release of anxiety feelings or with strong drives? How did they become so bound up, and how, if at all, can the bonds be loosened? What attitudes and habits are not involved with drives or anxiety release and hence are relatively more susceptible to change? Can existing beliefs be utilized to give support to desirable economic changes? What kinds of economic development can

4. This outline follows that used by A. Kardiner and Associates, *The Psychological Frontiers of Society* (New York: Columbia University Press, 1945).

and should be carried out within the confines set by existing beliefs, attitudes, values?

Here is a field where development planning and administration obviously require the closest co-operation among the administrator, the technical expert, and the social scientist. Given the general lines of development desired by the nation concerned and given the existing economic and social determinants (of which Joseph Spengler in a recent article distinguishes some twenty)[5] of the nation's present industrial status, these three persons must jointly work out their judgments concerning the kind and timing of changes needed. The participation of nationals, preferably representing all three of these interests or skills, is of course an absolute requisite in any such development planning.

The particular task of the social scientist is to consider each proposed change in technology, investment, or institutions; to consider probable subsequent induced changes where these can be predicted; to identify the particular traits of the particular groups of people who would be affected by these proposed changes; to advise about the resistances to or support for these changes likely to be found in the local culture and society; and to recommend modifications in the proposed program of development or in the proposed methods of introducing changes.

This is a somewhat idealized conception of a work process, perhaps. It may promise more than the social scientist is yet ready to deliver, and it certainly is not a process that can work well unless the social scientist is prepared to work on the actual scene of operations where he can personally observe both the culture and the proposed technological changes. The only way to find out how effective such a co-operation might be is to try it out in the field for a while.

The World Health Organization has already had some experience with this and feels that the social scientist involved (in this case a cultural anthropologist) made a great contribution.

5. Joseph J. Spengler, "Economic Factors in the Development of Densely Populated Areas," *Proceedings of the American Philosophical Society*, XCV, No. 1 (February, 1951), 20–53.

We are working out arrangements to do the same thing in some of our United States government programs. Some of the kinds of problems on which such joint field action would be especially helpful can be inferred from the following examples of traits that are likely to affect development.

There are frequent reports of the "natural conservatism" of the peasantry, of businessmen, of the rich.[6] This really needs very careful analysis. If it is conservatism because change would impinge on deeply held beliefs or status-determining relationships, that is one thing; if it is conservatism because change involves risk, that is another. When farmers hesitate to adopt new strains of seeds or new methods of cultivation, it may well reflect the fact that a crop failure would mean starvation for their families, not just an experiment to be repeated under different conditions. This is not something to be risked on the say-so of some upstart "expert" who comes to the community with new ideas but without taking responsibility for any failures that may occur. Finally, if it is conservatism because the gains to be achieved by the change are not very highly valued, that is a third. The term "conservatism" probably obscures analysis and understanding rather than contributing to it.

A fairly general attitude in the underdeveloped areas that hampers development programs is distrust of government. Government is looked upon as a tax-collector only, or as a traditional but necessary evil represented locally by rapacious troops and corrupt officials. It is not easy in such circumstances to be asked to believe that suddenly one's government is interested in the welfare of the people and is to be represented by public-spirited and competent officials. Government may be the only suitable agency to carry out public health, educational, agricultural, housing, or other programs, but government must in many areas break through a thick crust of suspicion before the confidence necessary for real co-operation can be generated.[7]

6. See, e.g., H. B. Allen, *Come Over into Macedonia* (New Brunswick: Rutgers University Press, 1943), and his *Rural Education and Welfare in the Middle East* (London: His Majesty's Stationery Office, 1946).

7. Justice William O. Douglas, "Strange Lands and Poor People," *Life*, XXX (June 18, 1951), 120 ff.

A third general characteristic in many underdeveloped countries is discrimination based on sex, race, religion, occupation, etc. This may pose a major obstacle to the vertical and horizontal mobility needed to maximize creativeness and effort (both essential for economic development) and yet is extremely persistent in any society. Where such discrimination becomes embodied in a system of caste or class, it may present a rigid barrier to the changes needed for economic and social progress.

Related to class and caste discrimination is a fairly frequently occurring attitude of disdain of work in general and particularly disdain of manual work. As a recent International Labor Office document puts it:

The prestige which by social tradition attaches to cultural subjects in some countries of the East has long deterred and still does many young men and women of the middle and upper classes from engaging in studies for acquiring practical knowledge and still more a manual skill, even though they may be better fitted to succeed in such work and so to contribute more fully to be development of their country.[8]

In a number of Near Eastern countries there are apparently plenty of technically competent personnel in the professions; what is lacking and what most hinders economic development is the lack of the great middle group of foremen, supervisors, etc., who have enough training to follow the directions of highly trained engineers but who are also willing to get their hands dirty in actually getting a project under way. In a number of Latin-American countries the same general prejudice against work, especially manual work, exists.[9] One gains prestige by delegating work to others. If one has been fortunate enough to get advanced training, especially abroad, one at once becomes too good for one's past job or for any job that takes one out of one's clean office.

Finally, mention may be made of one other general attitude—the attitude toward honesty. This varies greatly throughout the world, and there is in most areas little comprehension of the

8. Marguerite Thibert, *Training Problems in the Far East* (Geneva: International Labor Office, 1948), p. 115.

9. See, e.g., Caroline F. Ware, "Technicians' Report on Proposed Community Service Program for Venezuela" (New York: American International Association for Economic and Social Development, 1948). (Mimeographed.)

vital role that honesty plays in economic development in an exchange economy. There is an interesting story about the mission sent out in 1871 by Emperor Meiji of Japan to discover the secrets which had enabled Westerners to humble the imperial Japanese. According to Condliffe, the mission carried out a very penetrating investigation, "but one important fact they failed to grasp. They reasoned correctly that the naval and military power of the western world rested upon science applied to industry, and that industry rested upon credit. But they did not realize that fundamentally credit rests upon good faith and individual and collective honesty . . . the moral basis of the western civilization."[10]

Let us now turn to the major aspects of economic activity in the underdeveloped areas and consider some of the traits influencing their development.

Farmers and farming methods are of top importance for the development of underdeveloped areas, as agriculture constitutes some three-quarters of the economic activity of these areas and agricultural methods are frequently so primitive that better techniques requiring relatively little research and relatively little capital investment can apparently very greatly and quite quickly increase production. Psychological and cultural traits that affect agriculture are therefore of particular importance to the Point IV program.

In Iran, as in many other countries, some agricultural practices are closely bound up with religion and related "projective systems." A recent writer points out that "to peasants who believe that raising chickens may call a divine curse upon them, that planting vegetables may destroy fertility, modern agricultural technics are mentally inaccessible."[11] This may be somewhat exaggerated, for Point IV experts now in Iran are finding great acceptability for some kinds of improved practices. There are indications that the paucity of return to the peasant, the small portion which he himself gets out of any improvement in

10. J. B. Condliffe, "The Unbalance of Our World," in *International Cooperation or World Economic Development* (Berkeley: University of California Press, 1950), p. 14.

11. Heshmat Ala'i, "How Not To Develop a Backward Country," *Fortune*, August, 1948, p. 147.

his technology and increased production, is much more of a barrier to economic development than are religious beliefs. Nevertheless, there *are* religious obstacles, and social scientists might be very helpful in finding a way around them.

In India one of our Point IV agricultural experts reports that the farmers were recently troubled by thousands of wild antelopes. As the common name for these antelopes was *neilgai* (literally, "blue cows"), and as cows are sacred to Hindus, orthodox Hindus would not kill them, and they became a serious pest. They were really not cows, however, and a government decree was promulgated changing their name from *neilgai* to *neilghora* (literally, "blue horses"). Hindus then felt free to shoot them, and their numbers have been greatly reduced.

Here was an instance where religious beliefs could be disentangled fairly easily from an objective economic problem needing solution. Of course there remains the problem of the sacred cow itself, an animal that sometimes outnumbers the people of Indian villages and everywhere eats much that could otherwise feed the people. Is there not a good deal, however, that can be done to increase the milk production of these cows and thus convert them from economic liabilities into economic assets without any offense to an old and venerated religion?

In Africa one of the persistent problems of colonial administrators is that "the natives do not plant in straight rows, easy to cultivate and to spray or otherwise treat, but that they plant their trees at odd places surrounded by other growth. Consequently, processes which might be applicable to well organized white labor plantations are not applicable to native planting." This is reported in a dispatch from our scientific attaché in London. It simply states a problem, however; it does not divulge the significance to the African natives of their customary methods of planting trees. Investigation and analysis by a social scientist might uncover ways in which tree-planting in rows might be made culturally acceptable.

A final example is the familiar story of the introduction of the telephone in Saudi Arabia. According to reports, the king wished to connect the capital with certain other cities, but the tribal chiefs would have none of it. The Koran contained no mention of the telephone, and it must therefore be the work of the devil. The king then pointed out that the devil would be unwilling to transmit the words of the Prophet, and, see, the telephone lines carried the sacred words of the Koran perfectly. The chiefs were thus convinced that the telephone was all right for them to use.

These are relatively superficial examples. They do not require elaborate analysis—simply an acquaintanceship with a culture and a certain amount of imagination and intelligence. But they do make a point. The administrator of an economic development program must be continually alert to note cultural or psychological resistances and to seek ways around them or, better, to find positive support in existing psychological and cultural traits. Obviously, an expert in the field can be expected to do a better job of this than can the nonexpert, especially when the latter is plagued by the administrative problems of a going program.

In many parts of the world it is the land-tenure institutions that raise some of the most important obstacles to economic development. The incentive of personal gain becomes diluted in any system where the effort, initiative, and often the capital expense of one person are rewarded by only a small part of any resulting increment in production. Where tenure is insecure there is little incentive to make capital improvements, such as irrigation ditches, buildings, and fertilizer, the returns from which are received over several years, for the tenant making such improvements may not remain on the improved land long enough to reap the increased crops.

Where patterns of inheritance have resulted in many small holdings of land, so that one farmer may be cultivating several separate plots of land, some consolidation of holdings and some basic modification in the institution of inheritance itself may be necessary before substantial improvements in technology will be worth introducing. Where some landlords hold very large estates, their income may be already so large relative to their needs that they have no particular incentive to increase their capital investment or change their technical methods. Rich men in these countries often may not desire to keep on accumulating wealth indefinitely; they may feel that "enough is enough," so why bother?

In all these situations, existing institutions dampen the incentive that might otherwise bring about capital investment and technical change. If it is culturally and politically feasible to change these institutions, economic development can be given a strong push even without any kind of aid from outside. The social scientist may well devote a good deal of attention to the feasibility of changing such institutions. If they are so rooted in psychology and culture or so buttressed by economic and political power that change in the institutions themselves is excessively difficult, some way must be found to introduce into the existing institutions alternative arrangements that will result in effective incentives to economic development.

Perhaps the greatest force behind economic development in the United States has been the initiative, the energy, the imagination, and the venturesomeness of the independent farmer and businessman. Farmers and businessmen could do much to step up economic development in the underdeveloped areas; certainly much more than can be done by experts from outside the country. But the enterprising spirit as we know it in this country is usually rare in underdeveloped countries. Why it is rare is something that urgently needs investigation, but that it is rare seems to be agreed on all sides.

As Van Mook says of Southeast Asia:

The age-long influence of the West . . . failed, with only few exceptions, to instill its economic activity and enterprise into the minds and habits of these peoples. The Western apparatus of finance, commerce, and production remained an alien, undigested and indigestible element in Southeast Asia. It had created institutions, means of production and communication and a stability far beyond the achievements of the past, but it had hardly awakened a new economic initiative or industry. . . . The social solidarity, the public spirit, and the economic energy that were necessary for a vigorous resurgence were lacking.[12]

This is true of much of South Asia, Latin America, and the Near East as well (with some notable exceptions). For various

12. Hubertus J. Van Mook, "The Needs of Underdeveloped Areas," in *International Cooperation for World Economic Development*, p. 20.

reasons, some needing a good deal of analysis, owners of capital in these countries tend to hoard their wealth in the form of jewels and precious metals, to "invest" it in rural land and urban real estate, or to deposit it in foreign banks in the form of currencies believed safer than their own. They seem very reluctant to invest in capital equipment to build up the production of their own enterprises and extremely reluctant to invest in the enterprises of others.

Part of their reluctance to improve their own enterprises derives from attitudes toward business alien to the main tradition of American business. They have a large-profit, small-volume, monopolistic, consumer-be-damned philosophy that puts little faith in improved products, lowered costs, larger sales, etc. Their whole disposition is to find noncompetitive methods of maintaining or improving their market position and to limit investments to those that, by making excessively large profits, can be liquidated within two to three years.

All these attitudes may turn out to be logical deductions from historical experience and existing institutions, or they may be habits carried over from previous eras, or they may be rooted in projective systems involving personal anxiety feelings. Perhaps the most important contribution social science could make to our understanding of economic development and our formulation of programs to accelerate such development would be to investigate and analyze the factors influencing entrepreneurship in the major underdeveloped areas.

Another field of economic activity that requires a good deal of social science analysis, both because of its importance for economic development and because it is so intimately tied up with personality and culture traits, is the broad field of consumption, with which I shall, for obvious reasons, bracket the related activities of health habits and procreation.

The quantity and composition of goods and services consumed reflect the values, customs, and habits of a particular society and are limited by the volume and kinds of production the society is able to carry out. Although production limits consumption, it is not the only determinant by any means. In India a great potential food supply (in the form of cattle) roams the countryside while millions starve. In Moslem countries pork may not be consumed. In much of Asia (as in the United States) polished rice is eaten, although whole rice would be far more nutritious and healthful. Even where there are no religious or attitudinal barriers, most peoples in the underdeveloped areas get less nutrition than they might from the food available to them. Nutrition research and teaching can help considerably, but their effects are likely to be slow, because food habits are usually imbedded deeply in a society's traditions and customs, with many overtones of religious or status significance. Moreover, it is much harder to demonstrate the advantages of an improved diet than it is to demonstrate, for example, how fertilizer increases crops. Consumption of other kinds, whether of clothing, housing, health supplies and facilities, recreation, transportation, or religion, is similarly difficult to influence.

Analysis of the factors influencing consumption is important because changed habits may mean gaining greater satisfaction from the consumption of a given amount of resources. It is important also because, by and large, consumption competes with investment for the same economic resources. Hence, the potential pace of economic development is in good measure directly dependent upon a society's success in holding consumption below production and thus enabling saving and investment to take place.

How a society with an already very low per capita income, particularly when it ardently desires immediate and marked improvement in its standard of living—how such a society can actually be enabled to engage in substantial saving—is a problem of the greatest importance and urgently needs much social science investigation and analysis.

This points up the special importance of the population problem in the general problem of economic development. It is quite true that a good many countries are relatively underpopulated today and that others have populations that bear some reasonable relationship to their resources, but a number of countries are already suffering severely from overpopulation; and it is probably true that in any of the underdeveloped countries today population increases take place at the expense of the standard of living. For countries that fervently desire better standards of living, and for us who believe that the world's and our own interests would be served if those countries were able to enjoy improved conditions of life, this poses a major problem.

Without getting into the question of what actions governments, especially foreign governments, can appropriately take to solve this problem—although the question of suitable government activity in this sphere would be fascinating for the social scientist to investigate—there is a potentially fruitful area of research for the social scientist in investigating the factors in each society that affect its fertility rates and in appraising the likelihood of introducing into that society the elements that have been important in reducing fertility rates elsewhere.

It seems to be agreed that in western Europe

the primary factors in the decline of birth rates were social rather than physiological. Urban life put heavy economic penalties on the large family by limiting the income contributed by children, increasing the costs of child maintenance and greatly extending the range of advantages that parents aspired to give their children. General literacy instilled new wants and brought freedom from old taboos. City life gave new importance to the individual as compared with the larger family group and stimulated his hopes for his own and his children's advancement. It greatly changed the role of women by extending the range of activities that took place outside the home and these activities were therefore less compatible with continuous child-bearing. Moreover, the anonymity of city life weakened the traditional controls of the community on familial and individual behavior.[13]

Urbanization, education, industrialization, and higher incomes are all apparently important factors in diminishing fertility. Even such a simple change as bringing electricity to a densely populated slum (as in San Juan, Puerto Rico) has been followed by a very marked drop in the birth rate. Some of these changes will be necessary elements in any substantial program of economic development, and such programs therefore can be expected to have by-products in the form of some reduction in fertility rates.

Should certain changes then be stressed because they will affect fertility? Should the decline of fertility rates be hastened by introducing other elements, such as social security legisla-

13. M. C. Balfour, R. F. Evans, F. W. Notestein, and I. B. Taeuber, *Public Health and Demography in the Far East* (New York: Rockefeller Foundation, 1950), pp. 9–10.

tion, to reduce the dependence of parents on their children, child-labor laws that diminish the income families get from their children, encouragement of education for women and opening up desirable occupations to them so that they could find interest and prestige in ways other than by bearing children, or establishment of birth-control clinics?

These are questions both for the social scientist, as technician, and for the society affected, as judge of its own values. Unless the leaders and people of an underdeveloped area consider high fertility rates to be a problem for which they want to find a solution, there is little point in asking social scientists to analyze the factors bearing on fertility (except perhaps to aid in long-run predictions of the effects of changes introduced for other purposes). If a nation does explicitly desire to bring about a reduction in fertility rates, however, there may be much that the social scientist can discover on this frontier of social science and much assistance that he can render in adapting development programs to serve this objective as well as the other expressed objectives of the nation concerned.[14]

I shall say little about the next major field of economic activity where social science investigation and analysis can contribute importantly to Point IV. This is the field of working for wages—the field of industrial employment broadly defined. Dr. Wilbert Moore has published two excellent articles covering this field and will soon bring out a book on it. In his published articles he reviews the psychological and cultural factors that act as barriers to or propellants toward industrial employment and that determine morale and efficiency on the job.[15] While there is quite a voluminous literature touching on this problem, it is again a problem that so importantly affects the actual impact of our technical aid programs that it urgently requires social science field work, in the areas where economic development is taking place, in order to get practical guidance for development aid programs.

14. Balfour et al., op. cit., pp. 111–22. Cf. Kingsley Davis, "Population and the Further Spread of Industrial Society," Proceedings of the American Philosophical Society, XCV, No. 1 (February, 1951), 8–19

15. Wilbert E. Moore, "Primitives and Peasants in Industry," Social Research, XV (1948), 44–81; and "Theoretical Aspects of Industrialization," ibid., pp. 277–303.

So far I have discussed primarily the private sectors of the underdeveloped economy—the behavior of private individuals in their various roles as farmers and businessmen, investors, consumers, and parents, and employees. The activities pursued by individuals playing these private roles are those to which most social science attention has thus far been given. But there is another sector of the economy, and one that is of relatively much greater importance in the underdeveloped countries than it is, for example, in the United States. This is the governmental sector.

In most underdeveloped countries governments get right into enterprise themselves. They buy and sell, manufacture, cultivate, mine, and, in one country or another, engage in practically every kind of activity that private enterprisers undertake. Moreover, governments are the channels through which other governments necessarily work in carrying on programs of aid to economic development. Both intergovernmental loans and international programs of technical co-operation are carried out with and through the governments of the underdeveloped countries. It is with governmental and other leaders that most contacts in a technical co-operation program take place.

The attitudes, motivations, competence, energy, and honesty of government officials—legislative and judicial as well as executive—are therefore of the utmost importance in determining the success of development aid programs in particular and in determining the pace of economic development in general. Merely to mention this fact is enough to indicate a major area where social science guidance is needed.

In many countries, unfortunately, "the basic problems . . . are those of securing a professional administration from a non-specialized society in which primary loyalties are likely to be personal or familial or to run to the community or the caste."[16] What kinds of development programs can be expected to have the support of governments that are dominated by feudal land-holding families, if these families have little interest in greater productivity (because they have all they need themselves), and little sympathy with the aspirations of the people as a whole,

16. Balfour *et al.*, *op. cit.*, p. 116.

or may even have some fear that economic development will produce new groups whose power will threaten theirs? What about countries where there is a tradition of political instability so well established that government office is sought and held only for the opportunities it offers for a big profit, quick enough to beat the next revolution? Even where there are relatively public-spirited, relatively honest, relatively stable governments, the kinds of development projects emphasized may reveal admixtures of motives that are not conducive to obtaining the greatest gain in gross national product resulting from each development expenditure.

Many development programs include projects for heavy industries that are considered to bring prestige, even if quite unjustifiable on economic grounds; public works designed more as personal monuments than for their public service value; and projects that somehow get located in the home districts of particular ministers, although economic considerations would dictate their location elsewhere. Let no one think that politicians change their personalities when they concern themselves with economic development programs!

This problem is particularly acute in those countries that do not have well-established and reasonably well-paid civil services. This includes most of the underdeveloped countries, for such countries usually are characterized by underdeveloped governments.

It is all very well to launch out upon a program of co-operation in economic development, perhaps with the enthusiastic indorsement of the top government officials of a country. But it is easy to understand how quickly the energy of the really public-spirited official gets dissipated if the bureaucracy that must carry out such a program is predominantly composed of friends, relatives, or supporters of successful politicians so underpaid that they rely on a substantial "squeeze" just to keep their families alive, so proud of their meager education and their status as government officials that they look down upon and readily victimize the people they deal with, avoiding any contact with manual labor because that would reflect on their prestige, afraid to leave their offices in the capital city to inspect rural areas and activities because their offices and jobs might be gone when they came back to town, believing that advancement or even continuation in their jobs is dependent on political favor rather than on competence in performance.[17]

Yet this is not a problem to be easy shrugged off. Perhaps there are motivations that can be tapped to energize the bureaucracy. Perhaps there are institutional changes that can be made so that existing incentives can lead to effective work. Perhaps there are kinds of selection and training that over a period of time will being a new spirit into being. These are problems for the social psychologist and the political scientist to tackle together. They are of great importance for economic development, for in most underdeveloped countries this must proceed as much from the top down as from the bottom up.

Most of the problems discussed so far have been those that appear in connection with the direct impact of developmental changes on the beliefs and customs of particular people, whether they be private individuals or government officials. There is a second level of impact, however, indirectly resulting from changes in investment or technology and much more difficult to analyze as a basis for policy guidance.

Change in one aspect of a society inevitably generates changes in others. What happens to the existing social organization when capital formation and technological change begin to affect personal relationships, work habits, and the pattern of power? Will the family be strengthened or weakened? Will the authority of village and tribal chiefs continue to be respected? Will racial, caste, or other discrimination decrease or increase in intensity and pervasiveness? Will the community become less or more democratic?

These induced structural changes in the community are difficult to analyze and difficult to predict, and yet they are of the highest importance in tipping the balance toward gain or loss from economic development. Only if economic development programs are properly designed or appropriately supplemented

17. There is a suggestive discussion of the unlikelihood that any farm-raised man will become an official of the Department of Agriculture in an underdeveloped country, in *Experience with Human Factors in Agricultural Areas of the World* (Washington, D.C.: U.S. Department of Agriculture, 1950).

by measures in other fields can the maximum benefit be derived from them. Here is another area were social scientists may be able to make very great contributions to the administration of programs of economic development.

In most discussions of the process of economic development in underdeveloped countries, attention has been focused on the peoples experiencing the development. This is to be expected, for it is recognized that the major source and direction of development changes must be indigenous. Where foreign captial and personnel are involved, however, as they frequently are today, there is a second important area for social science analysis and advice. This is the area of the cultural and psychological traits of the people of the relatively industrialized countries, to the extent that they, too, participate in the process of economic development in the underdeveloped countries. Unfortunately this is rather a neglected area, but there is no reason why it should be. It is closer at hand, physically, psychologically, and culturally, and it is of great importance.

Why do (or do not) American investors invest in enterprises in Indonesia? That is a question that needs to be answered right along with the questions: Why is the rate of domestic capital formation so low (or so high) in Indonesia? And why do (or do not) Indonesians welcome American and other foreign private investment in their country?

Why do (or do not) American farmers, draftsmen, and businessmen emigrate to Paraguay to start a new life and build the country at the same time that they build up their own capital? This parallels the question: Why does (or does not) Paraguay make settlement there attractive to potential immigrants?

Why do (or do not) American voters and legislators support a continuing program of aid to economic development abroad? This parallels the question: Why do (or do not) the voters and legislators of underdeveloped countries adopt those policies and appropriate those funds that will contribute most effectively to their own economic development?

What personality and culture traits of American personnel predispose them to effectiveness when they participate in international technical co-operation programs? What kind, duration, and locale of training will produce the most effective Point IV experts? These are all questions that are right on our doorsteps. The answers will help greatly in administering the Point IV program.

Let us now turn our attention from the participants at both ends of the international flow of capital and technology, and let us consider certain psychological problems that arise out of the situations in which that flow takes place. There are five "type" situations that should be distinguished: (1) intergovernmental loans; (2) direct private investment; (3) grants-in-aid for development; (4) technical experts sent as advisers or participants; and (5) training programs.

By far the simplest situation is that of the intergovernmental loan. Here there are psychological problems that arise out of the necessity to justify the loan, its possible political connotations, control of expenditures and end-use inspection, and technical questions of interest rate, term of loan, and "Buy American" provisions.

Any of these may in a particular situation give rise to disagreement and may be distorted for political purposes. Moreover, there is implicit in the whole situation of being a borrower and having to meet certain conditions set by the lender a deflation of the national ego that is quite uncomfortable and can express itself in various unpleasant ways.[18]

On the whole, however, although intergovernmental lending probably gives rise to as much ill will as good will, the causes and forms of expression of the ill will are well enough understood and the concrete results of well-administered loans are so important (for reflating egos as well as for increasing production) that this does not represent the highest priority area for social science research and guidance, useful as this might be.

Direct investment is more complicated in terms of the international and intercultural contacts made and in terms of the

18. See, e.g., Harold Lasswell, *Psychological Aspects of Foreign Aid and Development Programs* (Washington, D.C.: U.S. Department of State, Foreign Service Institute, 1949); cf. Leslie M. Lipson, "The Political Framework for World Economic Development," in *International Cooperation for World Economic Development*, pp. 81–86, esp. p. 84.

number of people who experience some change in their work habits, status, and relationship to others. Almost always the top management in an enterprise in which foreign money is heavily invested will itself be predominantly foreign. The entrance of powerful foreigners into any community gives rise to changed relationships, feelings of importance, etc. Higher rates of pay for foreigners than for nationals are an added irritant. If these foreign managers make local allies and get involved in politics, there are more adjustments to make.

In any case, some of the resources of the community have come under foreign control, they are being "exploited" for foreign profit, and many local persons are subordinated to foreigners in the very process of employment by them. What can happen if these relationships are not intelligently and tactfully handled is evident today in Iran. It would be very instructive for social scientists to make a series of case studies of private direct investments in underdeveloped areas to discover the psychological and cultural factors making for success or failure of such enterprises.

Governmental grant-in-aid programs face some of the problems of both of the above types of capital investment abroad. Grants-in-aid are frequently looked upon as charity, and charity does not necessarily generate good will. Grants-in-aid must be "requested" and thoroughly "justified," which promptly punctures the pride of some officials. Grants-in-aid to the underdeveloped countries usually involve the participation of American experts, administrators, "inspectors," and program planners, who may be felt to be playing an unduly large role in the internal affairs of sovereign nations and who in any case get incomes and live on a scale far above those enjoyed by the nationals with whom they work.

Grants-in-aid often involve the setting-up of local funds which may be used for developmental purposes but only with the agreement of American authorities. Again this may be looked upon as a derogation of sovereignty. Finally, grants-in-aid programs usually have training or demonstration activities through which American technicians become the teachers of many nationals. Much as the teaching may be desired, any teaching situation among adults is a fairly delicate one, and, when it involves adults of different cultural backgrounds, the chances for misunderstandings and deflated egos are many.

A similar situation arises when the only contribution of the transmitting country is the services of technicians which it provides (along with necessary equipment and materials). This is the typical technical co-operation project carried on by the Technical Co-operation Administration of the Department of State, and by the various United Nations agencies that provide technical assistance to governments of underdeveloped countries. Here frictions may develop out of interpersonal relationships, heightened by gross differences in income and scale of living and by the adviser-advisee or teacher-student status relationship; but the feeling of accepting charity or financial aid is probably a good deal less than in either the loan situation or the grant-in-aid situation, especially as technical co-operation projects usually require the local government to put up substantial sums of its own funds and the services of numerous personnel as its contribution to the joint venture.

Finally, there are the training programs, particularly those carried on away from home and perhaps in a different culture altogether. One recent study of Latin-American students, before and after they had spent a year in the United States, cast grave doubts on the belief that any real increase in good will toward the United States resulted from the training experience.[19] The lonesomeness engendered by distance from families and friends, the unfamiliarity of the new environment and culture, the occasional discrimination, the limited social contacts, the inability to understand United States institutions the language difficulty and the frustration and low quality of work resulting from it, the shock and envy aroused by the unbelievably high standards of living—all combine to produce an unfavorable reaction that frequently may outweigh the pleasant times and favorable impressions experienced. Training programs, because they can be pretty much modified to take into

19. Charles P. Loomis and Edgar A. Schuler, "Acculturation of Foreign Students in the United States," *Applied Anthropology*, VII (1948), 17–34.

account the recommendations of social scientists, are a particularly appropriate subject of investigation and analysis.

Common to these several kinds of situation in which investment and technology are transmitted from one country to another are certain attitudes and reactions that are prevalent in large underdeveloped areas and that importantly influence the feasibility and necessary form of development aid programs. One of these is nationalism or anticolonialism. Related to it are antiforeignism and anti-Westernism and anti-white-race-ism. Some of the largest underdeveloped countries have only recently achieved their political independence of Western nations. During the period of their political dependence and particularly during the period when they achieved their independence, they developed highly emotional attitudes of opposition to every restraint on their national independence of action, to every symbol of foreign domination. Replacement of a foreign language by a native language is frequently an aspect of this nationalist purging and poses its own obstacles to economic development where the native language is unsuited to the needs of modern science, business, and government.[20]

Both in these newly independent countries and in many underdeveloped countries that have long been politically independent there continues to be an *economic* dependence on Western nations that is galling. It is a dependence on foreign capital, on foreign technology, and on foreign markets, and it is deeply resented. I shall leave the psychological analysis of this resentment to those who know the different cultures in which it appears, but the fact of this resentment and the difficulties it raises to effective co-operation in development aid programs are plain to see.

There are many instances of resistance to improved technology merely because it is foreign in origin or because a foreign adviser suggests its adoption. There are suspicions and even charges that Point IV is a vehicle for a new kind of colonialism

20. Both Indonesia, which is replacing Dutch with Bahasa Indonesian (a modernized Malay), and India, which is replacing English with Hindi, face this problem currently and find it a major obstacle to even the maintenance and utilization of the technology they already have obtained (cf. Thibert, *op. cit.*, p. 114).

utilizing technical advisers to exercise influence over economic development and political alignments. (The newspapers recently reported the decision of the Syrian government, on these grounds, not to request any Point IV assistance from the United States.) There is also a pervasive and persistent belief in some countries that our development aid programs have been undertaken in order to enlist the underdeveloped countries on our side as pawns in the "cold war." Finally, as mentioned above (p. 226), a kind of ego deflation is a frequent concomitant of an aid program. It is not at all rare for these apparent inferiority feelings to find expression in hostility toward Americans, in derision of American "materialism" or "barbarianism," or in imputation of motives of exploitation.

Where these beliefs and attitudes exist, they markedly limit the possibilities of co-operative action to promote economic development, not because that development is inconsistent with psychological or cultural traits of that society, but because the aid is proffered by a country whose motives are suspect or because the very process of accepting aid implies that one party is inferior and the other superior.

This is a situation that poses very delicate problems of mutual understanding. We try to meet it by jointly defining what are the common goals of our country and of the country with which we are co-operating in development programs, explicitly stating our own interests in achieving goals in which both countries have a common interest and drawing up project agreements in which the equality of status and the jointness of interest and contribution are apparent. Whether we can be successful in holding off these suspicions long enough so that our actions will engender real confidence still remains to be seen.[21]

This paper has touched on some of the major areas where psychology and culture influence the process of economic development, especially where investment and technology are transmitted from one country to another. In so doing, it has suggested areas of particular importance for co-operation between social scientist and program administrator. These areas include the behavior of farmers and businessmen, investors,

21. Cf. Condliffe, *op. cit.*, p. 15.

consumers, employees, government officials, legislators, voters, teachers, and students, not only in the underdeveloped countries but often in the capital-exporting and technology-exporting countries as well. They are areas that obviously require combined investigation and analysis by economists, social psychologists, cultural anthropologists, political scientists, sociologists, historians, etc.

The need for such a combined attack to understand the process of economic growth seems more readily understood for underdeveloped economies than for our own. Perhaps this is because the underdeveloped economies have moved less far along the road toward a money-exchange–dominated market economy than we have. Perhaps it is because anxiety feelings and status relationships in our own professional lives keep our academic disciplines segregated and prevent us from adopting the changed attitudes and methods of work that might forward the development of a more integrated social science.

In any case, the need for integrated social science research on the problems of economic development abroad is obvious to all. It can contribute importantly both to the administration of programs of aid to economic development and to the development of social science itself.

THE POINT IV PROGRAM OF THE
UNITED STATES

By KONRAD BEKKER

WE HAVE now considered the role of technical aid in the progress of underdeveloped countries as anthropologists, economists, historians, area specialists, administrators, and in the many other capacities represented in this group. But we have yet to take a close look at the Point IV program of the United States. In presenting the opening statement on this subject, I propose that we reverse the approach we have been taking so far. Instead of formulating theoretical propositions and then measuring the program against them, I suggest we place ourselves in the role of the programming agency and look from there at the problems. The people who plan and carry out Point IV projects meet the whole complex of economic, anthropological, political, and moral issues as they move along, and they see them in a context in which some problems seem less, others more, important than they do in theory. Moreover, the need for decisions covering the whole field of technical assistance brings out many gaps in our theoretical coverage that might otherwise get by unnoticed. The necessary integration of government operations and academic research must come about through the continuing informal and spontaneous co-ordination of work in both fields. Common ground must be approached from both sides, and we have so far approached it from the academic side only.

I shall begin with a brief description of the Point IV program of the United States as it stands today. Next I shall take up some of the problems that seem to be less difficult in actual experience than our discussions up to now would suggest. Finally, I shall turn to a number of points of theoretical interest that emerge in the operation of the program but to which ready answers do not seem to be available.

THE POINT IV PROGRAM

When President Truman lifted technical assistance from comparative obscurity and proclaimed it as a major element in American foreign policy in January, 1949, Point IV type operations had been in progress for ten years in Latin America. They lacked systematic integration and certainly an elaborate theory, but they had thoroughly established their usefulness. The test was that they were being taken over and expanded by the Latin-American countries.

Today, the Technical Co-operation Administration in the Department of State—with which, by the way, I have no official connection—is the focal point of the Point IV activities of the United States, but its own operations cover only part of the ground staked out by the President as the province of Point IV. TCA has completely absorbed the staff and the responsibilities of the oldest of the technical assistance agencies, the Interdepartmental Committee on Scientific and Cultural Co-operation, which was set up in 1938 to work with Latin-American countries but was freed of this geographical limitation in 1948.

TCA has also acquired jurisdiction over the Institute of Inter-American Affairs, a wartime creation. The Institute is still a unit within TCA. It co-operates with the other twenty American republics in the fields of public health, agriculture, and education. It works characteristically through *servicios*, that is, joint staffs, usually headed by an American and attached to a Latin-American ministry.

Aside from TCA, although co-ordinated with it, several other agencies carry on Point IV activities that outweigh in total magnitude the program controlled directly by TCA. The Economic Co-operation Administration has an extensive technical assistance program, even though its principal emphasis is on short-term rehabilitation and recovery programs. The Export-Import Bank renders technical assistance in connection with many of its loans. The educational foundations set up under the Fulbright Act meet a need that is closely related to Point IV, and the State Department's role in working out treaties of friendship, commerce, and investment is in part a Point IV function.

This is by no means an exhaustive list, and to it must be added the technical assistance rendered through the United Nations and its various subsidiary agencies, in many of which the United States participates directly.

A word about the development of the present program. The authorization act under which TCA operates was passed in June, 1950, and funds were not appropriated until September, 1950, or more than a year and a half after the President's inaugural address. The 1952 program has just gone to Congress as part of the Mutual Security Program. In the meantime the United States has signed Point IV general agreements with twenty-seven nations and has begun operations in thirty-five countries. In June, 1951, about 350–400 technicians were abroad under TCA proper. It is proposed to increase this number to about 2,000. Agricultural, health, and education projects account for about 87 per cent of the current program, with about 45 per cent of the funds devoted to agriculture alone. Fifty-four nations participate in the United Nations program.

The Mutual Security Program for 1952 does not show technical assistance as a separate category, but it is estimated that about eighty-five million dollars can be considered as technical aid under TCA. While this represents a substantial increase over last year's appropriation of thirty-four million dollars, a meaningful comparison should take into account the amounts administered by other agencies, particularly ECA. If that is done, technical assistance may amount to between two hundred and fifty and three hundred million of the new program. This is a substantial increase over last year's program but does not double or triple it, as TCA's own program would make it appear. And, of course, it is a small fraction of the Mutual Security Program of eight and a half billion dollars.

During the initial period of operations a good deal of experience has been gained. The present organization has been found workable, although it pleases nobody completely. Technicians have proved to be available in most fields but not always at the terms which the government can offer. The delays in present hiring practices are more than many good men will put up with. Funds as related to demand have not been too inadequate so far because of the late start of the program, but with operations now well under way the organization will be able to meet only part of the constructive requests it is receiving.

Servicios have not yet been set up in areas other than Latin America, although they have proved successful in every way and have even survived forcible changes in the local governments. Three joint planning commissions have been organized, but this is not a particularly significant new departure.

Both TCA and ECA have found it useful to operate through contracts with private United States and foreign organizations. In that way they can delegate responsibilities and tap sources of personnel that would not otherwise be available. Contracts can also take the curse of official involvement from operations where that is important, and they are useful in bringing about mutuality in technical assistance among participating countries.

Abroad the response to the program has been positive with a few exceptions. There was a good deal of hope that Point IV meant large-scale capital assistance, and those hopes are disappointed. Institutional resistance and oppositionof vested interest may yet be felt more strongly, but there are usually enough projects of a noncontroversial nature—such as malaria control —to make a start. Existing fears of possible political interference or economic imperialism have in several instances been allayed very definitely, and it appears that the complex motivations that lead to the sponsorship of such a program by the United States are coming to be fairly well understood abroad.

Broadly, Point IV has come to mean government-sponsored technical co-operation for basic improvement in economic well-being as distinct from short-term relief, rehabilitation, recovery programs, military and capital assistance. The feeling that this is a major and distinct phase of our foreign policy underlies present efforts to keep the Point IV work separate from other economic aid programs. On the other hand, it can be argued that close integration of our foreign economic operations would be easier if all their aspects were handled by one agency. As you may recall, President Truman stated in the Mutual Security Program he sent to Congress on May 24 that the merits of a possible transfer of TCA to ECA are now being studied by the Administration.[1]

If we wish to consider the descriptive material I have just presented to you on a loftier plane, we can think of it as a statement of how Point IV is being fitted into the American political system. The process is still going on. At this stage it seems highly unlikely that it will be reversed. Red tape, inconsistencies, and exasperation are an inevitable part of it. That may not be an excuse, but it is a reason for the slow and cautious manner in which the Administration has been feeling its way in the wake of the initial public enthusiasm.

I now turn to the second point which I proposed to take up: the fact that some of the issues we have been discussing appear to cause less difficulty in practice than in theory. I shall take my examples from South and Southeast Asia because I am relatively familiar with that area and because it illustrates what I want to show.

I am taking you to unfamiliar territory. The peoples to whom we are extending Point IV aid in Southeast Asia live in a no-man's land of the social sciences. The anthropologists have studied the Veddas in Ceylon, the Ifugaos, Igorots, Kalingas, and Bontoks in the Philippines, and other remote tribes elsewhere. The economists have studied European colonization by Portuguese, Spanish, Dutch, British, and French. But neither group has paid much attention to the Singhalese, the Tagalogs, or the Visayans—the groups who are the economic leaders of their countries.

The social scientist's pat answer is, of course, that he is studying his problems in their pure form. I doubt that the excuse holds, because these societies have dimensions not found among primitive peoples and at the same time they have features that cannot be described in the terms of an economic theory oriented toward Western economies. To be specific, if our Point IV man

1. The Mutual Security Act, passed since this paper was written, provides that TCA shall remain in the State Department but that its activities shall be co-ordinated with those of other agencies by a director attached to the executive office of the President. It is probable that, under the new act, TCA will be assigned responsibility for economic aid programs which go beyond the limits of technical assistance and include capital aid in countries that are not scheduled to receive military assistance.

in Thailand is to be aware of the social consequences of his program, he ought to know something about Thai history—including Thai-Chinese, Thai-British, and Thai-French relations—about Buddhism, about Indian art, about the economic geography of the Far East, and about a lot of other subjects in which the competence of any one social scientist cannot be presumed.

Clearly, the man we need must be a general practitioner who does not mind the sneers of the specialists. In the particular instance of Thailand he will have the benefit of two good anthropological studies that should help him in at least 10 per cent of his area of responsibility. He will also find several good books on Thailand written for the general public and quite a few travelogues and government documents. He will have to write the rest of the social sciences off as too under- or overdeveloped to be of much use.

Happily, some of his anticipated problems recede as he starts operating. One such is the choice between evolution and revolution. Since the program for better or for worse operates through government-to-government agreements, the choice reduces itself to the more pedestrian alternative of whether or not an agreed Point IV program is feasible in a given country or not. That may of course mean that the problem of institutional resistance and vested interests is deferred rather than solved.

A second problem of little practical concern at this stage is the imposition by Americans of modern industrial patterns on native workers against their will. The top item on the list of priorities of the typical underdeveloped country is a steel mill, and the first task of the Point IV official is to suggest that the local people apply to the International Bank rather than to him for it. There seems to be little prospect that industrial development around the world will proceed at the pace that all of us desire. Much less is industry likely to outrun the chances for social adjustment in local societies.

The problem of conflicting systems of values does not vanish, but it loses some of its sting. Of true value conflicts so many striking examples have been given in these meetings that I will say no more about them than that I have yet to see the Point IV official who is insensitive to the problem. If there is one, he will have to be fired.

But there is a class of pseudo-values that is easily confused with the real thing. If a Burmese feels that his malaria is due to supernatural causes, that does not indicate that his mind is on things of the other world but that he does not understand the nature of the disease. This is not a problem of metaphysics but one of information and communication, which is not to say that it may not be a difficult one. The eminently successful experience of public health programs all over the world has demonstrated that an intelligent approach with indigenous cooperation will bring disease within the realm of facts with which people feel they can cope. There need be no damage to the traditional system of values because disease was never one of them.

Generally, a look at the culturally developed but economically underdeveloped countries in which most of the Point IV programs operate—say, Pakistan, India, Ceylon, Burma, Thailand—suggests that these countries are highly sophisticated in dealing with the West. They themselves have diverse existing value systems and long histories of coping with conflicting and demanding foreign cultural influences. Our Point IV program is in fact quite out of keeping with their experience because it is so timid, considerate, and permissive. If we were to learn from history by analogy, we might take the successful and largely nonviolent proselytizing of the Hindus, Buddhists, and Moslems in that area as our example. These great cultural movements not only expected the local people to adopt their political and value systems, lock, stock, and barrel, but on top of that asked them to forget their literature and art and start over again with the study of an ancient foreign tradition transmitted in a foreign classical language. Our approach is different. But we want to be sure that our respect for other peoples' values cannot be misunderstood as lack of belief in our own, and that goes particularly for political values.

To summarize, let us leave their rightful place in the anthropology textbooks to the shrinking-violet cultures of primitive peoples. Most of the underdeveloped countries are not of this type, and our program can operate successfully in them if it is conducted with a reasonable amount of tact and common sense.

There are, however, enough problems that remain which are of importance to the program and for which guidance must come from the academic professions. I shall take some of them up in turn, starting with the more general and moving on to the more specific. This is, of course, a field in which different people will ask different questions, and mine cannot be more than samples.

First we might ask the economic theorist what an underdeveloped area is, why it is underdeveloped, and what lines its development might follow. It is not easy to find answers to these questions that seem to apply to South Asia. If I remember my principles of economics, underdeveloped countries such as the ones in South Asia should not exist. But, granted that an irrational history has brought them into being, they should have large trade deficits due to a rapid influx of capital. Private American firms should be eager to send experts and machinery to them, but the United States government might come under pressure from many quarters to step in and prevent this from happening. Assuming the presence of adequate resources, the opportunities for progress should be the greater the more underdeveloped a country is. Foreign trade alone should have an equalizing function that would raise South Asia's economic levels. To make the actual economic stagnation of underdeveloped countries in South Asia compatible with our theoretical framework, we have to impute to them extremes of poverty in land and natural resources, population pressures, an irrational orientation toward work, and an inability to raise capital which are often not borne out by the facts.

Let us look at some of the facts. From 1900 to 1940 the countries of Southeast Asia had a total export surplus of ten billion dollars. For the nineteenth and eighteenth centuries the data are incomplete, but there is little doubt that all these countries always had export surpluses. Since these surpluses were far larger than any possible payments for services, Southeast Asia must have exported capital all along. This was true in periods when there were no problems of transfer, no political unrest, and no shortages of supplies. And we find that many of these underdeveloped countries have returned to having export surpluses within the last year and that they are increasing their holdings of foreign exchange in spite of their crying need for economic development and in the absence of an imperialist exploiting power.

Is this situation due to rigid resistance to economic expansion? It is true enough that there are many examples of apparently quite irrational failure to utilize economic opportunities. But there are important examples to the contrary, too. One of these is the spread of native rubber production, which has been rapid throughout the area in spite of official discouragement. The similarly rapid spread of peanut cultivation for the market is further confirmation that there is no absolute resistance throughout these countries to involvement in innovations or in a money economy.

If we tend to assume that Southeast Asia is an overpopulated area and that its low per capita product might be due to pressure of the population on the land, we again come up against data that seem to dispute that point. Over the whole area, some 50 per cent of the land surface is arable but only some 10 per cent is under cultivation. Much of the uncultivated arable land is accessible, and vast additional areas are becoming accessible with present methods of malaria control. Analogies from China and India will not fit.

Historically, some of these countries appear to have been able to invest in public works of astonishing magnitude, and, indeed, if we make a common-sense estimate of their ability to save not in terms of money income but in terms of labor availability, it is obviously substantial. And we find that there are several forms in which this resource has in the past been tapped and is still being used.

Our common-sense estimate might start out with the fact that throughout the area agricultural producers seem to be able to produce about twice as much rice as they consume. In many instances the remainder is taken away from them in one form or another, and much of it is converted into money through exports. If these amounts could be mobilized for investment, they would permit a prodigious rate of increase in capital formation. But all I want to suggest at this point is that we should not conclude from the low absolute level of income in these countries that the producer's margin above consumption must be small. Percentagewise I suspect it may be greater than ours, and it is wrung from him through various gimmicks in the price system, by inflation, by land taxes, by duties, and by the use of physical services. It is reflected in the export surplus and in the large amount of luxury consumption of these areas, but even so most of it goes to support inefficiencies in social organization among which the maintenance of the underemployed is probably the most costly.

These brief remarks will sufficiently illustrate the point that many of our stereotypes do not apply in some underdeveloped countries, although they may apply in others. The lack of a more thorough analysis of the deviant situations is a serious handicap in dealing with their problems. It leads us to think in terms of our own solutions in situations where they do not apply. We may, for example, be unable to visualize any system for the mobilization of rural savings other than an expansion of the banking system, we may completely ignore the possibilities of capital formation by the improvement of farm property, and we may, in fact, focus our attention exclusively on problems of investment when there is room for progress along other lines.

Assuming, however, that we have enough of a general understanding of conditions in an underdeveloped country to see our way clear to recommending a program, how shall we determine priorities? Is technical assistance without capital assistance likely to be useful? If so, in what fields? Should it be government or private? It was said here that underdeveloped countries are likely to suggest a hodgepodge of projects that come out of the newspapers. Some, I might add, stem from the prestige needs of the different government offices in a fashion reminiscent of our own value systems. But can we do better? Can we at present honestly say more than that agriculture is obviously paramount but that public health is good too, and then suggest 90 per cent for agriculture and 10 per cent for public health?

Our own society has developed techniques for dealing with technological progress that range all the way from an elaborate system of technical education to collective bargaining and patent laws. We are catching up with our inventors with fairly well-determined lags. The underdeveloped countries, on the other hand, are surrounded by a technological environment which is a hundred years ahead of their present situation. Has technological progress become so much a monopoly of highly advanced countries that it can only spread by transfer from here to underdeveloped countries? Or are the problems of development, for instance, of alternative emphasis on the factors of production, such that underdeveloped countries will have to do their own inventing?

It is clear that we cannot answer any of these questions by referring to the criterion that has broadly guided our economic aid policy in Europe: the balance of payments of the recipient country. Underdeveloped countries should ideally have large imports of development goods balanced by an influx of foreign capital. But the import surplus is not desirable for its own sake; it is the kind of goods imported and the use made of them that matter. Many technical assistance projects and much internal development will not affect the balance of payments at all. We must look for criteria in the underdeveloped countries themselves.

Perhaps we could agree that an increase in labor productivity is the broadest measure of what we are aiming at. But if we want to use this term in underdeveloped areas, we have to qualify its meaning. We are not aiming at a rise in output per worker if that rise is attained at the expense of the total volume of employment. And we have to keep in mind that most underdeveloped countries today suffer from widespread unemployment and underemployment.

Perhaps our own preoccupation with technological change and increased productivity of labor deflects our attention from the large possibilities of horizontal expansion at the existing level of technology. Most economists are quick to dismiss horizontal expansion of subsistence agriculture as a palliative that must soon be offset by population growth. Before so dismissing it, we should investigate the magnitudes involved. A breathing space of a generation may be all that is needed to break the vicious circle of poverty and population pressure in which some of the areas are caught. Temporary relief in one area may present an opportunity for advance that will later affect the areas initially left behind. But even if nothing were to be gained but temporary relief, the cavalier attitude with which social scientists dispose of the matter would not become the practitioner. After all, we ourselves do not disdain to eat because it would only postpone our death.

There are great opportunities for horizontal expansion in most of Southeast Asia and even in more densely populated countries like India. We tend to underestimate the large spontaneous migrations, involving not hundreds of thousands, but millions, which are going on unaided. But even greater opportunities for the expansion of subsistence agriculture by the use of a nominal amount of technical assistance are constantly being created. The amount of arable land available in a country is itself a function of many variables. It may expand rapidly with improved malaria control, cheapened transportation, better surveys, and other steps in economic progress that leave agricultural technology itself unaffected.

Ordinarily, of course, our interest is focused on changes in techniques of production rather than on the expansion of those already in general use. Where does the introduction of an improved technology have the greatest merit from a purely economic point of view?

There are some very practical, measurable, short-range criteria such as the attainment of a balance in current payment which I mentioned before, the covering of a short-term food deficit, or the increased production of scarce commodities. Depending on the circumstances, these may legitimately be of primary concern in a technical assistance program. But they fall short of providing for the basic improvement in economic well-being which we defined as the broader aim of Point IV. The criteria for progress toward this goal are more difficult to formulate. A new technology, to be useful, should probably be (1) capital extensive; (2) easily transferable; (3) productive of realizable results; (4) geared to the most underutilized resources; and (5) flexible. Let me comment briefly on these points.

A shortage of capital is almost by definition a characteristic of underdeveloped areas, and it is axiomatic that what capital there is must be made to go as far as possible. Capital extensive industries should be given preference over capital intensive ones. Can we reconcile this admitted truth with the emphasis on hydroelectric power and the provision of overhead capital and social services in most development programs? Perhaps we could arrange all our projects along a scale reaching from the proverbial steel mill at one extreme to agricultural extension at the other and measure their merit in terms of capital extensiveness at the point where their end products reach the consumer. We might then find that hydroelectric power was one of the more capital extensive industries because of the vast amounts of other factors associated with its end use.

But we have to take into account not only the vertical flow from power source to consumer goods but also the horizontal association of industries. In that sense we could think of a project as more capital extensive if a maximum of other resources tended to be associated with its operations rather than with the use of its output. As an example I might mention the establishment of a canning plant that may open up opportunities for the employment of land and labor in the production of crops that would not otherwise have been grown.

Not every technique, regardless of how capital extensive it may be, lends itself equally well to a transfer abroad. One of the most serious drawbacks to private economic development in underdeveloped countries is the lack of the complementary industrial facilities that are available in advanced countries. Access to supplies of materials and equipment of all types, labor technical skills, transportation facilities, professional and government services, and organized markets are part of a technological environment on which Western industries depend. But they do so to a greater or less extent, and some of them are for that reason more readily transferable to underdeveloped areas than others. The cement industry seems to be a good example of an industry that can be fitted into the resource and requirements pattern of countries of different levels of economic development. The reasons seem to be that the industry's raw materials are widely distributed, its machinery and operation are relatively simple and not subject to rapid changes in technology, and its output feeds into a wide variety of local purposes. Moreover, transportation costs give a local mill a sufficient margin to offset minor differences in efficiency. Few other industries have this combination of advantages.

The points just mentioned are closely related to a further principle of selection that may at times clash with the criterion of capital extensiveness. Given a limited amount of resources that can be concentrated in any one point, most underdeveloped countries must seek to apply these resources in a way that will yield not only a maximum return in benefits but a return that can be mobilized for further development. From this point of view, an increase in crops produced for the market, for example, and particularly for export, may deserve preference over a greater increase in crops consumed at the farm.

The criteria mentioned so far relate to the characteristics of the new technology to be introduced in an underdeveloped country. But it may well be argued that the matter should be approached from the opposite side: from an analysis of the existing pattern of resource utilization. It is from this point of view that I referred earlier to the existing opportunities for horizontal expansion by the extension of subsistence farming to new land. But there are more striking illustrations of the problem involved. In areas where there is widespread underemployment there may be strong justification for the utilization of an even less advanced technology than is generally applied in the area. Individuals, of course, act accordingly in the conduct of their private economy when they employ periods of enforced idleness to improve their property. In areas where, on the average, half of the agricultural labor force may be idle the potential gain to the community from employing this available manual labor by the use of a simple technology requiring a minimum of equipment may far outweigh the results that can be attained by the introduction of advanced techniques.

Underdeveloped countries, then, are likely to continue, as

they do now, to employ a wide range of less and more advanced technologies side by side. Because of the relative immobility of their resources, and particularly in the initial stages of their development, that range is likely to be far greater than in advanced countries. Furthermore, if an underdeveloped country is successful in its program for economic development, the most economic combination of factors in many of its industries is likely to change as the initial handicaps are overcome. This suggests that the opportunities for technological progress may be greatest in those fields where alternative techniques can be introduced with a great deal of flexibility.

This point is of considerable practical interest. It so happens that the industries which provide, for example, Southeast Asia's greatest immediate opportunities for translating its margin of unutilized labor into exports—and thereby potentially into imports of capital goods—are not very susceptible of technological progress. This is true of the cultivation of rice, coconuts, rubber, and pepper, to name some outstanding examples. The reasons are very different in each case, but they are cogent. Rice is already one of those capital intensive industries in which the effort sunk in permanent investment prevents a shift to new methods. Moreover, the social implications of increased rice production for a market are in a large part unfavorable, since for good reasons large rice surpluses often come from areas of tenancy, exploitation, and waste of human resources. In the case of copra and rubber, technology has little to offer. And pepper-growing is a craftlike labor-intensive industry.

The absence of technological opportunities for improvement in these fields which constitute direct economic links with the outside world may be in part responsible for Southeast Asia's failure to show the explosive rate of development for which we might be looking.

All I have said so far has related to the technology of physical production. But there is a vast field for technological advance which we tend to forget because it does not offer some of the difficulties connected with capital investment. I am speaking of the broad range of services—from government to the professions. It is characteristic of the economic advance of underdeveloped countries that the proportion of their population which is engaged in services increases rapidly. But ordinarily we consider this trend as a by-product of advance in other fields rather than as a goal in itself. There is little excuse for this point of view. The services of the barbershop may be unessential, but such services as education are among the most crucial requirements of economic progress. We could indeed extend our scale of capital extensivencss to cover government, education, and public health, and we might find that these fields far outrank all others in the breadth of their contribution to economic well-being.

The principal resource these services require, personnel, is often available and can be expanded rapidly with technical assistance. The utilization of this resource is a problem of institutional arrangements that has been solved in the past. It need not necessarily be thought of in terms of raising taxes in a largely nonmonetary economy. The countries that have a Hinayana Buddhist culture used to have, and some of them still have, highly developed systems of education, with an adult literacy ranging upward of 50 per cent—systems that were not paralleled by anything in the Western world until the nineteenth century. Education was supported by a progressive income tax levied in kind upon the population, turned over in the form of alms to the Buddhist monks. The system provided schooling for the children along with other religious and community services. Our own time may call for a more secular arrangement. But it does demand an at least equivalent community effort along similar lines.

The various aspects of technical aid to underdeveloped countries which I have just mentioned do not add up to the integrated conceptual framework we need, but I think they must be among its elements. If we had a more complete system of criteria, our next step would perhaps consist in scheduling our priorities not only according to the comparative individual merit of the projects but also according to their proper tie-in over a period of time. We might work out a system of time discounts of anticipated results that would permit us to equate the merits of a river valley development program with those of a fertilizer import program. I do not think that we would want to carry this sort of thing to extremes of mathematical precision or substitute it for the exercise of judgment. But we would want our judgment in these matters to be as informed and deliberate as possible. We would certainly get away from the simplistic contrasts between agriculture and industry, light and heavy industry, and consumer and producer goods industries that now beset our thinking in these matters. Even the incomplete list of criteria I have suggested above makes it clear that in a given situation industry may qualify where agriculture does not, and heavy industry may qualify where light industry does not.

Perhaps we would also be able to say more about the opportunities for private as compared to government projects than that we want a maximum of private initiative, but we also recognize the role of the state. The area of risk-bearing, the cost structure, and the relationship to public services of private industries in most underdeveloped countries are very different from those of similar industries in economically advanced countries. If we understood these differences better, we might be able to treat as a technical problem what now appears as a political issue.

One of our principal gains from a good conceptual framework would be an increased ability to see facts. Many of the issues we have to deal with are now beclouded because we see only so much of them as our statistical tools can grasp. Take the instance of national income. The customary disclaimers of the experts to the contrary, we do in fact use national income data concerning underdeveloped countries and compiled by Western methods for international comparisons and as indicators of standards of welfare. Yet these measures are meaningless unless the country to which they apply has an integrated price system and unless its market sector is reasonably representative of the whole economy. If these two conditions are not met—as is true in many underdeveloped countries—substitute measures should be developed that would cover what national income statistics cover in advanced countries: substantially the whole output of the economy measured by some relevant uniform monetary standard. That can be done. But it requires a recognition of the fact that we have to recast our intellectual routines in dealing with underdeveloped areas.

It has been my task to give you a picture of bewilderment, and I trust that I have done so. Fortunately we are not often confronted with absolute choices that require a precise theoretical answer. The issues I have raised are finding empirical solutions a good part of which will probably stand up under critical analysis. Programs operate on a broad front rather than in a narrow field. Most important of all, there is opportunity for progress along so many lines that few if any efforts in technical assistance are likely to be wasted. But the task set to the Point IV program is of vast proportions, and the resources are very small. We need all the advice that can make the program more effective.

Our questions should not be addressed to the economist alone. We need to learn more from the anthropologist about the loose or rigid integration of the societies with which we deal in order to know how they will respond to Point IV assistance. We ought to learn from the political scientist how to recognize trends toward or away from democratic controls when they appear in unfamiliar institutional guises. The answers we need must be at the level of generalization—or lack of it—at which Point IV decisions are made. That means that the social scientist will have to immerse himself deeply in subject matter that is at present still poorly analyzed. In so doing, he may find new theoretical insights, or he may at least be able to communicate the existing ones to us.

ECONOMIC DEVELOPMENT AND
PUBLIC FINANCE

By H. S. BLOCH

THE economic policy of underdeveloped countries is generally determined by the shortage of capital and skilled labor. The difficulty in obtaining foreign capital makes capital savings devices more important than labor-saving devices. This calls in some instances for methods of production which would appear inefficient in developed countries. Giving priority to capital savings devices frequently results in relatively larger-scale domestic spending than the emphasizing of labor devices would produce. Since development is financed both from foreign and from domestic sources, a close correlation between foreign and domestic fiscal policy must exist. The bulk of both types of financing coming currently from public rather than from private sources, the problem becomes a major element of governmental policy. While it is axiomatic to minimize the foreign and to maximize the domestic part of the spending volume, it is also clear that the foreign spending by itself is not inflationary, while the domestic spending is inflationary in nature.

The inflationary trend has a direct effect on the balance-of-payments position for the following reasons: (1) it makes prohibitive the investment of foreign capital because of unfavorable exchange rates and encourages capital flight; (2) it reduces export possibilities by creating a high internal price level; and (3) it diverts production to nonessentials.

There are a number of countries which have suddenly achieved a relatively sound fiscal position because they have been able to export raw materials for which there is a high level of demand on the world market and the producers of which (frequently foreign entrepreneurs) are the chief contributors to government financing. In these cases the fiscal problem may be quite easy, although the physical problem of development may be far from being solved. Such cases apply, for instance, to oil-, tin-, copper-, and nitrate-producing countries as well as to economies which are big exporters of rice (e.g., Thailand and Burma), coffee, wool, sugar, and rubber. In fact, the financial situation of many Latin-American countries is eminently sound in a strictly fiscal sense. Deficit countries have become surplus countries due to war and postwar demand and recently as a result of developments in the Far East. This has led to a high degree of solvency for countries which are producers of critical raw materials. Their position is much sounder than that of certain Middle Eastern and Far Eastern countries which have had only a temporary improvement in their fiscal position because of the wartime accumulation of sterling balances which are now being drawn down very rapidly where they have not yet completely disappeared.

The countries in Latin America and Asia which rely on the export of raw materials are exceedingly vulnerable in the long run because they depend entirely on the demand fluctuations of the world market. They are especially vulnerable because they usually have only one or a very few commodities to offer, depending upon specific situations. All these resources are exhaustible and therefore cannot be counted upon permanently to support the finances of a country.

Some of these raw-material-producing countries, especially Venezuela, which is a major oil producer, use financial resources obtained from exhaustible natural resources to engage in the process of industrial diversification. They here devise a fiscal policy which is designed to utilize the foreign exchange gained from the sale of their exhaustible resources, or from the taxation of profits made by the companies exploiting them, for the purpose of financing new industries. By the process of industrial diversification they are thus making their economies less vulnerable to the unavoidable results of exhaustion and also to the fluctuations of the world-market price structure.

Countries which are producers of one or a few raw materials yielding relatively important financial results usually have a tax structure geared to tap primarily this source of revenue.

Such a tax structure is either based on export taxes, because these products are usually exported, or on royalties or franchise fees. Thus, as new enterprises are established under the diversification program, the old tax structure fails to reach the new industries. Economic development manifested through industrial diversification, therefore, requires immediate tax reforms which take into account such new industrial developments. This is an example of how it is possible and in fact necessary to build a fiscal structure which already takes into account the next stage of industrial development. Indeed, it is harder and takes longer to develop industrially than to set up the machinery for such a measure as a corporate income tax which is applicable to a variety of industries. It is necessary that the fiscal reforms both in the legislative and in the administrative aspects do not lag behind the industrial development but that they anticipate it, so that no revenue is lost to the state because of lack of adaptation of institutions and policies to new conditions.

This applies with even greater force to those countries which do not now have a sound "financial" situation. A sound "financial" situation, as reflected in a balance-of-payments surplus or, even more so, as reflected in a domestic financial surplus, does not necessarily indicate a general economically sound situation. The latter is rather shown by the extent of the road network, the public utilities, transportation facilities, level of literacy, methods of agriculture, and industrial development in in general. It is also indicated by the amount of value added to the raw materials which are exported. Thus, a country which exports refined sugar or alcohol draws much greater advantage from its position than a primitive country which sells sugar only in the raw stage. The fiscal problem of countries which do not have any critical raw materials at their disposal is more difficult. A country which does have such resources can at least accumulate foreign currency reserves for a long-run development program, even if it is not able or if for policy reasons it may not be advisable to expand such a program at an exceedingly rapid pace. There are even instances where, in a period of boom, development programs must be postponed in order to produce a maximum amount of material to be sold at high prices and in order to avoid highly inflationary pressure.

The country without raw materials must concentrate on prospecting for such materials through geological and agricultural surveys and on the utilization of its labor force to add value to raw materials which it may have to import. This requires a fiscal machinery of a very advanced type. It also requires aid from abroad in one form or another. An underdeveloped country cannot afford to let the fiscal structure lag behind the industrial and economic development, especially since the increase in the development program brings about an automatic increase of public finances (even in countries where private enterprise plays an important role) because it involves road-building, port-building, and the creation or expansion of public services of various types.

It also clarifies the point that in underdeveloped countries, even more than in developed countries, fiscal measures are too blunt to stem inflation all by themselves. The basic cause of inflation is the poverty of the country, the inability to produce or import enough consumers goods. The answer to this problem is economic development, but economic development necessitates large-scale operating. The excess spending power which must be mopped up in inflationary periods is more sporadically and more unequally distributed in underdeveloped than in developed countries and as a rule confined to the urban areas, although notorious exceptions have occurred in times of famine or near-famine.

The first and foremost task is to plan an expenditure program as to volume, character, and timing. This is important for both raw-material-exporting and non-raw-material-exporting countries, because the former may have to utilize all available resources for the production of the materials during a period of boom and to use the available cash balances for their internal development in a period of declining prices.

As the fiscal objectives become larger, expenditure planning becomes more significant. This requires the creation of budgetary machinery. It necessitates an approval to budgeting which takes into account long-run economic development plans. The annual budget often becomes the tactical implementation of a developmental strategy which is expressed in multi-annual plans. Financial reporting becomes then a necessity, and with its perfection a new type of financial control is created. Special financial machinery is necessary for governmental production, trading, and financial operations, and the flexibility required for such operations calls for new forms of financial organization and management. Daring and generosity instead of parsimony must prevail, even through inflationary periods, on the expenditure side, unless private industry can take care of the basic requirements for economic development which is practically nowhere the case. As the expenditure program becomes larger, boldness and vision must also be applied to the revenue system.

Taxation is usually the major method of mobilizing domestic savings in countries with a low level of national income. That is particularly the difficulty in countries which have no major raw materials to export. Normally taxation is the only really anti-inflationary instrument of financing at the disposal of governments. In countries where a large number of people are outside the money economy and where others are close to the subsistence level or even below the subsistence level, mass taxation is either antidevelopmental or altogether impossible. This creates the need for an approach to taxation which in some instances requires new fiscal techniques. Naturally, the choice of methods is a problem which arises in the field of public finance as in any other one.

It has been stated at this Institute, as also in other places, that a new economic theory is needed for underdeveloped countries. In my opinion, the available tools of economic theory are just as adequate for underdeveloped as they are for developed countries, and recommendations by theorists can be just as fatal or as beneficial for underdeveloped as for developed countries. What is required as a basic understanding of the policy determinants and of the institutional framework and the knowledge that all policy recommendations are time bound and area bound.

As stated above, the policy determinants involve choices between capital and labor-saving devices which would appear as a dichotomy in a developed country. They also require careful analysis of the financial resources. They require, moreover, a diagnostic approach to the institutions of the countries concerned.

A highly developed industrial economy may still have a very backward fiscal system, yet it is much easier to adjust a backward fiscal system to an advanced industrial structure than it is to develop a backward industrial system. Examples of the former can be found among American states and cities. Higher stages of institutional development can, however, be more rapidly reached if a careful diagnosis of local conditions is undertaken.

The underdeveloped countries have the extraordinary misfortune of having had their fiscal structure implanted from abroad. It is easier to transfer technological processes from one country to another than to transfer fiscal techniques which are part of the governmental process and intimately tied up with the entire political, social, and economic framework. What has happened in practice is that bits and pieces of various systems have been transferred, and, as they have been transferred, they have very often been transformed.

Financial institutions are an element of the political structure. Professor Opler has said during the present Institute session that if we asked an Indian what the most important reform is that has taken place in India since independence, he would say that it is the unification of the princely states. He would not say that it is the creation of the Dhamadar Valley Authority, which is the most significant economic development program the Indian Union has undertaken. Now, it is very likely that the Dhamadar Valley Authority could not have been created without the unification of the princely states. As a matter of fact, the planning of the Dhamadar Valley Authority is based on the cooperation of the princely states with the Indian Union.

The same is true of the railway system. The railway privileges of the Indian princes had to be given up in order to have a national railway plan, and therefore the unification of the princely states was more important than anything else, because there would not have been a Dhamadar Valley as it is now, and there would not have been a unification of the railroad projects.

The institutional changes which emerge with a development program sometimes lead to new forms of government activity such as the control of money supply and circulation through central banking institutions. Such institutions are quite recent even in developed countries but are now being organized at fairly early stages of economic development in a number of Latin-American and Asian countries.

With the growing complexity of a developing economy, numerous organs grow up which may have varied functions in the monetary and fiscal field. Co-ordination of their activities often is a complicated process which reaches across central into provincial and local government activities and which sometimes necessitates politically difficult synchronization of the policies of various autonomous and semiautonomous agencies. Very often, the problem of co-ordination is made almost impossible to solve, because of lack of consolidated information. The task of proper and adequate over-all reporting requires comparability of data. The comparability becomes more difficult as the process of development leads to a greater diversity of financial organization.

The development of the fiscal structure is, however, not merely limited to structural or managerial aspects of the governmental organization but often cuts rather deeply into the social structure. Where the taxing rights are taken away from feudal lords, a government makes always a basic incision in existing social relationships. Similarly, if a tax reform is undertaken which changes the relationship between landlords and tenants, it has significant redistributive effects and is already the beginning of an over-all land reform.

A distinction must be made here between those types of fiscal reforms which affect elements of the social structure as such and those which affect only financial institutions, even if these financial institutions are very important. The taxation of land is always closely linked to the agrarian structure as a whole. Changes on the tax side alone are not decisive as long as there is a land-tenure system which is unsuited to proper economic development. Yet tax changes and tenure changes must be interrelated in order to produce the kind of change in agrarian policy which is necessitated by growing development problems.

Techniques in land taxation are harder to transfer from one country to another than techniques in taxing corporations, because the taxation tool as it affects agriculture is closely intertwined with the governmental process on the local and provincial levels.

The taxation of corporations, however, affects the same type of financial institution in developed and underdeveloped countries and frequently is applicable to new and often foreign organizations engaged in rather similar types of activity. In fact, care must be taken to consider business corporations engaged in agricultural activity rather similarly to those operating extractive industries and not to confuse the former with the "nonbusiness-like" agricultural operations of local farmers and tenants. This applies particularly to large-scale sugar plantations and rubber plantations.

As far as taxation of corporations is concerned, there are certain technical problems which require adjustment of such existing taxes as export taxes to the marginal producer. The adjustment of export industries to marginal producers may especially benefit the local operator who, on a similar scale and with less capital than the foreign enterprise, must mine low-grade ores. Then there is a question of transforming specific taxes, especially customs duties, into an ad valorem basis if the inflationary process has led to such frequent price rises as to make speedy adjustment of specific industries impossible. The ad valorem taxes have been introduced in many countries only recently, and thus the collection system has lagged behind the inflationary process, and the governments have lost significant amounts of revenue.

Fiscal systems have often been transferred for political reasons or reasons of cultural affinity. The most typical instance is the transfer of British fiscal systems to the colonies.

First of all, the British system as it appears in the colonies has rather basic differentials from the system used in the home country. Second, it has sometimes been transferred without taking into account the social structure of the countries to which it has been exported. A typical example for the first instance is the fact that the period prescribed for debate of estimates in the British Parliament is much longer than that prescribed in those colonial countries to which the system has been transferred. For the second instance, there is the example of India, where the income tax of the British type was introduced in the 1860's, but when the application to the Hindu "Undivided Family," which is a special form of social organization typical of India, was only introduced in 1936—this was several decades after these "undivided families" had expanded their activities beyond rural into commercial and industrial endeavors.

Latin-American countries have generally the Franco-Spanish tax system which is based largely on indirect taxation, especially stamp taxes, and which also includes the so-called "schedular income taxes." Still today many of the stamp taxes, which have fallen by the wayside in France, continue to exist in Latin America. In some cases it has already been proved that it is perfectly possible to introduce immediately a so-called "global income tax" which is not based on different proportional rates for various types of economic activity but which introduces progressive scales operating on the same pattern for every economic activity. Yet some experts have maintained that "Latin systems" operate better on the classical schedular pattern or else that the evolution away from this pattern must be a slow one.

Now, it happens to be a fact that in underdeveloped countries agriculture especially needs a treatment different from other types of economic activities and that something resembling a schedular treatment is necessary even with the application of the so-called "global income tax" of the American-British type. Nevertheless, there is hardly ever a justification for different proportional rates for various types of economic activity, although the base may be calculated according to differing methods. As the system becomes more equitable in its impact upon various types of economic activity, one of the original arguments for differential treatment is automatically eliminated. A synthesis of patterns rather than a complete transfer appears as a desirable form of transferring techniques.

The main difficulty in transferring techniques from one country to the other consists in the continued evolution of the transferred techniques in the "mother-country," while the same evolution often does not take place in the underdeveloped countries to which the techniques have been exported. The schedular tax system, for instance, which has been transferred from France has undergone very significant changes in the 1948 tax reform in that country. Similarly, the British system has seen the addition of certain forms of taxation and also a number of basic modifications which have not been transferred to those countries abroad which operate on the basis of the original British system. This does not imply that all new developments in Britain should necessarily be reflected in countries to which the British fiscal system has been applied, but part of the changes are merely technical improvements which merit comparative evaluation.

Thus, as the fiscal systems continue to develop, it must be ascertained whether their organic growth has kept up with the modern trends in various countries in which they have been operating.

In this field almost everybody is a beginner, but it already appears that the future leaders in the field will be advanced experts from less-developed areas who understand not only the systems but the institutions to which they are to be applied.

The Technical Assistance Program of the United Nations is multinational in the sense that it gives technical assistance to itself. It is admittedly poorer and smaller than most of the bilateral programs. It is not accompanied by financial grants or loans.

It bases its work not only on the sending of experts but on the granting of fellowships and scholarships to persons from underdeveloped countries so that they themselves may implement the reforms which are called for by the development process. Backing up the programs of experts, fellowships, and scholarships is the research program of the Secretariat directed at a variety of national devices, systems, and methods the applicability of which is constantly tested against a diversity of levels of political, social, and economic development. One of the newer methods of testing is the seminar composed of experts from developed and underdeveloped countries who together evaluate the effectiveness of the various devices which have been recommended and which have already stood the test of practical application. Thus the UN program is one of learning together rather than teaching one another.

TECHNICAL AID FROM THE VIEWPOINT OF THE AID-RECEIVING COUNTRIES

By GEORGE HAKIM

A T THE outset I would like to restate a proposition which has been stated many times before and to which everybody agrees but which is sometimes forgotten. Technical aid is not an end in itself but is only a means to an end, which is the raising of the standard of living of the peoples of underdeveloped countries. Some of us are often so engrossed with the means we are studying and debating that we tend to forget the ends which these means are intended to serve. Technical aid is of no special significance in itself. In fact, the adoption of new technology by the underdeveloped countries is a painful process to which there is generally much cultural and economic resistance. But the new technology is a necessary means, though I would not say a necessary evil, without which increased production and higher standards of living cannot be attained. It is not, however, an all-sufficient means. By itself it does not necessarily lead to higher standards of living. There are other supplementary means which have to be used in the process of economic development so as to achieve the desired end of higher standards of living. This process may be long and arduous, for the road that has to be traveled between the application of the necessary means and the attainment of the ultimate aim is a rugged road with numerous pitfalls. Raising the standard of living of the peoples of underdeveloped countries requires long and strenuous efforts for the solution of difficult problems of organization and adaptation of modern technology to wholly new social and economic situations.

There follow from this simple proposition two self-evident conclusions. The first is that any technical aid which does not reach the majority of the people who are the producers of wealth will fail to bear its fruits in increased production and better standards of living. Technical assistance which remains in the form of reports, recommendations, programs, and blueprints of economic development which are not translated into new productive techniques adopted by the people engaged in the production of wealth will fall short of its purpose and will amount to a waste of effort and resources leading to frustration and disillusionment. The new technology which is so highly productive does not only need to be exported by the advanced countries but should become part of the economic life of the peoples of underdeveloped countries. It is not something which can be passed on from one government to another but something that should enter into the ways of living and working of the masses of the people. The second conclusion is that, even if the new techniques of production are adopted in agriculture and industry as a result of technical assistance, unless the resulting increase of wealth is shared in by the majority of the people, technical aid will fail to achieve its purpose. If the building of factories, hydroelectric plants, and irrigation systems and the use of fertilizers, insecticides, and machinery in agriculture only result in increasing the wealth of a small minority of the people, leaving the large majority as poor as they were before, technical aid will fall short of its aim to raise the standard of living of the people. In fact, the per capita income of an underdeveloped country may rise, and it may be said that the average standard of living is higher. But unless the higher income per capita means a higher standard of living for the majority of people, the aim of economic development will not be achieved. The result will only be to widen the gap between the rich minority who have grown richer and the poor majority whose poverty would then appear all the more glaring and all the more burdensome. Raising per capita income is not enough. The rise in national income must express itself in better food, clothing, and shelter, better health, better education, and a more decent and active life for the great majority of the people. These two conclusions are sometimes lost sight of by persons concerned with programs of technical aid for economic development. We must therefore constantly keep in mind and emphasize the raising of the standard of living of the majority of the people as the ultimate and necessary aim of economic development.

The main question for us, then, in considering technical aid from the viewpoint of the aid-receiving countries, is how this aid will affect the peoples of these countries, their productive activities as well as their living conditions. When we think of underdeveloped countries receiving technical assistance, we should think not only of their governments but also and mainly of their peoples. The term "country" vaguely refers both to government and to people. Those responsible for the administration of technical aid usually give consideration to the viewpoint of governments. This is both reasonable and proper, since they have to deal with governments; but they should not overlook the viewpoint of the people, whose attitude ultimately determines the success of all aid programs. In matters of economic development governments and peoples cannot always be considered identical. It would surely be an understatement to say that the governments of underdeveloped countries are not always, to use Lincoln's words, "governments of the people, by the people, and for the people." There is frequently a gap that separates the governments of these countries from their peoples. It is therefore a mistake to give too much attention to governments representing forces which are sooner or later destined to disappear and too little attention to the people. This mistake has often been committed in the past by governments of the advanced countries. In dealing with colonial and semicolonial territories, they have sought to win over a small minority group or class, strengthen it in its domination over the people, and allow it to reap the benefits of economic development, while the majority of the people remain in poverty and degradation. But even in the case of independent underdeveloped countries, the tendency of the Western powers as well as their private organizations and corporations is still to bolster up existing feudal and reactionary regimes rather than to help the progressive forces in opposition to them. But what does it profit you to win all the governments of the underdeveloped world and lose the people?

Bearing in mind this important distinction between governments and peoples, let us now consider technical aid not only from the viewpoint of governments of aid-receiving countries but also, where the distinction is significant, from the viewpoint of their peoples. The governments of underdeveloped countries have on various occasions expressed their appreciation of technical assistance programs and have welcomed offers of aid through the United Nations or directly by governments of advanced countries and, in particular, the United States government. These programs, however, have been slow to get under way and have not been on a scale that is anywhere adequate to meet their urgent requirements for foreign technical and capital resources. There has, therefore, been some impatience on the part of governments of underdeveloped countries not with the principle of technical aid but with its application. They have tended to regard the assistance offered as "too little and too late." In spite of the warning often repeated that the primary responsibility for economic development lies on the governments of underdeveloped countries themselves and that foreign assistance is intended only to help underdeveloped countries in helping themselves, many governments have found it difficult to face the overwhelming task of development and have tended to look for help from the advanced countries as the main element in the solution of the problem. They have therefore been generally disappointed that, after all the discussion and all the excitement, technical assistance programs seem to be so inadequate.

Governments of underdeveloped countries have also expressed doubts as to the efficacy of technical aid as it has so far been put into practice. It has consisted so far mainly of words leading to too little or no action. A great volume of words in the form of records of international debates as well as reports and recommendations of experts has been presented to government administrations totally unprepared to deal with them. Even the more detailed surveys and programs of development that have been prepared have usually gone into the files of governments unable to put them into execution. When the time comes to start operations, it may be found that the older plans are out of date or insufficient and that more reports and surveys are needed. This is exceedingly frustrating, not only to the authorities of the underdeveloped countries, but also to the experts and international organizations responsible for the preparation of surveys and the recommendation of development projects. The spectacle of foreign experts traveling to an underdeveloped country, staying there for a few weeks or months, and going back home while leaving everything exactly as it was, except for a few more files hidden away in some government department, strikes people as wasteful and futile, not to say ridiculous. While recognizing the value of reports, recommendations, and development plans, the responsible authorities of underdeveloped countries would like to see concrete results in the form of new methods of production, new factories, new enterprises, and new irrigation systems and hydroelectric plants. It is true that these things take time, money, and effort. But, if the means to bring them about are not available, the preparation of reports and plans would seem to have been so much wasted effort.

These considerations have led governments of underdeveloped countries to emphasize the great importance of capital in addition to technical aid as a necessary and basic element in the process of economic development. The provision of capital involves the availability not only of financial resources but also of capital goods for new investment. The new technology to be applied in increasing production for raising standards of living must embody itself in durable capital goods and other producers' goods to be utilized in the productive process. It is impossible to separate capital from technology. They are basic elements which should be applied jointly in the process of production. Technical aid therefore will be sterile without financial aid with which to secure the material means of production. Where capital exists in the undderdeveloped countries or can be easily made available from foreign sources, technical assistance will be very valuable in helping to make the best use of available resources. But in most underdeveloped countries domestic capital is not sufficient and foreign capital is not available to fill the breach. In such cases it is necessary in order to avoid waste to see to it that capital resources are made available together with technical aid.

Another question about which governments of underdeveloped countries are concerned relates to the type of development which is to be promoted. From the viewpoint of these countries, the major aim of economic development is industrialization. They are therefore disturbed when they find evidence of lack of enthusiasm for this aim, not to say opposition to it, on the part of the industrialized countries, which seem to lay the main emphasis on development of production of primary products including food and industrial raw materials and particularly strategic materials. It is significant, for example, that a very high proportion of United States foreign investments has gone into mineral production. In recent years 70 per cent of the capital invested in foreign countries has gone into petroleum development. The underdeveloped countries believe that in the long run no appreciable rise in the national income can be achieved without a substantial development of manufacturing industries. In fact, in some of the densely populated countries of Asia and the Middle East which have considerable underemployment in agriculture, industrialization is the only method of achieving a significant increase in national production by utilizing the surplus labor that can be withdrawn from agriculture without reduction in output. It is also the only way of finding employment for a growing population in countries where the possibility of extending cultivation to new land is extremely limited. For these and other reasons underdeveloped countries are anxious to see the major part of technical and financial aid directed toward industrial development.

Governments of aid-receiving countries have also had their doubts as to the purposes of foreign aid, whether technical or financial. This aid is being offered by powerful countries with economic and political interests throughout the world. These countries have been associated in the experience of underdeveloped countries with imperialist domination. This historical experience cannot be easily forgotten. In fact, imperialism is still practiced in one way or another in certain underdeveloped and colonial areas. It should not be difficult, therefore, to explain and to understand the fears of certain governments whose experience with imperialism is not too remote in the past and who can still see it practiced not very far from their borders. These governments are only prepared to accept foreign economic assistance if it is offered without any strings attached. But, even where it is so offered, they are afraid that there will be some political interference in practice. This principle of non-interference, however, may sometimes cover the opposition of existing governments to any radical social and economic changes which may undermine their authority. It is here that a divergence may appear between the interests of a minority group or class and the majority of the people.

This point provides us with an appropriate transition from the viewpoint of governments of aid-receiving countries to the viewpoint of the peoples of these countries. In many underdeveloped countries the nationalist movement for liberation from imperialist rule and domination has successfully mobilized the patriotism of the people against foreign rule or interference. With the successful achievement of independence, however, the woes and sufferings of the people attributed to the foreign imperialists have not come to an end. The nationalist leaders have found it difficult to eliminate the basic evils besetting their people and are gradually losing the confidence of the majority of the people, who are slowly waking up to their misery. It is true, of course, that the task of raising the level of large populations is a formidable one and that existing governments cannot be rightfully blamed for failing to accomplish it in a short period of time. The main reason, however, for their failure even to make a beginning to the solution of the problem is that they have proved incapable of carrying out the basic reforms and institutional changes without which the task of economic development can never be accomplished. One of the most important of these basic reforms is land reform to provide the institutional framework within which technological advance and productive investment in agriculture would become possible. It is futile to expect the share tenant in some underdeveloped countries to adopt new techniques of cultivation and to make investments on the land. Land reform is therefore essential for any appreciable increase in agricultural productivity.

The failure of many existing governments to carry out a program of social and economic reform is to be explained by the existence within them of reactionary forces whose interest is to maintain the existing economic and social structure. The mentality of these reactionary elements is such that they cannot realize the dangers which threaten their countries and themselves as a result of the failure to deal with the basic social and economic evils from which the majority of their people suffer and which may finally call for extremist revolutions. The more liberal and forward-looking elements in existing governments seem to have become captives of these reactionary forces and of existing institutions. It is doubtful that they have enough power to maintain their authority and impose basic reforms against the forces opposing economic and social progress. Gradually therefore they accept compromise and content themselves with superficial and ineffective solutions which are incapable of meeting the challenge of the great problems with which they are faced. They tend, therefore, to turn away from the basic solutions required and to seek foreign technical and financial assistance to help them in the difficult situation in which they find themselves. The moment, however, that such foreign assistance seeks to find the basic evils and to introduce basic reforms, the reactionary forces cry out against foreign interference which has long been the familiar slogan of the struggle against imperialist domination. In the new era of national independence, however, this outcry often has a false ring in the ears of the people, who are beginning to lose confidence in their old leaders. But the people themselves are confused and sometimes even ignorant of their best interests. Their most characteristic attitude is one of indifference and skepticism. The indifference is bred out of a long experience of oppression or, to say the least, of mere neglect. The skepticism results from the long absence of any genuine and serious attempt to improve their economic and social condition.

In spite of this attitude of mind, however, the common people would slowly respond to any genuine effort that would result in concrete benefits to them. It is true that both by nationalism and by economic interest they will resist attempts at imperialist intervention and domination. But they are coming slowly to realize that there is no hope for them from the small reactionary minority which maintains its domination over them. They are also waking up to the fact that imperialism helped fasten the rule of this minority over them in the past. Therefore, they would not like to see foreign assistance now used to strengthen the power of this minority.

What, then, would be the attitude of the people of underdeveloped countries to programs of technical and financial aid? To begin with, one would expect an attitude of waiting to judge by concrete results. But, aside from this passive and noncommittal attitude, the people cannot fail to respond favorably in the long run to genuine efforts to improve their condition. If such efforts take the form of foreign assistance directed toward securing basic reforms in the social and economic structure which would evidently lead to a betterment of their condition, the people would not only accept such assistance but would welcome it as a contribution toward raising their standards of living. To give a simple example, the landless agricultural workers and share tenants of underdeveloped countries would not fail to welcome assistance to implement a program of land reform which would give them land and would set them up as independent family farmers. In fact, the peasant class has more than once been won over by movements which make precisely such promises. There is no reason, therefore, for governments of advanced countries which wish to render assistance for economic development to shy away from measures wrongly regarded as interference in the affairs of other countries as long as they are directed toward the raising of living standards which is a recognized aim of the United Nations. For under a policy of so-called noninterference, technical and financial aid may result in benefits to a reactionary and corrupt group or class and leave the majority of the people in poverty. It would then amount in practice to a kind of interference which would bolster up corrupt regimes that might be overthrown by the people without foreign aid. In fact, the choice, in many cases, is not really between interference and noninterference but between interference in the interest of reaction and interference in the interest of progress. And, if foreign aid is to be successful, it must always be in the interest of progress.

What is important is to win over the people and not minority reactionary groups or classes which would ultimately be swept away in the march of progress. This can be done only by giving help and support to the progressive forces which can lead the people in a movement of social and economic reform without which economic development leading to higher standards of living is impossible. Ways and means can be found to give this help and support to the progressive forces in the underdeveloped countries without causing friction between governments. An aid-giving country should be free to adopt and proclaim the policy of giving technical and financial aid for the promotion of particular objectives such as land reform or rural education. The rejection of such aid by a government of an underdeveloped country would weaken it among the people and would strengthen the progressive forces in their struggle for social and economic reform. In order to avoid friction between aid-giving and aid-receiving governments, the United Nations and its affiliated international organizations may serve as the proper agencies to help bring about progressive social and economic development But whether through the United Nations or through direct assistance, all help must be given to the progressive forces in the underdeveloped countries on which falls the primary responsibility to undertake and bring to fruition the great tasks of social and economic progress.

In the present world situation there is one problem which seems to overshadow all others and which has a heavy impact on all programs of aid for economic development. I am, of course, referring to the present world political and ideological struggle. Many governments of underdeveloped countries are afraid of involvement in this struggle and are anxious to maintain a position of neutrality between the two powerful camps engaged in it. This neutralism can be understood as a manifestation of military weakness and of a desire to avoid the terrible destruction that may result from participation in the struggle. For countries which have little power with which to defend themselves and the homes of their people, there is an understandable tendency to avoid getting involved in a conflict over which they have little control. People all over the world want peace more than anything else, both for self-preservation and as a necessary condition for economic development. They cannot therefore agree to participation in the world struggle as a price for foreign economic assistance. Nor should that price be required of them. On the contrary, economic assistance by the advanced countries to the underdeveloped must have its own rewards in that it not only would help to raise standards of living but also would help to bring about international stability and peace. A higher standard of living for all human beings is certainly important in itself. But it is also essential for the preservation of peace and freedom. It is only when people have a decent way of life to defend that they will struggle to preserve it. But, if they are poor and miserable, they will be indifferent to the world struggle and can easily be led to participate in any movement that promises improvement of their condition.

The ultimate reward of economic assistance must be that, through the economic development to which it would contribute, it would bring about the basic conditions necessary for world stability and world prosperity. It is these two parallel objectives, peace and social and economic progress, which are consecrated in the Charter of the United Nations. They can be best achieved through a vigorous United Nations in which all peoples participate in the construction of a peaceful and prosperous world.

EFFECTS OF INDUSTRIALIZATION ON THE MARKETS OF INDUSTRIAL COUNTRIES

By Albert O. Hirschman

B EFORE tracing the history of ideas in this field I shall present a short analytical discussion of the agreements at stake. Industrialization of new areas has two effects on the markets of the old industrial countries. We may call them the market-destroying and the market-creating effects.

The market-destroying effects.—It is easy enough to understand how industrialization of new areas can be harmful for the established industrial countries. Certainly the local refining of ores and canning of food will take work away from the refineries and canneries of the countries that previously imported materials and foodstuffs in their raw state. No doubt the setting-up of cotton mills in the developing countries reduces the market of the old-established cotton industries.

It is also possible that the country with the newly established industries may eventually compete successfully with the older industrial countries in third markets, and we cannot even exclude the possibility that it may do so in the market of the very country that originally supplied it with finished goods as well as with the capital necessary for industrialization. Is it not natural enough, then, to cast the industrializing country in the role of the snake reared and nursed at the bosom of the older industrial countries?

The strength of this argument lies in its simplicity and directness. In this it has a striking affinity to the early arguments against the introduction of labor-saving machinery. The counterarguments are very similar in both cases. It is shown, first, that the harmful direct effects described above are more than compensated by a number of beneficial indirect effects. Second, it is argued that the incriminated process is already under way, that it cannot be halted, and that therefore it is far better to lead it into beneficial or at least innocuous channels rather than futilely to oppose and bemoan it.

The market-creating effects.—The first market-creating rather than market-destroying effect of industrialization (here again the analogy with the argument for the introduction of labor-saving machinery is obvious) relates to the demand for capital goods in the newly industrializing country. This demand clearly has been for some time of the greatest importance for the continued vitality of the exports of older industrial countries. Nevertheless, in itself the new demand for, say, textile machinery cannot lastingly compensate for the loss of old markets for finished textiles.[1]

The second and more powerful market-creating effect of industrialization rests on its income-generating aspects. It is easily shown how for many countries a soundly conceived process of industrialization is a necessary component of any development that would lift these countries to higher levels of real income. These increases in income will result in higher demands for all kinds of goods including imports. In this fashion new markets will be created all around, and in the end the older industrial countries will find that they can export new varieties of manufacturers in far greater quantities than previously.

The statistical evidence.—These arguments are valid enough, and they are made even more convincing by the statistical evidence that has been accumulated in their support. The statistical material has brought out the following facts:

1. Not only do imports of all kinds show a universal tendency to rise with per capita income,[2] but imports of manufactured goods have generally increased in countries progressing along the road of industrialization.

The increase in imports of manufactures generally lagged be-

1. A. J. Brown, *Industrialization and Trade* (London, 1943), pp. 36–39.

2. With respect to the United States, for instance, it has recently been calculated that from 1936 to 1940 "the people of the well-developed areas bought from the United States on the average $5.80 worth of goods per person per annum; the people of the intermediate areas bought on the average only $1.25 worth; and those of the underdeveloped areas only 70¢ worth" (Department of State, *Point Four* [Washington, 1950], p. 10).

hind the increase in local manufacturing, but it is worthy of note that imports of manufactures generally showed a tendency to rise most in countries where a rapid process of industrialization took place.

This relationship is illustrated by Table 1, taken from the

TABLE 1

COUNTRY	1926/29 AS PERCENTAGE OF 1891/95	
	Manufacturing	Imports of Manufactures
Japan...............................	1,932	628
Finland.............................	583	473
United States......................	436	230
Sweden.............................	405	480
Italy...............................	394	189
Germany............................	279	185
France.............................	260	127
United Kingdom and Ireland...	143	195

League of Nations report on *Industrialization and Foreign Trade.*[3]

2. World trade is not by any means confined to the exchange of manufacturers against foodstuffs and raw materials. This "traditional type of interchange," in fact, amounts to only about one-third of total world trade; the remaining two-thirds consist of the exchange of some foodstuffs and raw materials against other foodstuffs and raw materials, on the one hand, and, on the other, of the exchange of some manufactures against other manufactures. It has been shown that approximately one-half of the manufactures entering world trade are exchanged against other manufactures and only the other half against foodstuffs and raw materials.[4] In a more detailed way, it has been shown that many countries "export and import what are apparently the same commodities," whereas, in fact, they

3. (Princeton, 1945), p. 93.

4. A. O. Hirschman, *National Power and the Structure of Foreign Trade* (Berkeley 1945), pp. 117–57.

are only broadly similar but differ in quality, price, design, and in other respects.[5]

These statistical findings show only that *on balance* industrial countries have nothing to fear, and much to gain, from the industrialization of other countries. Naturally they do not and cannot show that there will be no harm to any industry or firm. It is clear that industrialization will mean smaller markets and more competition for *some* industries of the old industrial countries.

Eugene Staley has stressed that, in order to maximize the net gain to be derived by the industrial countries from the industrialization of underdeveloped countries, the old industrial countries must strive to fulfil three conditions: (1) The exports of these countries should specialize as much as possible in such lines as are likely to be benefited, rather than hurt, by industrialization abroad. These lines are capital goods and such consumers goods whose production is rather complex and whose consumption is sensitive to rises in income. (2) These countries must actively develop new and improved processes and products so as to maintain their trade position with as little disturbance as possible. (3) Finally, these countries must maintain a sufficient degree of mobility and adaptability in their economy so as to be able to shift resources away from those branches which are threatened by foreign industrialization.[6]

Given these conditions, it is clear that the picture cannot be entirely bright for all countries. In fact, I believe that, when a number of countries have reached an advanced degree of industrialization, far-reaching institutional changes will be required to maintain among them a division of labor whose prime determinants are no longer differences in climate and natural resources.

International trade in an industrialized world.—A division of labor based essentially on differences in skill and on the past history of industrial development is likely to be more unstable than

5. H. Frankel, "The Industrialization of Agricultural Countries," *Economic Journal*, LIII (June–September, 1943), 188–201.

6. *World Economic Development* (Montreal, 1944), pp. 159 ff.

the simple and "natural" division of labor between industrial and agricultural nations. Countries with an established system of industry, with a good transportation system, and with a pool of engineers and technically skilled workers can usually graft additional lines of output onto their existing industrial structure without too much difficulty. In every single instance the loss from the pre-existing international specialization is likely to be small, although in the aggregate these losses may be quite considerable. For this reason, disintegration of the finely wrought international division of labor which we have in mind here is dangerously likely as long as nations remain entirely free to pursue autonomous domestic economic policies, as long as sectional interests can push for special advantages under the cover of national interest, and as long as the special risks affecting international as opposed to internal trade have not been eliminated.[7]

One example may perhaps make clear this proposition. Typewriters are produced in the United States today almost exclusively in the Northeast, while Hollywood has a virtual monopoly on the production of movies. This division of labor is based more on historical accident than on any basic difference in the distribution of natural or human resources. Nevertheless, it is presumably beneficial to both movie-goers and typewriter-uses, and there is little prospect that Los Angeles will add the production of typewriters and New York State or Massachusetts that of movies, thereby destroying these benefits. But would this still be the case if a national boundary line were drawn tomorrow somewhere down the middle of the country? Is it not likely that at one time or the other the West Coast state would then experience balance-of-payments difficulties with the East Coast state and would restrict the importation of typewriters? Would not, then, a profitable internal market be created in the West Coast state for the "domestic" production of such machines just as, in the absence of European imports

7. D. H. Robertson diagnosed this danger in his article, "The Future of International Trade," *Economic Journal*, XLVIII (1938), 1–14, reprinted in *Readings in the Theory of International Trade*, eds. H. S. Ellis and L. A. Metzler (Philadelphia, 1949), pp. 505–6.

during World War II, California was quick to build up a ceramics industry? And, once such an industry had come into being, would it not be likely to be protected by the West Coast state, to "safeguard employment" and for similar well-known reasons, even after the balance-of-payments difficulties have long been overcome? Are we not then confirming, through a slightly more sophisticated route, the very thesis which we thought we had refuted, namely, that world-wide industrialization makes the future of internationl atrade dark and hazardous indeed?

In answering this question, we must first repeat that this danger is remote insofar as the undeveloped countries are concerned. It has taken on actuality only for the small but important group of countries formed by the United States and western Europe. Within this group we have indeed already experienced a substantial regression from the delicate integration that existed within it before the first World War or again in the twenties. But within this group also we are now witnessing the beginning of a major effort to reverse this process by changing the institutional framework within which the intertrade of the group operates. By creating closer forms of economic association, it is hoped that serious divergences of national economic policies can be avoided, that sectional interests can be held in check, and that the special risks affecting foreign trade can in general be reduced.

It remains to be seen to what extent this aim can be achieved through co-operation in the economic field alone. Closer forms of political association may be required to convert what is today international trade into the interregional trade of tomorrow.

Thus, provided we retain flexibility in our economic structure and do not consider existing political institutions as immutable, we need not fear even a very much more advanced process of industrialization than any in immediate prospect as the result of the development of underdeveloped countries. The opposite belief, however, has had a long history and has at times importantly influenced the attitudes and policies of governments. I shall now review a number of manifestations of this belief, particularly on the part of European industrial countries, and shall then contrast the American with the European attitude in this respect.

Attitudes of European industrial countries toward industrialization abroad.—"Is Export of Machinery Economic Suicide?" This succinct question was the title of a little tract published at the beginning of the century by one of the lone free-trade economists of imperial Germany.[8] The tract ably answered the question in the negative, but its publication was symptomatic of the widespread alarm that was felt at the time in Germany about the industrialization of new areas of the world and about the "suicidal," though, in the meantime, highly profitable help in this process extended by the older industrial countries.

In truth, the technically more advanced countries have been remarkably inconsistent in their attitude toward the less advanced countries ever since the rise of manufacturing: they have alternatively and often simultaneously helped, feared, and attempted to block the efforts of these countries to acquire industrial techniques and equipment. The most consistent attempt at blocking was made during the mercantilist period when all manufacturing nations issued prohibitions against the exports of machinery and the emigration of skilled artisans; these regulations could not be enforced with the coming of the industrial age, and evasions became so widespread that they either fell into disuse or were formally repealed, as happened in England a century ago.[9] But while England did nothing to prevent the

8. Heinrich Dietzel, *Ist Maschinenausfuhr volkswirtschaftlicher Selbstmord?* (Berlin, 1907).

9. "The export of machines was prohibited because it was feared that this would help a competing industry in another country. One of the first examples of this was the export prohibition . . . against stocking frames in England (1695/96), followed by a similar measure in France in 1724. About this time there was also a considerable fine in France on the export of textile implements in general. In various other ways, too, every possible obstacle was placed in the way of this export. At the beginning of the 1720's, Jonas Alstromer, the most enthusiastic protagonist of manufactures in Sweden in the 18th century, experienced the greatest of difficulties in smuggling from France and Holland the equipment which he needed for the formation of the Alingsas textile works. In England it was not until a somewhat later date (1750 and 1774) that the export of various textile machines and instruments was forbidden and there soon followed similar prohibitions against the export of iron-producing machinery (1781). Once this policy had been set going it was elaborated on all sides and pursued for a considerable time. In England, the country where an independent machine industry

spreading of industrial methods to other nations that marked the second half of the nineteenth century, this development did not fail to arouse many misgivings. No less an economist than Stanley Jevons warned in 1865 that the emigration toward the United States would "develop, or rather complete, abroad systems of iron and steel industry in direct competition with ours."[10] Even earlier, a similar concern about foreign industrialization can be found in Torrens' writings.[11] Some of the classical economists may have been led to take this position because they tended to think rather rigidly in terms of the two-country, two-commodity model of international trade. (It might give some comfort to the anthropologists in our midst if the economists admitted freely that, in the theory of international trade, this model is the economist's equivalent for the Hopi Indians.) If one reasons about the process of industrialization with this model in mind, a pessimistic outlook for the future of international trade is inevitable. Another reason for the concern shown by some of the nineteenth-century economists was the way in which the law of diminishing returns was expected to operate in reducing the profitability of agriculture in the food-exporting countries.

The rapid rise of German and American industry benefited the British economy in many respects but at the same time alarmed British opinion. An extensive literature grew up toward the end of the century describing in particular the disastrous dangers of the German trade rivalry.[12]

But the fears of the industrialization of undeveloped countries found their most outspoken expression in Germany itself; with rather bad taste, that country had hardly joined the small band of industrialized countries when it was already intent on

---

originated, the prohibition against its export was not abandoned in effect before 1825, while officially it persisted until 1843" (Eli F. Heckscher, *Mercantilism* [London, 1934], II, 147).

10. *The Coal Question* (3d rev. ed.; London, 1906), p. 424.

11. As quoted by Jacob Viner in "The Prospects for Foreign Trade in the Postwar World," *Transactions of the Manchester Statistical Society* (1946), reprinted in *Readings in the Theory of International Trade* (Philadelphia, 1949), p. 520.

12. Ross J. S. Hoffmann, *Great Britain and the German Trade Rivalry, 1875–1914* (Philadelphia, 1933).

slamming the door behind it in the face of any additional new-comers.

German writers taunted Britain for the "short-sightedness" with which she had helped—through large-scale capital export as well as by what we call today "technical assistance"—her future competitors to grow. Thus a German writer of the historical school, whose comprehensive treatment of British foreign-trade policy was translated into English, exclaimed:

> The question arises as to whether English investments of capital abroad are, economically speaking, altogether advantageous. They most certainly are not, if a competing industry is thereby supported abroad.[13]
>
> Is it, for instance, really advantageous, from the economic point of view, when a well-known English politician, formerly a cotton spinner in England, invests his whole fortune in spinning wheels in Saxony, and becomes an active competitor on Continental and other markets with the home industry? It may be said with truth that the rapid industrial growth of the Continent and the United States which has overthrown England's industrial hegemony, has been, to a great extent, made possible and even promoted by English capital.[14]

German policy did its best not to repeat what it deemed to have been the British mistake. Export of capital was to serve well-defined, national interests, and the close collaboration among industry, the banks, and the government made foreign investment, in the words of Feis, into an "integral part of the German outward thrust."[15] Moreover, the record of Germany's foreign economic policy before both World Wars I and II actually contains several instances of direct attempts at preventing industrialization of other countries.[16]

With the possible exception of their own colonies, it proved, however, generally impossible for the older industrial countries to prevent the spread of industrialization to other countries, and, once this was clear, every industrial country wished for its own manufacturers to capture the profitable market in capital

13. C. J. Fuchs, *The Trade Policy of Great Britain and Her Colonies since 1860* (London, 1908), p. 208.

14. *Ibid.*, p. 210.

15. Herbert Feis, *Europe: The World's Banker, 1870–1914* (New Haven, 1930), p. 188.

16. For German policy prior to World War I see Jacob Viner, *Dumping: A Problem of International Trade* (Chicago, 1924), p. 52. Literature on Germany's foreign economic policies before World War II in this respect is too voluminous to be quoted here.

goods that was the consequence of world-wide industrialization. Nevertheless, opinion in the industrial countries always remained apprehensive about the ultimate outcome of the process. The effect in the interwar period of the Japanese trade expansion on specific old-established industries such as the British cotton mills seemed to justify the many pessimistic forecasts.

The United States attitude.—Among the many expressions of these gloomy views, one voice is almost consistently absent: that of the United States. Indeed, once this country turned its attention to the problem, it was in order to foster the development of undeveloped countries through the promotion of the International Bank for Reconstruction and Development, through the development loans of the Export-Import Bank, and, finally, through the elaboration of the Point IV program. It is of considerable interest to analyze the probable reasons for the apparent absence of concern in the United States over any untoward effect of foreign development and industrialization on the United States economy. For, in the course of this analysis, not only will we discover why we have been traditionally exempt of a fear that has afflicted most other industrial countries but we will also find out whether we have any reasons to change our traditional outlook on this problem.

Possibly the most important reasons for our lack of concern about industrialization abroad is the composition of our exports. In contrast with a country such as the United Kingdom, our exports of manufactures consist typically of articles that are geared either to increases in production (machine tools and other capital goods) or to high and expanding levels of income (automobiles and other consumers durables). For this reason our exports are not only not endangered by industrialization and development abroad but, on the contrary, stand to gain considerably from expanding production and rising incomes in other parts of the world. This is in marked contrast with those industrial countries whose exports were mainly based on such goods as textiles, hardware, glassware, etc., the production of which is usually among the first undertaken by newly industrializing countries. Moreover, the United States also exports substantial quantities of industrial raw materials, such as cotton, petroleum, sulphur, etc., and these exports therefore are likely to gain directly from an expansion of manufacturing abroad.

The industrial countries of Europe, in particular England and Germany, viewed with concern and alarm the building of foreign industries not alone because of the prospective competition for their own export industries; there was the additional fear that, once the foreign markets were lost, they would not have any countervalue to offer for the foodstuffs and raw materials on whose massive imports they had come to rely for the sustenance and employment of their people. Actually, the "fear of becoming a predominantly industrial state," often voiced in Germany during the period of rapid industrialization toward the end of the nineteenth century, had in part its roots in this vision of a country that finds itself suddenly deprived of the essential supplies because it can no longer market its manufactures abroad. Such apprehensions gave considerable impetus to the German policies of agricultural protection and of colonialism.

In the United States such fears could never become very oppressive, for the dependence of our economy on foreign supplies has always been quantitatively and qualitatively of a much smaller order than that of the western European industrial countries. There would be no starvation in the United States even if we were to be cut off overnight from our foreign sources of supply as a result of industrialization abroad.

There are other less tangible factors that are equally important in explaining the United States attitude toward foreign development. After all, the differences in foreign-trade structure between Germany and the United States, important as they are, are not so great as to explain why Germany should have been generally alarmed and the United States largely unconcerned by industrialization abroad. For if the United States had good reasons for its attitude, the German fears were largely unfounded. Even some contemporaries pointed out, statistics in hand, that industrial countries usually are each other's best customers. The truth is that German writers took a certain delight in showing that the industrial countries were digging their own grave through the export of machinery and industrial techniques. This propensity for discovering apocalyptic historical vistas has been a general trait of German historical and sociological writing since the nineteenth century. It can for, example, also be found in the familiar Marxist analysis which showed how capitalism was preparing its own destruction through the creation of a proletariat and how competition was destined for extinction because of the way in which the competitive struggle led to monopoly. These numerous prophecies of doom do not teach us so much about the real nature of industrialism, capitalism, and competition as about the state of mind of their intellectual authors, ill at ease in the industrial age, and therefore inordinately fertile in finding proofs for its inevitable dissolution.

The fundamental reason why these theories have never gained much credence or influence in the United States is to be found in the absence of the many conflicts and strains—deeply imbedded in history—that in Germany and many other European countries resulted in a widespread intellectual hostility toward industrial capitalism. In this country any difficulties accompanying our economic development were generally interpreted as difficulties of growth, remedies for which could readily be found from case to case, rather than as deep-seated cracks fated to bring about the collapse of our whole economic structure.

Instead of casting an uneasy eye toward the industrial advances of other countries, we have always believed in the possibilities of further economic and technological progress and in our ability to maintain industrial leadership. Moreover, our economic history testifies abundantly to the benefits of vigorous industrial expansion; and a theory maintaining that any further extension of industrialism, be it within or without our borders, is disastrous or even dangerous, is prima facie suspect to us.

These historical and psychological reasons are at least as important as the purely economic ones in explaining not only why we have practiced foreign economic and industrial development but why, unlike other industrial nations, we have generally not been alarmed by this practice and have lately taken the lead in advocating it as a matter of public policy.

In fact, it is not so much the advocacy of the Point IV program that testifies to the "carefree attitude" of the United States with regard to the fostering of foreign competition through capital export, but even more the aid that we have made available to the industrial countries of western Europe and to Japan over the past years. When we undertook to give large-scale aid to these countries, the threat of potential competition on their part lay not decades but just a few years ahead. Occasionally, of course, consideration was given to the question of competition with established American industry. A well-known instance is the building and modernization of oil refineries in Europe through ECA funds. While in such cases the point of view of our domestic industry was taken into account, the final decision favored a considerable expansion of European facilities. It is maybe significant that it was a European agency staffed primarily by European economists, the Economic Commission for Europe, that called attention to the fact that the United States was possibly doing a slightly foolish thing in building up European industry. It said in its *Economic Survey of Europe in 1948:*

> The United States is thus in the strange position of financing a programme which is directed largely towards the reduction of its own exports. It faces the anomalous prospect that, by the end of the programme, it will have surpluses and excess production capacity in commodities for which it has helped (directly or indirectly) to develop substitute sources of supply elsewhere; its own exports to Europe will be reduced below the depression-shrunk volume of 1938; and Europe nevertheless will still be short of dollars to cover its imports from the United States.[17]

These sentences are strangely reminiscent of the passage quoted earlier in which we saw Herr Fuchs shake his head about the way in which the British had built up their competitors a century ago.

In spite of the Economic Commission for Europe, the latest period of transfer of capital among the industrial countries will perhaps leave an imprint even on those countries that have

17. Economic Commission for Europe, *Economic Survey of Europe in 1948* (Geneva, 1949), p. 222.

traditionally shown most concern about industrialization abroad. It has been demonstrated to them that the only way in which any nation can hope to maintain industrial leadership is through a continuous process of economic growth and technological improvement.

All in all, it is therefore not surprising that our proceedings have focused almost exclusively on development and industrialization as viewed from the underdeveloped countries. Occasional doubts and objections have been raised in our meetings primarily because ill-conceived efforts at development would bring with them a number of undesirable effects on the stability and cohesion of native societies so that the process on the whole would do more harm than good. I believe that our present attitude does represent a genuine advance, provided that we do not pile up new imaginary dangers and obstacles in the way of foreign development that, just because they are not tainted by "selfishness," might be more effective than the older fears which we appear to have largely overcome.

APPENDIX

LIST OF PARTICIPANTS OF THE TWENTY-SEVENTH HARRIS INSTITUTE

ALLBAUGH, LELAND G., Rockefeller Foundation, New York, New York
AUBREY, HENRY G., Institute of World Affairs, New School for Social Research
BARENTS, J., Department of Political Science, University of Amsterdam
BEALS, CARLETON, Guilford, Connecticut
BEKKER, KONRAD, American Embassy, New Delhi, India
BLACK, HERMANN DAVID, University of Sydney, Sydney, Australia
BLOCH, HENRY S., United Nations, New York, New York
BONNE, ALFRED, The Hebrew University, Jerusalem, Israel
BROZEN, YALE, Department of Economics, Northwestern University
CALEF, WESLEY, Department of Geography, University of Chicago
CARSON, GEORGE B., Department of History, University of Chicago
CRANE, ROBERT I., Department of History, University of Chicago
EASTERBROOK, W. THOMAS, Department of Political Economy, University of Toronto
EGGAN, FRED, Department of Anthropology, University of Chicago
FRIEDENBERG, EDGAR Z., Division of Social Sciences, University of Chicago
GERSCHENKRON, ALEXANDER, Department of Economics, Harvard University
GLICK, M. PHILIP, Technical Co-operation Administration, Department of State
GOLDSCHMIDT, WALTER, Department of Anthropology and Sociology, University of California
GRODZINS, MORTON M., Department of Political Science, University of Chicago
GRUNEBAUM, GUSTAVE E. VON, Oriental Institute, University of Chicago
HAAS, ERNST, Department of Political Science, University of California
HAKIM, GEORGE, Legation of Lebanon, Washington, D.C.
HANDLIN, OSCAR, Department of History, Harvard University
HAYES, SAMUEL P., Technical Co-operation Administration, Washington, D.C.
HERSEY, ARTHUR B., Board of Governors of the Federal Reserve System
HERSKOVITS, MELVILLE J., Department of Anthropology, Northwestern University
HIRSCHMAN, ALBERT O., Board of Governors of the Federal Reserve System
HISSINK, KARIN, Frobenius Institute, Frankfurt/Main, Germany
HOSELITZ, BERT F., Committee on International Relations, University of Chicago
HUGHES, EVERETT C., Department of Sociology, University of Chicago
ISSAWI, CHARLES, United Nations
JANOWITZ, MORRIS, Department of Sociology, University of Michigan
JOHNSON, D. GALE, Department of Economics, University of Chicago

KINDLEBERGER, CHARLES P., Department of Economics and Social Science, Massachusetts Institute of Technology

KRUEGER, MAYNARD C., The College, University of Chicago

LAMB, HELEN BOYDEN, Research Associate in Economics, Massachusetts Institute of Technology

LAMB, ROBERT K., Department of English and History, Massachusetts Institute of Technology

LANTIS, MARGARET, Department of Hygiene, Harvard University

LEVY, MARION J., Department of Economics and Social Institutions, Princeton University

LINTON, RALPH, Institute of Human Relations, Yale University

McQUOWN, NORMAN A., Department of Anthropology, University of Chicago

MALENBAUM, WILFRED, Department of State

MEIER, RICHARD L., Department of Planning, University of Chicago

METZLER, LLOYD A., Department of Economics, University of Chicago

MINGES, ROBERT J., TCA Mission, Teheran

MORGENTHAU, HANS J., Department of Political Science, University of Chicago

MORIN, ALEXANDER, Agricultural Research Project, University of Chicago

OGBURN, WILLIAM F., Department of Sociology, University of Chicago

OPLER, MORRIS E., Department of Anthropology, Cornell University

PLATT, ROBERT S., Department of Geography, University of Chicago

PRITCHARD, EARL H., Department of History, University of Chicago

REDFIELD, ROBERT, Department of Anthropology, University of Chicago

REISS, ALBERT J., JR., Department of Sociology, University of Chicago

ROSEN, S. McKEE, Bureau of the Budget, Washington, D.C.

SACKS, MILTON, Department of Political Science, Yale University

SENIOR, CLARENCE, Research Associate, Bureau of Applied Social Research, Columbia University

SINGER, MILTON B., The College, University of Chicago

SMITH, WILFRED CANTWELL, Department of Comparative Religion, McGill University

TAX, SOL, Department of Anthropology, University of Chicago

THOMPSON, KENNETH, Department of Political Science, University of Chicago

UTLEY, CLIFTON M., National Broadcasting Company, Chicago, Illinois

VINER, JACOB, Department of Economics and Social Institutions, Princeton University

WATNICK, MORRIS, Department of State

WILSON, JOHN A., Oriental Institute, University of Chicago

WOHL, R. RICHARD, Research Center in Entrepreneurial History, Harvard University

WRIGHT, LOUISE LEONARD, Chicago Council on Foreign Relations

WRIGHT, QUINCY, Department of Political Science, University of Chicago

INDEX

INDEX

Adamic, Louis, 55 n.
Adams, John 37
Adloff, R., 163 n.
Africa, 92–108, 140, 146–47, 213–14
Agrarian reform, 157, 165
Agrarian revolts, 158, 166–68
Agriculture
  balance with industry, 14–15, 44
  planned development of, 103–4, 132,
    143–44, 212–15, 239, 243–44
  rehabilitation of, 132, 134, 210, 212,
    238, 243–44
  size of plot, 81–82, 109
  see also Agrarian reform; Agrarian
    revolts; Land
Ala'i, Heshmet, 212 n.
Allen, H. B., 210 n.
American Indians, 76, 80 (Navaho), 86,
  87 (Pueblo), 137–38 (Navaho), 141
  (Hopi), 142–43 (Athabaskan), 143–
  44 (Blackfoot), 148 (Hopi, Zuni,
  Ojibwa), 149 (Pueblo)
American Revolution, 30, 32, 36–39, 41,
  48–49
Anderson, Richmond K., 138 n.
Anglo-American Loan Agreement, 179–80
Anglo-French Commercial Treaty of
  1860, 10, 23
Arnold, Matthew, 24

Bacon, Francis, 207 and n.
Balfour, M. C., 218 n., 219 n. 220 n.
Banking, 10–13, 18–20
Banks
  commercial, 11–12, 21
  concentration of, 14, 20
  industrial, 10–12, 13, 20
  international, 10–11
Bardi (Florentine financial family), 33
Bauer, Otto, 153 n., 155 n.
Bazard, Amand, 22
Benedict, Ruth, 147 n.
Berthoff, Rowland T., 57 n., 58 n.
Bipolar world, 29, 30, 45, 50, 179–80,
  201–2, 268–69
Bloom, Herbert I., 56 n.
Bourbon (French royal family), 10
Bridge, James Howard, 59 n.

Bright, John, 24
Brown, A. J., 271 n.
Buckle, Henry Thomas, 24
Budget, 251–52
Buell, Raymond L., 146 n.
Bureaucracy, 49–50, 65, 221–22
Business cycle, 57–58, 196–97

Canadian-American relations
  economic, 61–62, 69–70
  political, 60–61
  with respect to Britain, 62, 64, 68–69
Capital
  export of, 181–85, 196, 224–26, 237,
    271, 276, 282–83
  formation by indigenous sources, 103,
    189, 238–39
  import of, 61, 82, 183, 240, 271–73
  mobilization for economic development,
    18–19, 188–89, 215, 238, 263
  see also Banking; Foreign-aid programs;
    Government; Industrialization;
    Technology; Transfer of technol-
    ogy
Catherine II, the Great, 28
Cattle and cattle-raising
  in Africa, 105–8
  in India, 128, 213
  in New Zealand, 141–42
Ch'en Tu-hsu, 163
Chevalier, Michel, 10, 23
China, 119, 123, 124, 152, 156, 160, 163,
  168–69, 171
Cobden, Richard, 10
Cocoa-growing, 102–3
Cole, Arthur H., 56 n.
Collier, John, 149
Commercial revolution, 32–34, 49
Communalism, 140, 142
  in Africa, 99–100
  in Russia, 47
Communication of ideas, 127–28, 227, 236
Communism
  in Burma, 163
  in China, 152, 160, 163, 168–69, 171
  and the colonial question, 161–65
  in India, 163

INDEX

INDEX

INDEX